RETIREMENT ISSUES, PLANS AND LIFESTYLES

RETIREMENT

ISSUES, BENEFITS AND DEVELOPMENTS

RETIREMENT ISSUES, PLANS AND LIFESTYLES

Additional books and e-books in this series can be found on Nova's website under the Series tab.

RETIREMENT ISSUES, PLANS AND LIFESTYLES

RETIREMENT

ISSUES, BENEFITS AND DEVELOPMENTS

THOMAS M. OSBORNE
EDITOR

snova
New York

Library of Congress Cataloging-in-Publication Data

ISBN: 978-1-53615-703-1

Published by Nova Science Publishers, Inc. † New York

CONTENTS

PREFACE

Strengthening the U.S. retirement system to be more accessible and financially sound is important to ensuring that all Americans can retire with dignity and security, and to managing the fiscal exposures to the federal government from various retirement-related programs. Currently, the U.S. retirement system, and many of the workers and retirees it was designed to help, face major challenges. Chapter 1 discusses (1) the fiscal risks and other challenges facing the U.S. retirement system, and (2) the need to re-evaluate our nation's approach to financing retirement. Chapters 2 and 3 discuss the Social Security full retirement age. Chapter 4 provides information on the benefits and disadvantages of alternate price indexes for measuring the cost of living for older Americans.

Chapter 5 examines (1) how much in retirement savings is transferred to states as unclaimed property and what happens to those savings once transferred and (2) the steps IRS and DOL have taken to oversee these transfers and what improvements are needed. Chapter 6 discusses the availability of enhanced retirement benefits for federal law enforcement officers (LEOs). Chapters 7 and 8 focus on the Railroad Retirement Board (RRB), an independent federal agency, which administers retirement, survivor, disability, unemployment, and sickness insurance for railroad workers and their families. Chapters 9 and 10 provide information on the military retirement system.

Chapter 1 - Strengthening the U.S. retirement system to be more accessible and financially sound is important to ensuring that all Americans can retire with dignity and security, and to managing the fiscal exposures to the federal government from various retirement-related programs. Currently, the U.S. retirement system, and many of the workers and retirees it was designed to help, face major challenges. This testimony discusses (1) the fiscal risks and other challenges facing the U.S. retirement system, and (2) the need to re-evaluate our nation's approach to financing retirement. It is based on a 2017 report, GAO-18- 111SP, on the nation's retirement system, with updated statistics when more recent estimates from publicly available sources were available.

Chapter 2 - The Social Security *full retirement age* (FRA) is the age at which workers can first claim *full* Social Security retired-worker benefits. Among other factors, a worker's monthly benefit amount is affected by the age at which he or she claims benefits relative to the FRA. Benefit adjustments are made based on the number of months before or after the FRA the worker claims benefits. The adjustments are intended to provide the worker with roughly the same total lifetime benefits, regardless of when he or she claims benefits, based on average life expectancy. Claiming benefits before the FRA results in a reduction in monthly benefits (to take into account the longer expected period of benefit receipt); claiming benefits after the FRA results in an increase in monthly benefits (to take into account the shorter expected period of benefit receipt). The FRA was 65 at the inception of Social Security in the 1930s. Under legislation enacted in 1983, the FRA is increasing gradually from 65 to 67 over a 22-year period (2000-2022). The FRA will reach 67 for workers born in 1960 or later (i.e., for workers who become eligible for retirement benefits at age 62 in 2022). Currently, the FRA is 66 and 4 months for workers who become eligible for retirement benefits in 2018 (i.e., workers born in 1956). Workers can claim *reduced* retirement benefits as early as age 62 (the *early eligibility age*). Spouses can also claim reduced retirement benefits starting at age 62. Other dependents, such as widow(er)s, can claim benefits at earlier ages. For workers with an FRA of 66, for example, claiming benefits at age 62 results in a 25% reduction in monthly benefits. For workers with an FRA of 67, claiming benefits at age 62 results in a 30% benefit reduction. A majority of retired-worker beneficiaries claim benefits before the FRA. In 2016, 39% of new retired-worker beneficiaries were age 62; almost two-thirds (66%) were under the age of 66. Workers who delay claiming benefits until after the FRA receive a *delayed retirement credit*, which applies up to the age of 70. For workers with an FRA of 66, for example, claiming benefits at age 70 results in a 32% increase in monthly benefits. For workers with an FRA of 67, claiming benefits at age 70 results in a 24% benefit increase. In 2016, almost one-fourth (23%) of new retired-worker beneficiaries were age 66; 11% were over the age of 66. Some lawmakers have called for increasing the Social Security retirement age in response to the system's projected financial imbalance, citing gains in life expectancy for the population overall. Other lawmakers, however, express concern that increasing the retirement age would disproportionately affect certain groups within the population, citing differences in life expectancy by socioeconomic groups. Differential gains in life expectancy are important in the context of Social Security because the actuarial adjustments for claiming benefits before or after the full retirement age are based on *average* life expectancy. Proposals to increase the retirement age are also met with concerns about the resulting hardship for certain workers, such as those in physically demanding occupations, who may be unable to work until older ages and may not qualify for Social Security disability benefits.

Chapter 3 - Social Security provides monthly cash benefits to retired or disabled workers and their family members as well as to the family members of deceased workers. The Social Security full retirement age (FRA) is the age at which retired workers can first claim full Social Security retired-worker benefits. The FRA was 65 at the inception of Social Security in 1935. As part of legislation enacted in 1983 (P.L. 98-21), starting with workers born in 1938, the FRA increased by two months every birth year until the FRA reached 66 for workers born in 1943 to 1954, and then increases again in two-month increments until the FRA reaches 67 for workers born in 1960 or later. Retired workers can claim retirement benefits as early as age 62 (the earliest eligibility age, or EEA).

Benefits claimed between age 62 and the FRA, however, are subject to a permanent reduction for early retirement. For each of the 36 months immediately preceding the FRA, the monthly rate of reduction from the full retirement benefit is five-ninths of 1%. For each month earlier than three years (36 months) before the FRA, the monthly rate of reduction is five-twelfths of 1%. Therefore, for a worker with an FRA of 65, claiming benefits at 62 results in a 20% permanent reduction in their monthly benefit; the reduction is 25% if the FRA is 66, and 30% if the FRA is 67. Workers who claim benefits after the FRA may receive a delayed retirement credit (DRC). The maximum age at which the DRC applies is age 70. Any further delay in claiming benefits past age 70 does not result in a higher benefit. Under current law, the amount of the credit varies based on the worker's year of birth. The credit for workers born in 1943 or later is 8% per year.

Chapter 4 - BLS produces four CPIs, including three official indexes published on its website and an experimental index that is available on request:

- CPI-W: The CPI for Urban Wage Earners and Clerical Workers. First published in 1921, it was the only national CPI when the Social Security Administration began indexing benefits in 1975. It represents the types of expenditures made by about 29 percent of the U.S. population.
- CPI-U: The CPI for All Urban Consumers. First published in 1978, when it became the headline index, it represents the types of expenditures made by about 93 percent of the U.S. population, including retired individuals.
- CPI-E: The CPI for the Elderly. Created in 1988 at the request of Congress, this index addresses spending patterns of those age 62 and older by shifting the weights for certain expenditures such as medical care and shelter. BLS considers this index experimental. It represents the types of expenditures made by about 21 percent of the U.S. population.
- Chained CPI-U: The Chained CPI for All Urban Consumers. It was first published in 2002 to address methodological concerns about

more fully capturing consumers' ability to buy different goods and services to adapt to changing prices. It represents the types of expenditures made by about 93 percent of the U.S. population.

BLS regularly reviews and revises the methodologies for producing indexes to improve their accuracy. Several federal retirement programs use COLAs that are generally based on third quarter averages of the CPI-W. This includes Social Security (the largest of these programs), Military Retirement, Railroad Retirement Board pensions, the Federal Employees Retirement System, the Civil Service Retirement System, and Veterans Affairs pensions. Price indexing also occurs in other federal programs not exclusively focused on older Americans, such as Social Security Disability Insurance, Supplemental Security Income, and the Supplemental Nutrition Assistance Program. In summary, we found the following:

- Using an alternate index would likely result in changes to benefits and program costs that accumulate over time. A switch to an alternate index for federal retirement programs' COLAs would likely create tradeoffs in regards to individual benefits and program costs. An increase in benefits would also mean an increase in program costs, and a decrease in benefits would mean a decrease in costs. We estimate that a switch to the Chained CPI-U would lower benefits through small annual changes that accumulate over time, relative to using the CPI-W, whereas a switch to the CPI-E would increase benefits in a similar manner. For example, if COLAs had been based on the Chained CPI-U or CPI-E over the 2003–2033 period, our analysis shows that the first year's adjusted monthly benefit in 2004 would change by a few dollars or less, relative to using the CPI-W, but after 30 years we estimate that the monthly difference would be $100 or more for a hypothetical beneficiary with earnings equal to the national average wage index.
- Changing to an alternate index would have the largest relative effect on those who receive benefits the longest and those with lower incomes. Beneficiaries who claim benefits over many years

and those with lower incomes would most strongly experience the effects of using an alternate index for federal retirement programs' COLAs. This is in part because changes to COLAs accumulate over time and because lower-income beneficiaries rely more heavily on federal retirement programs, such as Social Security. For example, after 30 years of Social Security COLA adjustments using an alternate index, we estimate that the total retirement income for a low-income household would decrease by about percent using the Chained CPI-U or increase by about 4 percent using the CPI-E, relative to the current index.6 In contrast, we estimate that this same change in COLA would affect the total retirement income of a high-income household by only about a 1 percent decrease using the Chained CPI-U or about a 1 percent increase using the CPI-E, relative to the CPI-W.

- Implementing an alternate index could pose issues regarding timeliness of data and cost. The Chained CPI-U data are preliminary and can be subject to significant revisions up to 1 year after they are initially produced. This may require agencies to determine how or whether to address these data lags. BLS considers the CPI-E an experimental index. According to 2017 estimates from BLS, it could cost about $5 million per year over several years to research it and, if BLS finds that the current CPI-E methodology is not sufficient, up to an additional $110 million per year thereafter to produce an official CPI-E. In addition to timeliness and cost issues, switching to an alternate index would require explanations to beneficiaries. Also, SSA officials indicated that any change to how SSA computes COLAs would require a legislative change.
- A change in certain indexes would affect other federal programs. While this chapter focused on federal retirement programs, the information is relevant for other federal programs as well. For example, by law the COLA for Social Security's retirement program applies to some other programs too. The COLA for Social Security retirement benefits is the same as the COLA for Social Security disability benefits, and changes to that COLA trigger

changes to the COLA for Supplemental Security Income, Railroad Retirement Board pensions, and Veterans Affairs pensions. The same issues could present themselves if other federal programs changed the CPI used for various program aspects, such as income eligibility levels or benefit amount.

Chapter 5 - Over the course of individuals' careers, their retirement savings can be spread across multiple retirement accounts and they can change jobs, both of which can cause their savings to become unclaimed and even lost. Prior GAO work has found that unclaimed retirement savings are sometimes transferred to the states. GAO was asked to review such transfers. This chapter examines (1) how much in retirement savings is transferred to states as unclaimed property and what happens to those savings once transferred and (2) the steps IRS and DOL have taken to oversee these transfers and what improvements are needed. GAO interviewed federal and state officials, industry representatives, and other stakeholders, and surveyed all 50 states and the District of Columbia (and received 22 responses). GAO also surveyed 401(k) plan service providers and IRA trustees regarding the volume of retirement savings transferred to states and their federal tax reporting and withholding practices for those transfers.

Chapter 6 - Federal employees who perform specific duties, as defined in statute, are classified as law enforcement officers (LEOs) for the purpose of federal retirement benefits. LEOs and a few legislatively designated groups, including federal firefighters and air traffic controllers, are eligible for enhanced retirement benefits under the Civil Service Retirement System (CSRS), for individuals hired before 1984, or the Federal Employees' Retirement System (FERS), for individuals hired in 1984 or later. The availability of enhanced retirement benefits for LEOs and similar groups is linked to an expectation of limited federal service. This limited service is due, in turn, to the rigorous physical demands of law enforcement duties and the mandatory retirement age to which these individuals are subject. LEO enhanced retirement benefits are designed to provide adequate retirement income for federal employees with careers that end at an earlier age with fewer years of service than regular civilian federal employees. In general, law enforcement personnel are subject to mandatory retirement at age 57, or as soon as 20 years of service have been completed after age 57. The maximum age of entry, which is intended to ensure full retirement benefits upon reaching mandatory retirement age, is typically age 37. Under both CSRS and FERS, law enforcement personnel are eligible for their enhanced benefits at the age of 50 provided they have completed the minimum requirement of 20 years of service. Under FERS, law enforcement personnel with 25 years of service are eligible for retirement regardless of age. Law enforcement personnel in CSRS and their employing agencies each contribute 7.5% of payroll. CSRS law enforcement personnel accrue benefits at the rate of 2.5% per year for their first 20 years of service and 2% for each year after the 20th year of service. Law enforcement personnel in FERS accrue benefits at the rate of 1.7% per year for the first 20 years of service and 1% per year for each year thereafter. FERS contribution rates vary by date of hire. Law enforcement personnel in FERS first hired before 2013 contribute 1.3% of pay (plus Social Security contributions), and their agencies contribute 30.1% of pay. Under P.L. 112-96, FERS law enforcement personnel first hired in 2013 contribute 3.6% of pay (plus Social Security contributions), and their agencies contribute 28.4% of pay. Finally, under P.L. 113-67, FERS law enforcement personnel first hired in 2014 or later contribute 4.9% of pay (plus Social Security contributions), but their agencies still contribute 28.4% of pay. FERS accrual rates remain unchanged for law enforcement personnel first hired in 2013 or later (including individuals first hired in 2014 or later). Many employees in law enforcement occupations are not recognized as LEOs by their agencies and OPM for the purposes of federal retirement coverage and, consequently, are not eligible to receive enhanced retirement benefits. Several employee groups and unions representing individuals in these occupations have sought enhanced retirement benefits through additional legislation. Recent Congresses have responded by introducing legislation that would provide enhanced retirement benefits to additional personnel. Though granting more groups such benefits may alleviate problems of attrition and perceived inequity across law enforcement occupations, it would also increase personnel costs for employing agencies as well as overall federal expenditures on civilian federal retirement benefits.

Chapter 7 - The Railroad Retirement Board (RRB), an independent federal agency, administers retirement, survivor, disability, unemployment, and sickness insurance for railroad workers and their families. During FY2017, the RRB paid nearly $12.5 billion in retirement, disability, and survivor benefits to approximately 548,000 beneficiaries and paid $105.4 million in unemployment and sickness benefits to approximately 28,000 claimants. Of the total $12.5 billion benefit payments in the same fiscal year, 60.0% was paid to retired workers, 8.0% to disabled workers, 14.4% to spouses, and 16.8% to survivors. The Railroad Retirement Act (RRA) authorizes retirement, disability, and survivor benefits for railroad workers and their families. RRA is financed primarily by payroll taxes, financial interchanges from Social Security, and transfers from the National Railroad Retirement Investment Trust (NRRIT). Railroad retirement payroll taxes have two tiers: the Tier I tax is essentially the same as the Social Security payroll tax and the Tier II tax is set each year based on the railroad retirement system's asset balances, benefit payments, and administrative costs. In FY2017, the gross RRA funding was about $12.7 billion. Railroad retirement annuities are also divided into two tiers. Tier I annuities are designed to be nearly equivalent to Social Security benefits and are based on both railroad retirement and Social Security-covered employment. However, Tier I annuities are more generous than Social Security benefits in certain situations. For example, at the age of 60, railroad workers with at least 30 years of covered railroad work may receive unreduced retirement annuities. Tier II annuities are similar to private pensions and based solely on covered railroad service. Tier II annuities are paid in addition to Tier I annuities. Railroad disability annuities may be payable to totally disabled railroad workers who are permanently disabled from all work and occupational disabled workers who are found to be permanently disabled from their regular railroad occupations. Eligible spouses and survivors of railroad workers may receive a certain portion of Tier I and Tier II benefits, but divorced spouses and surviving divorced spouses are eligible for only a certain portion of Tier I benefits. The Railroad Unemployment Insurance Act (RUIA) authorizes unemployment and sickness benefits for railroad workers. RUIA is financed solely by railroad employers, whose contributions are based on the taxable earnings of their employees. Eligibility for railroad unemployment and sickness benefits is based on recent railroad service and earnings. The maximum daily unemployment and sickness benefit payable in the benefit year that began July 1, 2018, is $77, and the maximum benefit for a biweekly claim is $770. Normal benefits are paid for up to 26 weeks in a benefit year. The railroad unemployment and sickness system remains affected by sequestration, as unemployment benefits will continue to be reduced through at least September 30, 2019.

Chapter 8 - The Railroad Retirement Board (RRB), an independent federal agency, administers retirement, survivor, disability, unemployment, and sickness insurance for railroad workers and their families. Railroad retirement payroll taxes include two tiers—Tier I and Tier II taxes. The Tier I tax finances the Tier I railroad retirement benefit that is equivalent to Social Security benefits and the Tier II tax finances the Tier II benefit, Tier I benefits in excess of Social Security benefits, and supplemental annuities. Since 2002, Tier II tax revenues in excess of obligatory RRB benefits and associated administrative costs have been invested in private stocks, bonds, and other investments. Prior to the Railroad Retirement and Survivors' Improvement Act of 2001 (RRSIA; P.L. 107-90), surplus railroad retirement assets could only be invested in U.S. government securities—just as the Social Security trust funds must be invested. The RRSIA established the National Railroad Retirement Investment Trust (NRRIT; hereinafter, the Trust) to manage and invest part of the RRB's assets in much the same way that the assets of private-sector and most state and local government pension plans are invested. The remainder of RRB's assets continues to be invested solely in U.S. government securities. Congress structured the Trust in an effort to ensure investment independence and limit political interference. It also aimed to increase railroad retirement system funding, add enhanced benefits, potentially reduce taxes, and protect system financing in case of market downturns.

The Trust's assets are invested in a diversified portfolio, both to minimize investment risk and avoid disproportionate influence over an industry or firm. The Trust is a tax-exempt entity independent of the federal government, and it is not subject to the same oversight as federal agencies. However, the RRSIA requires an annual management report to Congress. From its inception in February 2002 to September 30, 2017, $21.3 billion has been transferred to the Trust from the RRB and $21.1 billion has been transferred from the Trust to pay railroad retirement benefits. At the end of FY2017, the net asset value of the Trust was $26.5 billion. The Trust's investments have generally followed the markets' recent performance. From FY2003 to FY2017, the Trust's annual returns averaged 8.3%, slightly higher than expectations of the bill's drafters, who assumed nominal annual returns of 8.0%. As the Trust's investment portfolio diversified over time, its administrative expenses steadily increased, to 36 basis points in FY2011, but fell to 31 basis points in FY2017, and remain low when compared with other mutual funds. The combined fair market value of Tier II taxes and Trust assets is designed to maintain four to six years' worth of RRB benefits and administrative expenses. To maintain this balance, the Railroad Retirement Tier II tax rates automatically adjust as needed. This tax adjustment does not require congressional action. The Railroad Retirement Tier II tax rates increased in 2013 and most recently in 2015.

Chapter 9 - The military retirement system is a government-funded, noncontributory, defined benefit system that has historically been viewed as a significant incentive in retaining a career military force. The system currently includes monthly compensation for qualified active and reserve retirees, disability benefits for those deemed medically unfit to serve, and a survivor annuity program for the eligible survivors of deceased retirees. The amount of compensation is dependent on time served, basic pay at retirement, and annual Cost-of-Living-Adjustments (COLAs). Military retirees are also entitled to nonmonetary benefits including exchange and commissary privileges, medical care through TRICARE, and access to Morale, Welfare and Recreation (MWR) facilities and programs. Currently, there are three general categories of military retiree, active component, reserve component, and disability retiree. Active component personnel are eligible for retirement (i.e., vested) after completing 20 years of service (YOS). Reserve personnel are eligible after 20 years of creditable service based on a points system, but do not typically begin to draw retirement pay until age 60. Finally, those with a disability retirement do not need to have served 20 years to be eligible for retired pay; however, they must have been found unqualified for further service due to a permanent, stable disability. In FY2017, approximately $57 billion was paid to 2.3 million military retirees and survivors. Given the size of the program, some have viewed military retirement as a place where substantial budgetary savings could be made. Others have argued that past modifications intended to save money have had a deleterious effect on military recruiting and retention. Military retirees, families, and veterans' service organizations closely monitor potential changes to the retirement system. When considering alternatives to the current system, Congress may choose to consider the balance among the benefits of the military retirement system as a retention incentive, budget constraints, and the needs and concerns of their constituents.

Chapter 10 - The *Department of Defense Authorization Act of 1984* changed the method of military retirement benefit funding. Prior to 1984, military retirement benefits were funded on a "pay-as-you-go" basis. "Pay-as-you-go" basis is a method of funding where the costs of retirement benefits are paid for when owed to plan participants. The *Department of Defense Authorization Act of 1984* established an accrual funding system for the Military Retirement System. Accrual funding is a method of setting aside funds from current budgets for retirement annuities that eventually will be received by military personnel who are in current service. Military retirement pension benefits, including benefits for survivors of deceased servicemembers, are paid out of the Department of Defense Military Retirement Fund. Under the current accrual funding system, a percentage of the annual appropriation for basic pay for members of the armed forces is transferred to the Department of Defense Military Retirement Fund in order to defray the future costs of retirement benefits earned during the year covered by the appropriation. Funds transferred to the Military

Retirement Fund are invested until disbursed to plan participants. The *Department of Defense Authorization Act of 1984*, as amended also mandates the actuarial cost method for developing retirement contribution rates for funding the Military Retirement Fund. The law mandates that DOD utilize the "aggregate entry-age normal" actuarial cost method for funding. The law requires DOD to develop a single contribution rate across the department for active duty personnel and a single rate for reserve component personnel. The contribution rate is the estimated percentage of basic pay that must be contributed over the entire active career of a typical group of new entrants to pay for all the future retirement and survivor benefits of that group. Mathematically, a contribution rate is calculated by dividing the present value of future benefits for the entire cohort by the present value of future basic pay, evaluated at an assumed interest rate. In other sectors of United States employment—in particular, for private sector and state and local government sector pension plans—to the extent that use of a particular actuarial cost method is required, the actuarial cost method generally differs from that required to be used for funding the Military Retirement System. See Enclosure II for more information regarding United States pension requirements in the private, state, and local government sectors. In addition to DOD's contribution to the Military Retirement Fund, the Department of the Treasury is required to make an annual contribution to cover, over time, the fund's initial unfunded liability, the cost of changes to Military Retirement System benefit provisions, the cost of changes in actuarial assumptions and actuarial gains or losses, and the normal cost for "concurrent receipt" benefits. "Concurrent receipt" refers to Combat Related Special Compensation and Concurrent Retirement and Disability Pay program where certain retirees can receive both retirement pay and disability pay. The Military Retirement Fund's initial unfunded liability is equal to the amount of liabilities owed when retirement benefit funding changed from a "pay-as-you-go" basis to an accrual funding basis.

In: Retirement
Editor: Thomas M. Osborne
ISBN: 978-1-53615-703-1

Chapter 1

THE NATION'S RETIREMENT SYSTEM: A COMPREHENSIVE RE-EVALUATION NEEDED TO BETTER PROMOTE FUTURE RETIREMENT SECURITY*

Gene L. Dodaro

WHY GAO DID THIS STUDY

Strengthening the U.S. retirement system to be more accessible and financially sound is important to ensuring that all Americans can retire with dignity and security, and to managing the fiscal exposures to the federal government from various retirement-related programs. Currently, the U.S. retirement system, and many of the workers and retirees it was designed to help, face major challenges.

* This is an edited, reformatted and augmented version of United States Government Accountability Office; Testimony Before the Special Committee on Aging, U.S. Senate, Publication No. GAO-19-342T, dated February 6, 2019.

This testimony discusses (1) the fiscal risks and other challenges facing the U.S. retirement system, and (2) the need to re-evaluate our nation's approach to financing retirement. It is based on a 2017 report, GAO-18- 111SP, on the nation's retirement system, with updated statistics when more recent estimates from publicly available sources were available.

WHAT GAO RECOMMENDS

In the 2017 report, GAO recommended that Congress should consider establishing an independent commission to comprehensively examine the US retirement system and make recommendations to clarify key policy goals for the system and improve how the nation promotes retirement security.

WHAT GAO FOUND

Fundamental changes over the past 40 years have led to various risks and challenges for the three main pillars supporting the U.S. retirement system. For example, current projections indicate that by 2034, the Old-Age and Survivors trust fund for Social Security's retirement program—the first pillar—will only be sufficient to pay 77 percent of scheduled benefits, due in part to the aging of the population (see Figure). Other federal government retirement-related programs also face financial uncertainty. For example, the Pension Benefit Guaranty Corporation, which insures the pension benefits of most private sector defined benefit plans, estimates a greater than 90 percent chance the multiemployer program will be insolvent by 2025. Meanwhile, employer-sponsored plans—the second pillar—have experienced a shift from traditional defined benefit (DB) plans that generally provide set monthly payments for life, to defined contribution (DC) account-based plans, like 401(k)s. DC plans provide greater portability of savings that can be better suited to the needs of a more mobile workforce, but also require individuals to assume more responsibility for planning and managing their savings. While DC plans can provide meaningful retirement security for many, especially higher earners, lower earners appear more prone to having little or no savings in their DC accounts. Further, individuals' savings—the third pillar—may be constrained by economic trends such as low real wage growth and growing out-of-pocket health care costs. Combined with increased longevity, these challenges can put individuals at greater risk of outliving their savings and fiscal pressures on government programs will likely grow.

Congress generally has sought to address retirement-related issues in an incremental fashion. Also, no one agency is responsible for overseeing the U.S. retirement system in its entirety, so there is no obvious federal agency to lead a comprehensive reform effort. It has been nearly 40 years since a federal commission has conducted a comprehensive evaluation of the nation's approach to financing retirement. Without a more comprehensive re-evaluation of the challenges across all three pillars of the system, it may be difficult to identify effective, enduring solutions. Unless timely action is taken, many older Americans risk not having sufficient means for a secure and dignified retirement.

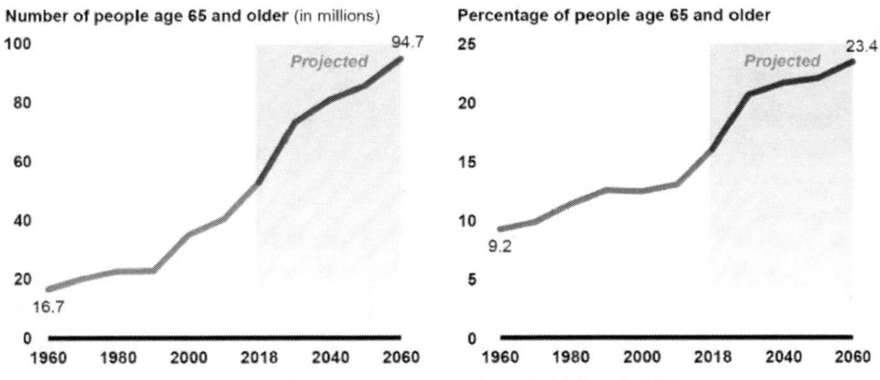

Source: GAO analysis of U.S. Census Bureau data. | GAO-19-342T.

The U.S. Population Is Aging.

Chairman Collins, Ranking Member Casey, and Members of the Committee:

Thank you for the opportunity to discuss the state of our nation's retirement system. Fundamental changes to the U.S. retirement system have occurred over the past 40 years. Traditional pensions have become less common, and the number of defined contribution plans, such as 401(k)s, has been growing. These types of plans can provide meaningful retirement security for many; however, the U.S. retirement system, and many of the workers and retirees it was designed to help, are facing major challenges. Social Security's financial outlook is threatened by demographic trends, certain large pension plans face insolvency, and individuals are increasingly responsible for planning and managing their own retirement accounts. Strengthening the U.S. retirement system to be more accessible and financially sound is important to better ensuring that all Americans can retire with dignity and security, and to managing the fiscal risks to the federal government from various retirement-related programs.

My statement today will focus on two topics: (1) the fiscal risks and other challenges facing the U.S. retirement system; and (2) the need to re-evaluate our nation's approach to financing retirement.

My statement is based primarily on a report we issued in October 2017.[1] For that report, we began with an examination of our recently published work and supplemented it with additional information from various federal agencies, organizations, and institutions. We also obtained insights from a panel of 15 experts that we convened in November 2016, representing a range of organizations, subject matter expertise, and views (see app. I for a list of the panelists). For this testimony, we updated statistics when more recent estimates from publicly available sources were available. A detailed description of the methodologies used is included in our prior report. We conducted the work on which this statement is based in accordance with generally accepted government auditing standards. Those standards require that we plan and perform the audit to obtain

[1] GAO, *The Nation's Retirement System: A Comprehensive Re-evaluation Is Needed to Better Promote Future Retirement Security*, GAO-18-111SP (Washington, D.C.: Oct. 18, 2017).

sufficient, appropriate evidence to provide a reasonable basis for our findings and conclusions based on our audit objectives. We believe that the evidence obtained provides a reasonable basis for our findings and conclusions based on our audit objectives.

BACKGROUND

Source: GAO. | GAO-19-342T.

Social Security has been the foundation of retirement security in the United States. Enacted in 1935, Social Security provides for the general welfare of older Americans by, among other things, establishing a system of federal old-age benefits, including a retirement program. Officially titled Old-Age and Survivors Insurance (OASI), the Social Security retirement program provides benefits to retired workers, their families, and survivors of deceased workers.[2] About 51 million retirees and their families received

[2] For more about Social Security, see GAO, *Social Security's Future: Answers to Key Questions*, GAO-16-75SP (Washington, D.C.: Oct. 27, 2015).

$798.7 billion in Social Security retirement benefits in 2017, according to Social Security Administration (SSA), which is responsible for administering the program.[3]

About 40 years after the creation of Social Security, landmark legislation was enacted in 1974 that has played a major role in establishing the structure for private sector employers' involvement in sponsoring retirement plans for their workers: the Employee Retirement Income Security Act of 1974 (ERISA). ERISA is a complex law administered by multiple federal agencies including the Department of Labor (DOL), the Internal Revenue Service (IRS) within the Department of the Treasury (Treasury), along with the Pension Benefit Guaranty Corporation (PBGC), and has evolved with many significant amendments over the years (see app. II).

ERISA was enacted, in part, to address public concerns about the security of pension benefits, including the prominent failure of a couple of large, private sector pension plans. The act, as amended, does not require any employer to establish a retirement plan, but those who do must meet certain requirements and minimum standards. For example, ERISA establishes certain requirements for all employer-sponsored plans, including responsibilities for plan fiduciaries (those who manage and control plan assets, among others), as well as minimum funding standards for defined benefit (DB) plans, which traditionally promise to provide a monthly payment to retirees for life. ERISA also established the PBGC, the government corporation responsible for insuring the pension benefits of nearly 37 million American workers and retirees who participate in nearly 24,800 private sector defined benefit plans. Under ERISA, tax-qualified DB plans (or the employers who sponsor them) may have to pay insurance premiums to the PBGC, based on the funding level of their plans. The IRS also administers the Internal Revenue Code (IRC), which has provisions that affect pensions and retirement savings.

---

[3] In addition, on the revenue side, about 174 million people were working and paying Social Security taxes in 2017. For more information, see The Board of Trustees, *The 2018 Annual Report of the Board of Trustees of the Federal Old-Age and Survivors Insurance and Federal Disability Insurance Trust Funds* (Washington, D.C.: June 5, 2018).

While SSA administers the Social Security program, and the DOL, PBGC, and IRS each are generally responsible for administering aspects of ERISA, several other agencies also have important roles in various parts of the retirement system. For example, the Department of Health and Human Services oversees the Centers for Medicare and Medicaid Services (CMS), which administers the major health care programs that provide coverage for retirees, as well as the Administration on Aging, which encourages and assists state grantees that provide services for older adults.

In addition, agencies such as the U.S. Department of Agriculture and the Department of Housing and Urban Development oversee food and housing programs for older adults. Other agencies also play a role in providing various services and supports for older adults. For example, the Department of Transportation administers a program that improves access and alternatives to public transportation for seniors and individuals with disabilities. The Consumer Financial Protection Bureau, as part of its mandate to provide financial literacy education, helps consumers navigate financial choices related to retirement. The Federal Trade Commission can have consumer protection and investor oversight roles and responsibilities related to individuals borrowing against their pensions. In addition, these federal agencies and others work together to help combat elder financial exploitation, which experts have described as an epidemic with society-wide repercussions. Citing our prior work on this topic, in October 2017, Congress enacted the Elder Abuse Prevention and Prosecution Act, calling on the Department of Justice to work with other federal, state, and local law enforcement agencies to improve data collection and provide technical assistance focused on combatting elder abuse.[4]

[4] Pub. L. No. 115-70, §§ 201-202, 131 Stat. 1208, 1211-12 (2017). For our prior work on this topic, see GAO, *Elder Justice: Stronger Federal Leadership Could Enhance National Response to Elder Abuse*, GAO-11-208 (Washington, D.C.: Mar. 2, 2011) and *Elder Justice: National Strategy Needed to Effectively Combat Elderly Exploitation*, GAO-13-110 (Washington, D.C: Nov. 15, 2012).

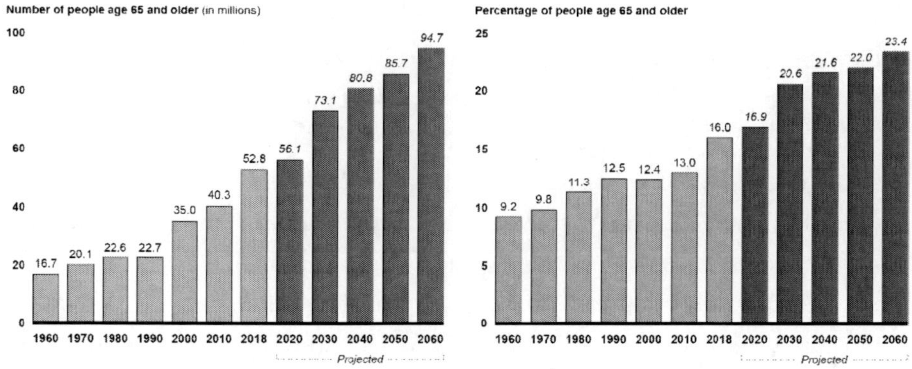

Source: GAO analysis of U.S. Census Bureau data. | GAO-19-342T.

Figure 1. The U.S. Population Is Aging.

The need for government services and support for older adults in retirement will continue to grow as the proportion of older adults in the United States continues to rise significantly in the future. In 1970, those age 65 and over accounted for about 10 percent of the population, but by 2060, they are expected to account for about 23 percent (see Figure 1). This reflects long-term decreases in birth rates and increases in life expectancy.

MAIN PILLARS OF THE U.S. RETIREMENT SYSTEM FACE FISCAL RISKS AND OTHER CHALLENGES

The U.S. retirement system is supported by three main pillars—Social Security, employer-sponsored plans, and individuals' savings—that serve as important sources of retirement income for Americans. Currently, each of these pillars faces various risks and other challenges. If left unchanged, these risks present the federal government with significant potential fiscal exposures, which may legally commit or create expectations for future federal spending.[5]

[5] Long-term fiscal projections show that, absent fiscal policy changes, the federal government is on an unsustainable path, largely due to a projected growing gap between federal revenues and

Pillar One: Social Security and Other Federal Programs

The first pillar, Social Security (specifically, Social Security's retirement program), is facing financial difficulties, as are other federal programs that provide essential supports to many older Americans, such as Medicare and the PBGC's insurance programs (see Figure 2). In addition, multiple federal agencies help fund a broad array of home and community-based services for older adults. As the number of older adults needing assistance continues to grow, the pressure to increase federal funding for these services is likely to increase.

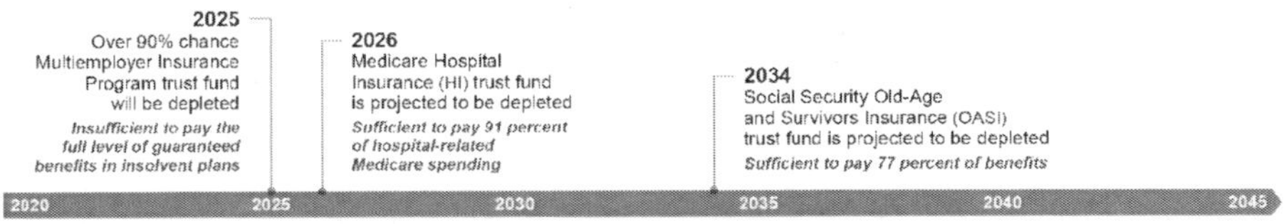

Source: GAO analysis of data from the Social Security Administartion, the Census for Medicare and Medicaid Services, and the Pension Benefit Guaranty Corporation. | GAO-19-342T.

Notes: The Pension Benefit Guaranty Corporation insures most private sector defined benefit plans under one of two programs: the Single-Employer Insurance Program or the Multiemployer Insurance Program. Social Security's Old-Age and Survivors Insurance is Social Security's retirement program.

Figure 2. Timeline of Projected Fiscal Risks for Certain Federal Programs.

Social Security

As the foundation of retirement security in the United States, Social Security's retirement program, financed primarily by payroll taxes, helps reduce poverty among beneficiaries, many of whom rely on Social Security for the majority of their income once they retire.[6] Our analysis of data from the Federal Reserve Board's most recent Survey of Consumer

expenditures, driven by demographic changes, health care costs, and interest costs on the public debt. For more information on the nation's fiscal exposure and fiscal health more generally, see GAO, *The Nation's Fiscal Health: Action Is Needed to Address the Federal Government's Fiscal Future,* GAO-18-299SP (Washington, D.C.: June 21, 2018).

[6] Old-Age and Survivors Insurance, also known as Social Security's retirement program, provides benefits to retirees as well as their survivors and dependents.

Finances (SCF) showed that in 2016, among households age 65 and over, the bottom 20 percent, ranked by income, relied on Social Security retirement benefits for 81 percent of their income, on average.

But Social Security is facing financial difficulties that, if not addressed, will affect its long-term stability. During the many years that the revenue for Social Security's retirement program exceeded costs, the program built up reserves in the trust fund. However, since 2010, Social Security has been paying out more in benefits than it received and has relied on interest income to help cover expenses. For 2018, the cost of the program was expected to exceed total income by $2 billion and, as a result, asset reserves were expected to decline. If no changes are made, current projections indicate that by 2034, the retirement program trust fund will only be sufficient to pay 77 percent of scheduled benefits.[7]

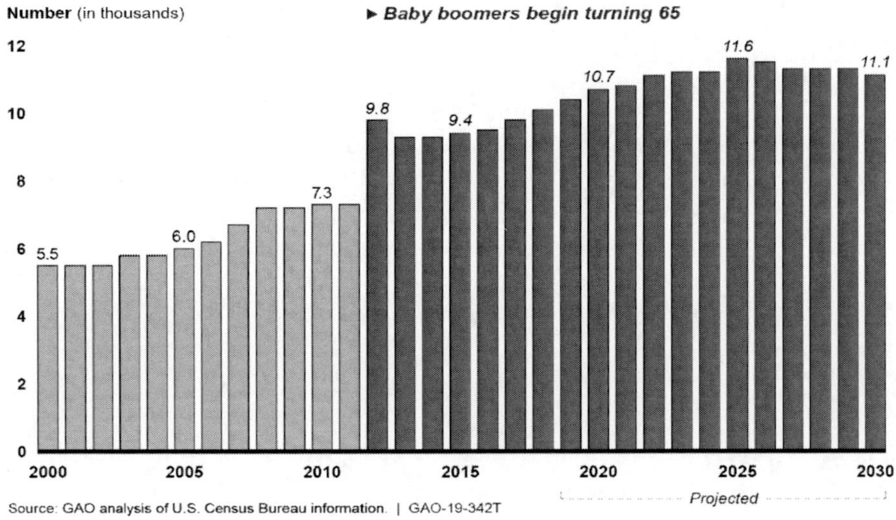

Note: Census data estimates of population are as of July 1 in each year. For baby boomers, born between 1946 and 1964, the age at which Social Security pays unreduced retirement benefits gradually increases from 66 to 67.

Figure 3. Average Daily Number of People Turning 65.

---

[7] The Board of Trustees, *The 2018 Annual Report of the Board of Trustees of the Federal Old-Age and Survivors Insurance and Federal Disability Insurance Trust Funds* (Washington, D.C.: June 5, 2018).

The underlying cause of Social Security's financial difficulties is the aging population, driven by lower fertility rates and increased life expectancy, and accelerated by the ongoing retirement of the baby boom generation.[8] The first baby boomers began receiving Social Security retirement benefits in 2008, and growing numbers will become eligible for Social Security benefits in coming years. Our analysis indicates that the number of baby boomers turning 65 is projected to increase from an average of about 10,200 per day in 2018 to more than 11,000 per day in 2029 (see Figure 3).

As with the Social Security retirement program, reserves had also built up over time in the trust fund for Social Security's disability program, but in 2005, the program began paying out more than it was taking in. To avoid benefit reductions, which were expected to begin in 2016, Congress passed a law in late 2015 that temporarily reallocated some payroll tax revenue from the retirement trust fund to the disability trust fund.[9] Even with this added boost, if no further changes are made, reductions in disability benefits are projected to be needed beginning in 2032, according to SSA's most recent report.[10]

For both the Social Security retirement and disability programs combined, the number of workers contributing to Social Security for each aged, disabled, dependent, or surviving beneficiary is declining, due to the aging population and other factors. While there are currently 2.8 workers

---

[8] One measure of an aging population is the portion of a population above a certain age, such as 65. Two key drivers of the proportion of a population above a certain age are fertility rates and longevity.

[9] According to the Social Security Trustees, in 2016 and 2017, non-interest income and total income from the DI Trust Fund exceeded benefit payments due primarily to the temporary reallocation of some of the payroll tax revenue from OASI to DI for the years 2016 through 2018.

[10] According to recent SSA data, applications for SSA's Disability Insurance program have declined steadily in recent years from a peak of 2.9 million in 2010 to 2.2 million in 2017. At the same time the number of individuals being awarded benefits has also declined from a peak of 1 million in 2011 to 762,000 in 2017. Possible explanations for these trends include better labor market conditions, the availability of health care through the Patient Protection and Affordable Care Act, and lower award rates at all adjudicative levels of SSA's disability determination process. For more information, see Social Security, *Annual Statistical Supplement to the Social Security Bulletin, 2017*. SSA Publication No. 13-11700 (Washington, D.C. March 2018).

contributing to Social Security per beneficiary, this ratio is expected to decline to 2.2 by 2035, and to 2.0 by 2095 (see Figure 4).

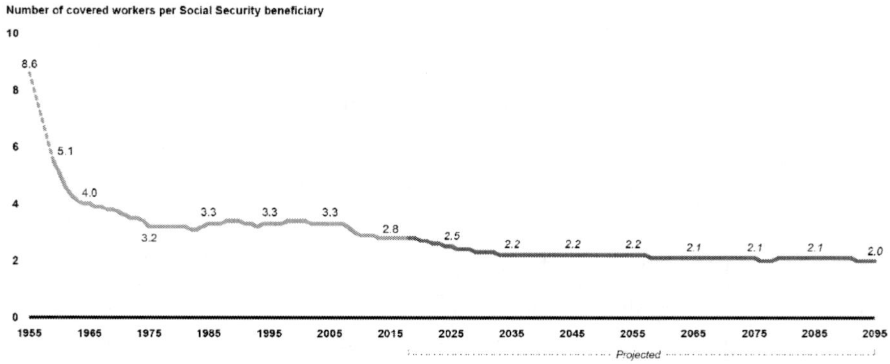

Source: 2018 Social Security Trustees' Report (intermediate assumptions). | GAO-19-342T.

Note: Beneficiaries include all those receiving benefits from Social Security's Old-Age and Survivors Insurance program and its Disability Insurance program combined. Data for the years between 1955 and 1960 are not available.

Figure 4. Past and Projected Social Security Covered Workers per Social Security Beneficiary.

It is difficult to predict exactly what would occur if either Social Security's retirement or disability programs were to become insolvent because the Social Security Act does not provide for any procedure for paying less than full benefits. According to SSA, benefits could be reduced across the board by a set percentage, certain benefits could be prioritized, or benefits could be delayed.

Medicare and Medicaid

The major health care programs that include coverage for retirees, Medicare and Medicaid, also face increasing financial challenges due to program and demographic changes. For example, over the years, Congress has made changes to Medicare so that more people have become eligible, even if under age 65.[11] Also, Congress has added two more parts to

[11] These changes included covering individuals with specific illnesses, such as end stage renal disease. In addition, Medicare beneficiaries also include individuals under age 65 who are

Medicare: one part allowing insurance under private plans approved by Medicare (Medicare Advantage),[12] and another part providing prescription drug coverage. As of 2017, over 58 million people were enrolled in one or more parts under Medicare. Projections indicate that in the coming decade, as more members of the baby-boom generation become eligible for benefits, the number of Medicare beneficiaries will rise to 75 million in 2027. Similar to the challenges facing Social Security, spending for Medicare Part A (Hospital Insurance) is projected to outpace revenue over time,[13] and the trust fund for Medicare Part A is projected to be unable to pay full benefits beginning in 2026. At that time, the Hospital Insurance trust fund will only be sufficient to pay 91 percent of hospital-related Medicare spending.[14]

Medicaid, which provides health care coverage and financing for millions of low-income individuals, including those age 65 or older, also faces financial challenges. Medicaid is the nation's primary payer for long-term services and supports, and the elderly—along with those with disabilities—are among the highest cost Medicaid beneficiaries. The federal government and states share in the financing of the Medicaid program, with the federal government matching most state expenditures for Medicaid services using a statutory formula. Estimated Medicaid outlays for fiscal year 2017 were $592.2 billion, of which $370.6 billion was financed by the federal government and $221.6 billion by the states. Over

receiving benefits from Social Security or the Railroad Retirement Board on the basis of a disability.

[12] Medicare Advantage Plans (also known as Medicare Part C) are a type of Medicare health plan offered by a private company that contracts with Medicare to provide certain benefits. Medicare Advantage Plans include health maintenance organizations, preferred provider organizations, private fee-for-service plans, special needs plans, and Medicare medical savings account plans.

[13] Medicare is funded primarily by payroll taxes, general revenue, and premiums paid by Medicare beneficiaries.

[14] The Boards of Trustees, 2018 Annual Report of the Boards of Trustees of the Federal Hospital Insurance and Federal Supplementary Medical Insurance Trust Funds (Washington, D.C.: June 5, 2018). GAO designated Medicare as a high-risk program in 1990 due to its size, complexity, and susceptibility to mismanagement and improper payments, and it remains on GAO's high-risk list for these reasons. See GAO, High-Risk Series: Progress on Many High-Risk Areas, While Substantial Efforts Needed on Others, GAO-17-317 (Washington, D.C.: Feb. 15, 2017).

the next 7 years, Medicaid expenditures are expected to increase significantly, reaching just over $1 trillion in 2026.

PBGC

The PBGC insures the pension benefits of most private sector DB plans through one of its two programs: the Single-Employer Insurance Program and the Multiemployer Insurance Program. The single-employer program is the larger of the two programs. As of the end of fiscal year 2018, the single-employer program insured about 26 million workers and retirees participating in about 23,400 private sector single-employer DB plans. As of the end of fiscal year 2018, the multiemployer program insured about 11 million workers and retirees in about 1,400 private sector DB plans created through a collective bargaining agreement between two or more employers and a union.

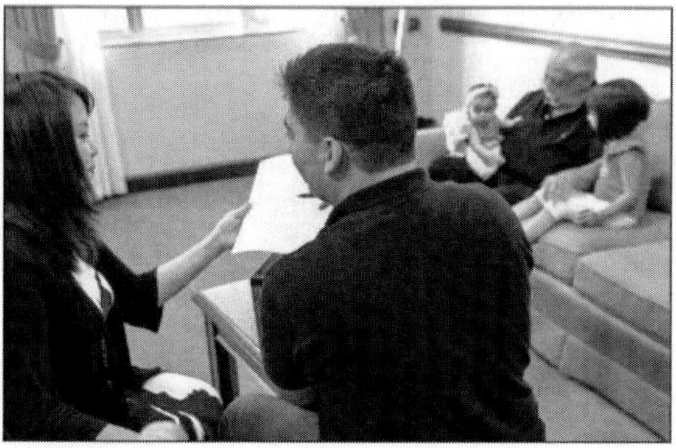

Source: GAO. | GAO-19-342T.

Although PBGC is one of the largest of any federal government corporations, with over $110 billion in assets, its pension benefit guarantees are increasingly at risk due to its substantial liabilities. At the end of fiscal year 2018, PBGC's net accumulated financial deficit was over $51 billion, and its exposure to potential future losses for underfunded retirement plans was estimated to be nearly $185 billion.[15]

[15] PBGC, *Annual Report 2018* (Washington, D.C.: Nov. 15, 2018).

We designated the single-employer program as high risk in July 2003 and added the multi-employer program to our high-risk list in January 2009. Concerns about PBGC's financial future have kept both programs on GAO's high-risk list. As long as PBGC's long-term financial stability remains uncertain, the retirement benefits of millions of U.S. workers and retirees are at risk of greater reductions should their benefit plans be terminated below PBGC's current guaranteed benefit levels.[16]

In contrast to Social Security, PBGC is not funded by tax revenues, but by the premiums paid by plans or their sponsors, the assets acquired from terminated plans, and investment returns on these funds. The primary drivers of the government's fiscal exposure related to PBGC's deficit are the collective financial risk of the many underfunded pension plans insured by PBGC and the long-term decline in the number of participants covered by traditional DB plans. Since 1985, there has been a 78 percent decline in the number of plans insured by PBGC and more than 13 million fewer workers actively participating in PBGC-insured plans. There has also been a recent trend of single-employer plan sponsors transferring the liability for some of their participants to insurance companies via group annuity "buy-outs," further reducing the number of participants in PBGC-covered plans. As a result of these trends, even though PBGC premium rates have increased significantly in recent years, PBGC's premium base has been eroding over time as fewer sponsors are paying premiums for fewer participants.

In addition, more recently, PBGC's net accumulated financial deficit has escalated dramatically due to the critical and declining status of a number of large multiemployer pension plans.[17] As we previously reported, PBGC's multiemployer plan is projected to become insolvent in approximately 6 years, and if that happens, participants in the insolvent multiemployer plans who rely on PBGC guarantees will receive only a

---

[16] For more information on PBGC and the high-risk list, see GAO-17-317.

[17] GAO, *Central States Pension Fund: Investment Policy Decisions and Challenges Facing the Plan*, GAO-18-106 (Washington, D.C.: June 4, 2018) and *Central States Pension Fund: Department of Labor Activities under the Consent Decree and Federal Law*, GAO-18-05 (Washington, D.C.: June 4, 2018).

small fraction of current statutory guarantees. According to PBGC, most participants would receive less than $2,000 a year, and in many cases less.

Social Safety Net Programs

Our prior work has found that federally-funded services for older Americans were not reaching many older adults who may need them, and that the funding for these programs had decreased while the number of older adults had increased.[18] The federal government helps provide state and local governments with funding for a broad array of home and community-based services for older adults through multiple federal agencies and programs.[19] In addition to long-term care services funded by Medicaid, these programs also include services funded under the Older Americans Act of 1965, as amended, which provides grants to states for such services as home-delivered and congregate meals, home-based care, transportation, and housing. In our 2015 report, we recommended that the Department of Health and Human Services (HHS) should facilitate development of a cross-agency federal strategy to help ensure that federal resources are used effectively and efficiently to support a comprehensive system of home and community-based services and related supports for older adults. While HHS agreed with our recommendation, the agency has yet to develop a cross-agency strategy involving all five agencies that fund these services.[20]

As the number of older adults needing assistance continues to grow, the gap in services can only be expected to widen. Absent any changes, state and local governments are facing—and will continue to face—a gap

---

[18] See GAO, *Older Adults: Federal Strategy Needed to Help Ensure Efficient and Effective Delivery of Home and Community-Based Services and Supports*, GAO-15-190 (Washington, D.C.: May 20, 2015); and *Older Americans Act: Updated Information on Unmet Need for Services,* GAO-15-601R (Washington, D.C.: June 10, 2015).

[19] GAO, *State and Local Governments' Fiscal Outlook 2018 Update*, GAO-19-208SP (Washington, D.C.: Dec. 13, 2018).

[20] GAO is currently conducting a study on the accessibility of home and community-based services in rural areas. The report is expected to be issued in Spring 2019.

between receipts and expenditures in the coming years, putting greater pressure on the federal government to increase funding.[21]

Pillar Two: Employer-Sponsored Retirement Plans

The second pillar of the U.S. retirement system, employer-sponsored retirement plans, is also an important source of income relied upon by many Americans in their retirement. However, not everyone has access to employer-sponsored plans, and among those who do, certain provisions and requirements of the plans can make it difficult for individuals to accumulate savings over time.[22]

Bureau of Labor Statistics data indicate that about one-third of private sector workers in the United States did not have access to an employer-sponsored retirement plan in 2016, and about two-thirds did.[23] Of those with access, the vast majority (about 76 percent) participated in the plan, either because they were automatically enrolled by the plan sponsor or they chose to participate.

---

[21] Since 2007, GAO has published simulations of long-term fiscal trends in the state and local government sector, which have consistently shown that the sector faces long-term fiscal pressures. For the most recent of these reports, see GAO-19-208SP.

[22] The challenges discussed here about employer-sponsored plans are applicable primarily to private sector workers, as the challenges faced by public sector workers are somewhat different. Virtually all public sector workers have access to employer-sponsored retirement plans, and in most cases, defined benefit plans. However, public sector plans are not governed by most of the substantive requirements under ERISA, including PBGC insurance.

[23] Bureau of Labor Statistics, *National Compensation Survey, Access, participation, and take-up rates for retirement benefits* (Washington, D.C.: July 2017. In this testimony, we define "access to an employer-sponsored retirement plan" to mean that a worker's employer is offering a plan and that the worker is eligible to participate in the plan. In our 2015 report on retirement plan coverage, we found similar results using Survey of Income and Program Participation (SIPP) data matched with W2 tax data. We calculated that 61 percent of private sector workers had access to an employer-sponsored retirement plan, while 39 percent did not. In addition, in our 2015 report, we estimated that another 15 percent chose not to participate, even though they had access so that, overall, about half of private sector workers lacked coverage from a workplace plan. See GAO, *Retirement Security: Federal Action Could Help State Efforts to Expand Private Sector Coverage,* GAO-15-556 (Washington, D.C.: Sept. 10, 2015).

Source: GAO. | GAO-19-342T.

Although individuals without access to an employer-sponsored plan can save for retirement on their own, having access to an employer-sponsored retirement plan makes it easier to save, and more likely that an individual will have another source of income in retirement beyond Social Security. Our prior work found that employees working for smaller firms and in certain industries, such as leisure and hospitality, are significantly less likely to have access to an employer-sponsored plan compared with those working in larger firms and in certain other industries, such as information services. Also, we found that low-income workers are much less likely than high-income workers to have access to an employer-sponsored plan.

Among those individuals who have access to employer-sponsored plans in the private sector, the structure of plans has changed over time, with a shift from traditional DB pension plans to defined contribution (DC) plans, such as 401(k)s, as the primary type of retirement plan (see Figure 5). DB plans are traditional retirement plans that generally promise to provide a benefit for the life of the participant, based on a formula specified in the plan that typically takes into account factors such as an employee's salary, years of service, and age at retirement. DC plans are employer-sponsored account-based retirement plans, such as a 401(k) plan, that allow individuals to accumulate tax-advantaged retirement savings in an individual account based on employee and/or employer contributions, and the investment returns (gains and losses) earned on the account. The amount of assets held in individual retirement accounts (IRA) also has increased significantly. Most of the assets in IRAs are funded by assets rolled over from DC plans, and sometimes DB plans, when individuals change jobs or retire.

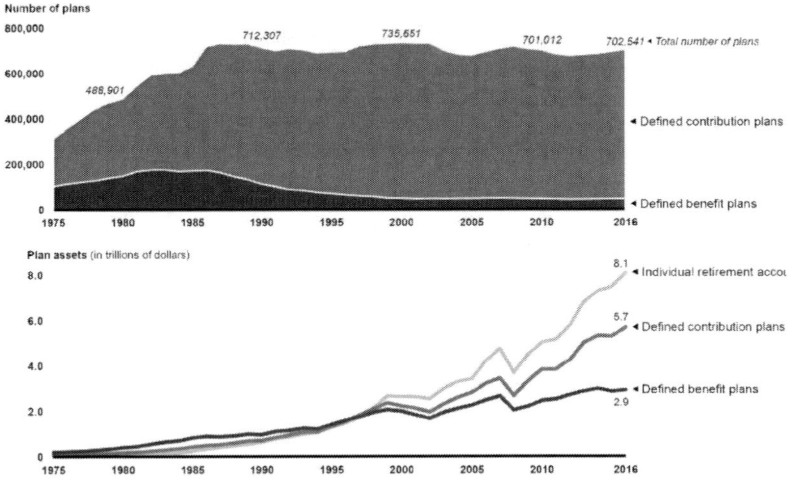

Source: GAO analysis of data from the U.S. Department of Labor and the Investment Company Institute. | GAO-19-342T.

Figure 5. Trends in Private Sector Retirement Plans since 1975.

With DB plans, participants can accumulate retirement savings simply by continuing to work for the employer offering the plan, and the employer is responsible for ensuring that the amount in the plan is sufficient to pay promised benefits at retirement. However, even when DB plans were more prevalent, many workers did not have access, and those with access to DB plans could still face challenges under certain circumstances. For example, when DB plan participants change employers, their accrued benefits are less portable than accrued savings in a DC plan. If the change in employers takes place before they have met vesting requirements, DB plan participants can lose all the benefits accumulated from employer contributions to that point, which in the private sector, generally means everything.[24] Also, for DB plans that base benefits on final average salary, benefit accruals are significantly "backloaded." As a result, if a DB plan participant changes employers mid-career, it could result in missing out on the time when the biggest benefit accruals would have occurred. In addition, when entering retirement, although those with DB plans can generally rely on receiving a set monthly benefit for life, they may still face challenges. For example, participants in certain financially troubled plans—such as those in the multiemployer plans discussed earlier—could see their benefits being suspended or cut. In addition, if a DB plan participant is offered and accepts a lump-sum payment in place of a lifetime annuity, the participant may face challenges similar to those with DC accounts in terms of managing the spend down of their retirement savings.

With DC plans, responsibility for planning and managing retirement savings is shifted from employers to employees. Participants in DC plans are often required to make complex financial decisions—decisions that generally require financial literacy and that could have significant consequences for their financial security throughout retirement. For example, workers with DC plans have to decide whether to participate in the plan, how much to contribute to their accounts and how to manage their investments to strike the right balance between risk and returns.

One way DC plan enrollment and contribution levels can be encouraged is by putting automatic mechanisms in place. For example, DC plan sponsors can encourage participation in the plan by adopting auto-enrollment, whereby eligible workers are enrolled into a plan automatically, unless they choose to opt out. DC plan sponsors can also encourage increases in contribution rates by adopting auto-escalation, whereby the employee's contributions are automatically increased to a predetermined level on a set schedule, unless they choose to opt out.

Participants in DC plans also have to decide whether to borrow from their accounts if other needs arise, or cash out their accounts when they

---

[24] ERISA requires that retirement plan participants' rights to their accrued benefit derived from their own contributions be nonforfeitable. However, as noted earlier, employees with private sector DB plans generally do not contribute to these plans, so, in most instances, all unvested accrued benefits would be lost when a change of employment takes place.

change jobs. When leaving an employer, those with DC accounts may be allowed to transfer their accumulated balances into a new employer plan or an individual retirement account (IRA), but they may also be tempted to their accounts, even though they may face associated tax consequences. Similarly, when entering retirement, those with DC accounts may decide to transfer the account balance into an IRA, or they may decide to receive the funds in a lump-sum payment. While some DC plans also offer monthly payments through an annuity, most do not provide lifetime income options or other options that can help participants draw down their retirement funds in a systematic way.

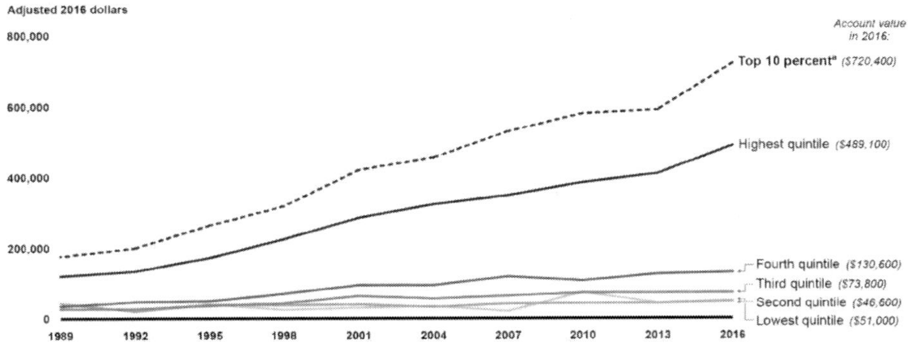

Source: GAO analysis of the Federal Reserve Board of Governor's 2016 Survey Consumer Finances Data. | GAO-19-342T.

Note: Retirement account balances include savings in individual retirement accounts as well as 401(k) or other defined contribution account savings. The changes over time are cross-sectional comparisons, not longitudinal ones—that is, the households in a particular quintile in one year may not be the same households in that quintile in another year.

[a] The top 10 percent is also included in the highest quintile.

Figure 6. All Households' Average Retirement Account Balances, by Income Quintiles, 1989-2016.

Findings from the most recent SCF indicate that an individual's ability to accumulate retirement savings depends on the individual's income level. In addition, the disparities in average account balances by income level have increased markedly over time (see Figure 6). For example, according to SCF data, households in the top 10 percent of income level appeared to be substantially better prepared for retirement than most others, with an average account balance of more than $720,000 in 2016. In contrast, households with below average income, in the second quintile, had an average account balance of about $47,000. Among lower-income households, our prior work suggests that cashing out accounts when changing jobs may be a significant drain on retirement savings, along with unexpected events that may also cause them to withdraw funds from their accounts prior to retirement.[25]

Retirement experts have posited a variety of reasons for employers' shift to DC plans. One oft-cited reason is that the structure of DC plans gives employers better control over how much they spend on wages and benefits packages. With DC plans, employers may choose whether to make contributions to participants' individual accounts; in contrast, DB plans promise a certain future monthly benefit to employees in retirement, and the employer must bear the risk of making adequate contributions to the plan to make good on that promise. Another reason retirement experts cite for the shift to DC plans was the introduction of 401(k) accounts in the Internal Revenue Code in 1978, which they credit with fostering the adoption of account-based plans by sanctioning the use of salary deferrals as a source of contributions. Some retirement experts have also suggested that employees' preferences and demands have changed over time, making DC plans more feasible and, in some respects, more appealing. For example, some analysts have noted that the portability of an account-based plan can be better suited to meet the needs of a more mobile workforce.

Pillar Three: Individuals' Savings and Other Resources

The third pillar of the retirement savings system—individuals' personal savings—is the remaining important source of retirement income, and it also faces certain risks and challenges. Personal savings can include a variety of assets, such as amounts saved from income or wages;

---

[25] GAO, *Retirement Security: Low Defined Contribution Savings May Pose Challenges*, GAO-16-408 (Washington, D.C.: May 5, 2016).

contributions to accounts outside of a retirement plan; non-retirement financial wealth that is inherited or accumulated over time; and equity from tangible assets such as a home. These savings are expected to augment any income from the first two pillars: Social Security and employer-sponsored retirement plans.

Over the past several decades, however, the personal saving rate—which is calculated as the proportion of disposable income that households save—has trended steeply downward, from a high of 14.2 percent in 1975, to a low of 3.1 percent in 2005, before recovering somewhat to 6.8 percent in 2018 (see Figure 7).[26]

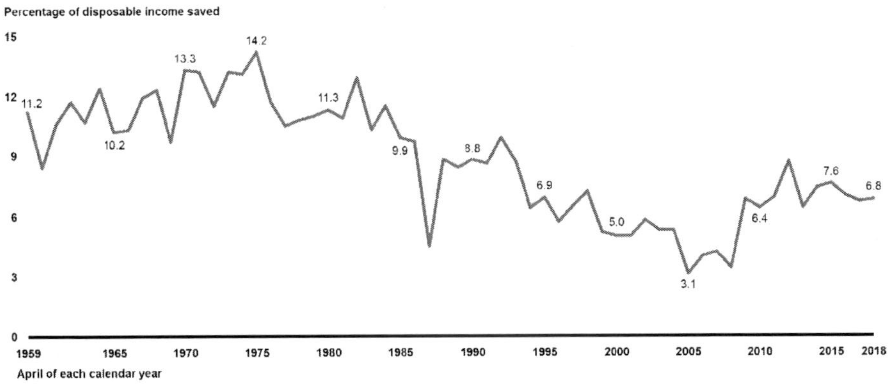

Source: U.S. Bureau of Economic Analysis. | GAO-19-342T.

Figure 7. Trend in U.S. Personal Saving Rate, 1959-2017.

While the specific implications of a historically low national saving rate on any current or future retiree are less clear, the decline in the U.S. personal savings rate over time is concerning and could have implications for retirement security, particularly when coupled with the recent trend of low wage growth. After accounting for inflation, average wages remain near the levels they were in the 1970s for most individuals (see Figure 8), adding to the difficulty of increasing their level of saving.

---

[26] It is important to note that the saving rate is an average, reflecting all households in the United States, across various stages of life.

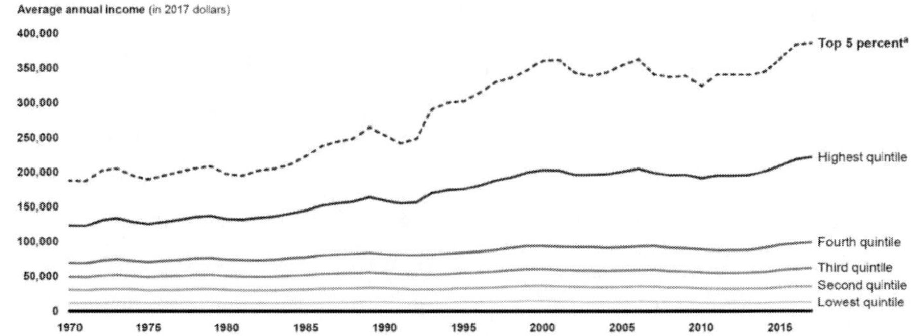

Source: U.S. Census Bureau. | GAO-19-342T.

Note: The changes over time are cross-sectional comparisons, not longitudinal ones—that is, the households in a particular quintile in one year may not be the same households in that quintile in another year.

[a] The top 5 percent is also included in the highest quintile.

Figure 8. Mean Household Incomes, by Quintiles and Top 5 Percent, 1970–2017.

In addition, many households have accumulated little wealth. SCF data show that among households in which the head of the household was working, the average value of all financial assets, excluding savings in retirement accounts, was $70,700 in 2016.[27] For households in which the head was retired, this average was $89,700.

For those who become home owners and build up equity in a home, this equity can serve as an important asset, providing a potential income source in retirement either by selling the home or obtaining a reverse mortgage. However, increased household debt levels may affect the amount of income available from this source, as well as from other assets. Data on the make-up of debt indicate that home ownership has been declining, while education debt has been rising, especially since 2013.

Another challenge with implications for individuals' ability to accumulate personal savings is that economy-wide, aggregate health care expenditures are projected to continue to grow as a percentage of the overall economy, and individuals have to contend with rising health care costs as they strive to save for retirement. CMS projections estimate that

---

[27] This estimate includes retirement savings, which cannot be easily separated out. All amounts are in 2016 dollars.

the annual growth rate of out-of-pocket health care spending for the U.S. population, per capita, will increase from 3.0 percent in 2018 to about 3.8 percent by 2026. While these costs are projected to rise for the population as a whole, individuals age 65 and over face the highest out-of-pocket health-related expenses. Further, health care expenses can be larger relative to other expenses for many retirees and hard to predict, making the amount of income retirees need to plan to spend on health care difficult to determine.

Simultaneously, trends in longer life expectancy have the potential to increase economic vulnerability for retirees. Specifically, life expectancy for those age 65 or older has increased significantly over the past century and is projected to continue to increase. For example, a man turning 65 in 2030 is expected to live to age 85.0, on average, an additional 5.3 years compared to a man who turned 65 in 1980, who was only expected to live to age 79.7, on average. A woman turning 65 in 2030 is expected to live to age 87.2, on average, an additional 3.5 years compared to a woman who turned 65 in 1980, who was only expected to live to age 83.8, on average.

Moreover, these life expectancies are averages, with some individuals living well beyond their life expectancy. As a result, people must now prepare for this greater longevity risk—that is, the risk that they will spend more years in retirement and potentially outlive their savings. For those who lack sufficient personal savings or other assets to augment their Social Security benefit or income from any employer-sponsored plan, the only option to maintain a desired standard of living may be to continue working past age 65. Our prior work has found that labor force participation among older workers has increased during the last decade and that, compared to current retirees, workers age 55 or older were more likely to expect to retire later and to work during retirement. Our prior work has also identified challenges maintaining retirement savings should older workers become unemployed.[28]

---

[28] See GAO, *Retirement Security: Most Households Approaching Retirement Have Low Savings*, GAO-15-419 (Washington, D.C.: May 12, 2015) and *Unemployed Older Workers: Many Experience Challenges Regaining Employment and Face Reduced Retirement Security*, GAO-12-445 (Washington, D.C.: Apr. 25, 2012).

Source: GAO. | GAO-19-342T.

THE NEED TO RE-EVALUATE THE NATION'S APPROACH TO FINANCING RETIREMENT

Over the past 40 years, the nation has taken an incremental approach to addressing the U.S. retirement system; however, such an approach may not be able to effectively address the interrelated foundational nature of the challenges facing the system today. Without a more comprehensive re-evaluation of the myriad challenges across all three pillars of the retirement system, identifying effective, enduring solutions may be difficult, and the consequences could be significant. Unless timely action is taken, many older Americans risk not having sufficient means for a secure and dignified retirement in the future.

Retirement Issues Have Been Addressed with an Incremental Approach

Congress has generally sought to address retirement-related issues and concerns one issue at a time. As highlighted in appendix II, at least 25 laws pertaining to retirement have been enacted since ERISA.[29] Some laws—such as the Social Security Amendments of 1983 and the Pension Protection Act of 2006—made large changes to the retirement system. Other laws were more targeted. For example in 1984, Congress amended ERISA to address concerns that women were not receiving their share of private pension benefits by, among other things, permitting certain breaks in service without loss of pension credits, and changing treatment of pension benefits for widowed and divorced spouses. Similarly, in 1996, Congress created a simplified retirement savings vehicle for employers with 100 or fewer employees to help address concerns that smaller employers were not sponsoring plans.

The number of agencies that play roles in the current retirement system has also contributed to the incremental approach to addressing concerns, with no single federal agency being responsible for taking a broad view of the system as a whole. As described earlier, there are at least 10 agencies that have a role in overseeing some part of the system, or that are involved in providing supports and services to older Americans. In addition to DOL, IRS, and PBGC, which are the agencies generally responsible for administering ERISA, SSA administers the Social Security program; and the Department of Health and Human Services oversees CMS, which administers the health care programs for retirees. In addition, various other agencies play a role in providing a range of services and supports to assist older adults through retirement.

Having multiple agencies involved in the system has also contributed to a complex web of programs and requirements. For example, our prior work identified more than 130 reports and disclosures stemming from provisions of ERISA and the Internal Revenue Code. Although each plan sponsor is required to submit only certain of these reports and disclosures, determining which ones can be challenging, and we found that the agencies' online resources to aid plan sponsors with this task were neither

[29] For further details and examples, see the chronology of retirement-related legislation since 1960 in app. II.

comprehensive nor up to date.[30] We made several recommendations to address these issues that have not been fully implemented.

Need for More Comprehensive Reform of the U.S. Retirement System

While three federal commissions have focused on various retirement issues (see app. III), it has been nearly 40 years since the last comprehensive evaluation of the nation's approach to financing retirement by a federal commission. The 1979 President's Commission on Pension Policy conducted a broad study of retirement-related issues and made a series of over-arching recommendations, such as creation of a minimum universal pension system that would provide a portable benefit for all workers that would be a supplement to Social Security. Other recommendations included federal protections for participants in state and local government plans, more consistent tax treatment of pension plans and retirement savings vehicles, provisions to strengthen Social Security, as well as proposals regarding employment of older workers and disability programs.[31] However, many of the commission's recommendations were not implemented.

The issues identified nearly 40 years ago by the 1979 commission's comprehensive re-evaluation of the U.S. retirement system continue to be issues facing the nation today. In fact, these issues have only become more complex and more urgent due to fundamental changes that have occurred since 1979—especially the growing fiscal exposure to the federal government and the shift from DB to DC plans, with its associated increase in risks and responsibilities for individual workers. Taken together, these changes may make it harder for retirees to achieve financial security in retirement, especially for those without access to employer-sponsored plans and at the lower end of the income scale.

---

[30] GAO, *Private Pensions: Clarity of Required Reports and Disclosures Could Be Improved*, GAO-14-92 (Washington, D.C.: Nov. 21, 2013).

[31] For more details on the 1979 commission, see app. III.

Source: GAO. | GAO-19-342T.

A panel of 15 retirement experts convened by GAO in November 2016 agreed that there is a need for a new comprehensive evaluation of the U.S. retirement system.[32] They noted weaknesses in the current system's ability to help ensure that all individuals can provide for a secure retirement. They also discussed the burden that the current system's complexity places on individuals, employers, and federal government. Although there was agreement among many panelists that a more comprehensive approach would be needed to provide a secure retirement for future retirees, opinions varied on the types of solutions needed. For example, some panelists suggested that a new government-sponsored savings vehicle should be created, while others supported modifying the existing employer-sponsored system to make any needed changes.

In addition, several panelists commented on how the current system can be overly complex and confusing for employers, especially small employers. They discussed how the current private sector system poses financial and litigation risk for employers, especially with respect to investment decisions, fiduciary duty, and fees. For example, one panelist suggested that DC plan sponsors may welcome the federal government providing more guidance on the types of investments that would be regarded as prudent and safe as a way to reduce their litigation risk.

Panelists also noted that the experiences of other countries can provide useful insights for ways to improve U.S. retirement programs and policies.

[32] For more information on the panelists, see app. I.

For example, some panelists described the approach being taken by the United Kingdom (UK) as a potential model for expanding access to retirement savings plans. In the UK model, universal access for workers was implemented by mandating that all employers automatically enroll employees in either their own or the government-sponsored retirement savings plan, the National Employment Savings Trust.[33]

Table 1. Policy Goals for Evaluating Potential Options for Reforming the U.S. Retirement System

Goals	Reasons for considering reform
Promote universal access to a retirement savings vehicle	About one-third of U.S. private sector workers do not have access to an employer-sponsored retirement plan
Ensure greater retirement income adequacy	Many Americans are at risk of relying solely on Social Security in retirement
Improve options for the spend down phase of retirement	Plans may not provide sufficient tools to aid retirees in the spend down of their savings, including the absence of lifetime income options in most defined contribution plans.
Reduce complexity and risk for both plan participants and plan sponsors	Decisions related to managing retirement savings and plan sponsorship have reached a level of complexity that participants and plan sponsors, respectively, find difficult to navigate
Stabilize fiscal exposure to the federal government	As the number of retirees increases, so does the financial stress on government programs serving the aging population

Source: GAO analysis. I GAO-19-342T.

In our 2017 report, we suggested five policy goals for a reformed U.S. retirement system as a starting point for discussion: (1) promoting universal access to a retirement savings vehicle, (2) ensuring greater retirement income adequacy, (3) improving options for the spend down phase of retirement, (4) reducing complexity and risk for both participants and plan sponsors, and (5) stabilizing fiscal exposure to the federal government (see Table 1 for more detail on these goals).

[33] For further discussion of NEST, see GAO-15-556.

Reforming the nation's retirement system to create a system that meets all of these goals, or others identified by the Congress, will require a careful and deliberative approach. For example, some type of consensus about the goals would need to be established as a first step. Broad questions are likely to be raised about how each of the goals should be achieved. The examination of relevant issues by past federal commissions, the discussions at our November 2016 panel, as well as what we can learn from the experiences of other countries, further illustrate how complex any reform effort is likely to be. Also, we recognize that some of these goals may compete with each other—in particular, ensuring greater retirement security and minimizing fiscal exposure to the federal government. Therefore, a balanced approach will be required, which can only result from a more holistic examination of the issues by those representing a broad range of perspectives.

As a result, we recommended that Congress consider establishing an independent commission to comprehensively examine the U.S. retirement system and make recommendations to clarify key policy goals for the system and improve the nation's approach to promoting more stable retirement security. We suggested that such a commission include representatives from government agencies, employers, the financial services industry, unions, participant advocates, and researchers, among others, to help inform policymakers on changes needed to improve the current U.S. retirement system.

Chairman Collins, Ranking Member Casey, and Members of the Committee, this concludes my prepared remarks. I would be happy to answer any questions that you may have.

We convened a panel of retirement experts in November 2016 to obtain their insights on the condition of retirement in the United States and various options for a new approach to help ensure that all individuals can provide for a secure retirement. This appendix provides a description of our methodology for selecting the panel. (See text box for final list of 15 experts participating in our panel.)

Appendix I: GAO's Expert Panel on the State of Retirement

State of Retirement Panel Participants (Positions are as of November 2016)	
William Bortz Michael S. Gordon Fellow Pension Rights Center **Phyllis Borzi** Assistant Secretary of Labor Employee Benefits Security Administration **Harry Conaway** President & CEO Employee Benefit Research Institute **Warren Cormier** CEO and Founder Boston Research Technologies **Teresa Ghilarducci** Professor of Economics and Director of the Schwartz Center for Economic Policy Analysis The New School for Social Research **Bill Hallmark** Vice President for Pensions American Academy of Actuaries **Will Hansen** Senior Vice President for Retirement Policy ERISA Industry Committee **Cindy Hounsell** President Women's Institute for a Secure Retirement	**Regina Jefferson** Professor of Law Columbus School of Law The Catholic University of America **David John** Senior Strategic Policy Advisor AARP **Melissa Kahn** Managing Director, Retirement Policy Strategist State Street Global Advisors **Hank Kim** Executive Director & Counsel The National Conference on Public Employee Retirement Systems **Diane Oakley** Executive Director National Institute on Retirement Security **Virginia Reno** Deputy Commissioner for Retirement and Disability Policy Social Security Administration **Sita Nataraj Slavov** Professor of Public Policy, Schar School of Policy and Government George Mason University

Source: GAO. | GAO-19-342T.

Methodology for Selecting the Panel and Analyzing Their Remarks

To identify the experts to invite to this meeting, we compiled an initial list based on interviews with experts conducted during recent GAO retirement income security work and the organizations invited to participate in a 2005 GAO forum on the future of the defined benefit system and the Pension Benefit Guaranty Corporation.[34] Potential experts were identified based on the following criteria:

- Organizational type: To ensure that we considered the unique roles or situations of various entities involved in retirement income policy, we selected panelists from the federal government, state or local government, research institutes or universities, advocacy or membership organizations, and financial services firms.
- Organizational reputation: To ensure that our panelists span political perspectives, we selected panelists from organizations known to be conservative, moderate, and liberal (to the extent the reputation for the organization could be easily identified).
- Subject matter expertise: To ensure that the discussion considered as many aspects of retirement income security as possible, we selected panelists with expertise across a range of areas, including defined benefit (DB) plans, defined contribution (DC) plans, individual retirement accounts (IRA), demographic trends, vulnerable populations, actuarial science, income in retirement, financial literacy, and behavioral finance.
- Range of views: To ensure that our discussion was inclusive of different philosophies regarding the role of government with regard to the population and the economy, we selected panelists to represent the viewpoints of individuals and business.

---

[34] GAO, *Highlights of a GAO Forum: The Future of the Defined Benefit System and the Pension Benefit Guaranty Corporation*, GAO-05-578SP (Washington, D.C. June 1, 2005).

- Representation of diverse groups: To ensure that the discussion benefited from different viewpoints, we selected panelists to reflect gender, racial, and ethnic diversity.

State of Retirement Expert Panel Agenda
Welcome and Opening Remarks

Session 1: How Well Is Our Current National Approach to Retirement Security Working?

Preamble: Retirement income sources in the United States have often been referred to as a three-legged stool – Social Security, employer-sponsored retirement plans, and personal savings.

1) Can the U.S, retirement system today still be accurately described by these three retirement income sources? Why/why not?
2) Are there aspects of our nation's approach to retirement income security that are working well? If so, are these aspects functioning well for all, or only for particular populations?
3) Are there aspects of our nation's approach to retirement income security that are concerning? If so, what are your biggest concerns?
4) Are there any specific populations you are particularly concerned about? If so, which ones and why?

Session 2: Reevaluating the Roles of the Federal Government, Employers, and Individuals

Preamble: Key actors in assuring a secure retirement have traditionally included the federal government, employers, and individuals, but their roles have evolved over time.

- Are there ways roles could or should be adapted or modified to address the strengths and weaknesses that have been identified for:
  - Federal government?
  - Employers?
  - Individuals?

Session 3: Reevaluating Our Nation's Approach to Retirement Policy

Preamble: Various proposals for a broader, more cohesive approach to retirement policy have been made over time.

1) Do you believe there is a need for some type of national retirement policy?
2) If such a policy were to be proposed--
   2a. What could or should be the primary goals of such a policy?
   2b. What could or should be the roles of key actors in achieving those goals?
3) What do you believe could be the greatest benefits of a national retirement policy?
4) What do you believe could be the greatest risks or potential downsides of a national retirement policy?

What barriers exist to creating a national retirement policy and how could the federal government best address these barriers?

Source: GAO. | GAO-19-342T.

An initial list of 41 potential experts was shared with GAO management officials with expertise in retirement issues, actuarial science, and strategic planning, as well as GAO methodologists, for their comments and suggestions. From this, we developed a shorter list eventually arriving at our final group of 15, listed above. These final 15 panelists were also evaluated for conflicts of interest. A conflict of interest was considered to be any current financial or other interest that might conflict with the service of an individual because it (1) could impair objectivity and (2) could create an unfair competitive advantage for any person or organization. All potential conflicts were discussed by GAO staff. The 15 experts were determined to be free of conflicts of interest, and the group as a whole was judged to have no inappropriate biases.

Panelists engaged in a day-long discussion about our nation's approach to retirement policy (see text box). The discussion was guided by a list of questions developed in advance, and the meeting was conducted by a GAO moderator to ensure that all panelists had an opportunity to participate and provide responses.

APPENDIX II: SELECTED FEDERAL LEGISLATION RELATED TO RETIREMENT SECURITY FROM 1960-PRESENT

The chronology highlights below selected federal legislation related to retirement security in the United States since 1960. It is based on a larger chronology included in our prior special product on the nation's retirement system (GAO-18-111SP). The chronology is intended to illustrate the incremental approach that the nation has taken to improving the U.S. retirement system and to convey the changes that the legislation enacted at the time. It is not intended to provide an exhaustive list of legislation that has impacted retirement in the United States, to make statements about current provisions of the law, or to provide comprehensive descriptions of each law.

Chronology of Selected Federal Legislation Shaping Retirement in the United States (1960–Present)	
1961	**Social Security Amendments of 1961** Selected provision: Enacted a provision for men, comparable to the provision enacted for women in 1956, concerning early retirement at age 62.
1962	**Self-Employed Individuals Tax Retirement Act of 1962** Selected provision: Imposed minimum distribution requirements for self-employed participants in a qualified plan generally beginning at age 70 1/2.
1965	**Social Security Amendments of 1965** Selected provisions: Enacted new titles to the Social Security Act for Medicare and Medicaid. Medicare provided hospital, post-hospital extended care, and home health coverage to almost all Americans age 65 or older; Medicaid provided states with the option of receiving federal funding for providing health care services to certain low-income and medically needy individuals.
1967	**Age Discrimination in Employment Act of 1967** Selected provisions: Made it unlawful for an employer to discriminate against any individual with respect to compensation, terms, conditions, or privileges of employment because of age; and required the Secretary of Labor to carry on a continuing program of education and information, which could include research with a view to reducing barriers to the employment of older persons.
1974	**Employee Retirement Income Security Act of 1974 (ERISA)** Selected provisions: Regulated private sector employers who offer pension or welfare benefit plans for their employees. • Title I: Imposed reporting and disclosure requirements on plans; imposed certain responsibilities on plan fiduciaries. • Title II: Strengthened participation requirements for employees age 25 and over; established vesting rules; required that a joint and survivor annuity be provided; and established minimum funding standards. In addition, provided individual retirement accounts (IRAs) for persons not covered by pensions. • Title IV: Required certain employers and plan administrators to fund an insurance system to protect certain kinds of retirement benefits (i.e., to pay premiums to the federal government's Pension Benefit Guaranty Corporation (PBGC)).
1978	**Revenue Act of 1978** Selected provisions: Established qualified deferred compensation plans called 401(k) plans after 26 U.S.C. § 401(k), which allowed for pre-tax employee contributions to such plans (known as elective deferrals).
1980	**Multiemployer Pension Plan Amendments Act of 1980** Selected provisions: Strengthened the funding requirements for multiemployer pension plans; authorized plan preservation measures for financially troubled multiemployer plans; and revised the manner in which insurance provisions applied to multiemployer plans.

Chronology of Selected Federal Legislation Shaping Retirement in the United States (1960–Present)	
1982	**Tax Equity and Fiscal Responsibility Act of 1982** Selected provisions: Reduced the maximum annual addition (employer contributions, employee contributions, and forfeitures) for each participant in a defined contribution (DC) plan; reduced the maximum annual retirement benefit for each participant in a defined benefit (DB) plan; introduced special rules for "top heavy" plans (i.e., plans in which more than 60 percent of the present value of the cumulative accrued benefits under the plan for all employees accrue to key employees, including certain owners and officers); and expanded minimum distribution requirements to all qualified plans.
1983	**Social Security Amendments of 1983** Selected provisions: Gradually raised the normal retirement age from 65 to 67, depending on an individuals' year of birth; expanded coverage; increased the self-employment tax for self-employed persons; subjected a portion of Social Security benefits to federal income tax for the first time; and changed how cost-of-living adjustments are calculated when trust funds are low.
1984	**Deficit Reduction Act of 1984** Selected provisions: Amended nondiscrimination testing requirements for 401(k) plans and required minimum distribution rules, and restricted prefunding of certain employee post-retirement welfare benefits (such as disability and medical benefits).
1984	**Retirement Equity Act of 1984** Selected provisions: Changed participation rules by lowering the minimum age that a plan may require for enrollment (from age 25 to 21), and permitted certain breaks in service without loss of pension credits. Also, strengthened treatment of pension benefits for widowed and divorced spouses.
1986	**Single-Employer Pension Plan Amendments Act of 1986** Selected provisions: Raised the per-participant PBGC premium from $2.60 to $8.50; established certain distress criteria that a contributing sponsor or substantial member of a contributing sponsor's controlled group must meet in order to terminate a single-employer plan under a distress termination; established certain criteria for PBGC to terminate a plan that does not have sufficient assets to pay benefits that are currently due (referred to as "involuntary terminations"); and created a new liability to plan participants for certain non-guaranteed benefits.
1986	**Federal Employees' Retirement System Act of 1986** Selected provisions: Established the Federal Employees' Retirement System (FERS). Unlike the existing Civil Service Retirement System (CSRS), retirement and disability benefits under FERS were structured to be fully funded by employee and employer contributions and interest earned by the bonds in which the contributions were invested. The DB under FERS was lower than under CSRS, but FERS also included a DC plan component: the Thrift Savings Plan.
1986	**Omnibus Budget Reconciliation Act of 1986** Selected provisions: Required employers that sponsor pension (DB plans) and retirement savings plans (DC plans such as a 401(k)) to provide benefit accruals or allocations for employees who work beyond their normal retirement age.

(Continued)

Chronology of Selected Federal Legislation Shaping Retirement in the United States (1960–Present)	
1986	**Tax Reform Act of 1986** Selected provisions: Established faster minimum vesting schedules; adjusted limitations on contributions and benefits for qualified plans; limited the exclusion for employee elective deferrals to $7,000; and amended nondiscrimination coverage rules. Also, restricted the allowable tax-deductible contributions to IRAs for individuals with incomes above a certain level and who participate in employer-sponsored pension plans, and imposed an additional 10 percent tax on early distributions (before age 59 1/2) from a qualified retirement plan.
1987	**Omnibus Budget Reconciliation Act of 1987** Selected provisions: Strengthened funding rules for pension plans and the level and structure of PBGC premiums.
1993	**Omnibus Budget Reconciliation Act of 1993** Selected provisions: Reduced compensation taken into account in determining contributions and benefits under qualified retirement plans, and expanded taxation of Social Security benefits.
1994	**Retirement Protection Act of 1994** Selected provisions: Strengthened funding rules for pension plans.
1996	**Small Business Job Protection Act of 1996** Selected provisions: Created a type of simplified retirement savings vehicle for small employers; added a nondiscrimination safe harbor for 401(k) plans; amended the definition highly compensated employee; and modified certain participation rules for DC plans.
1997	**Taxpayer Relief Act of 1997** Selected provision: Established Roth IRAs, under which contributions are after-tax, but distributions after age 591/2 are tax-free.
2000	**Senior Citizens' Freedom to Work Act of 2000** Selected provision: Amended the Social Security Act to eliminate the earnings limit for individuals who have reached their normal retirement age.
2001	**Economic Growth and Tax Relief Reconciliation Act of 2001 (EGTRRA)** Selected provisions: Increased the individual elective deferrals that may be made to a 401(k) plan; added "catch-up contributions" that allow individuals age 50 or older to make additional contributions; increased the maximum annual contributions to DC plans and individual retirement accounts; increased the maximum annual benefits under a DB plan; increased the compensation limit for qualified trusts; reduced the minimum vesting requirements for matching contributions; and changed the rules that permit plans to cash-out, without consent.

Chronology of Selected Federal Legislation Shaping Retirement in the United States (1960–Present)	
2002	**Sarbanes-Oxley Act of 2002** Selected provision: Added a new requirement that individual account pension plans provide notice to participants and beneficiaries in advance of periods during which the ability of participants or beneficiaries to take certain actions with respect to their accounts will be temporarily suspended, limited, or restricted (referred to as "blackout periods").
2005	**Deficit Reduction Act of 2005** Selected provisions: For plan years that begin after December 31, 2005, set the PBGC flat-rate premium for multiemployer plans at $8.00; and, for each plan year that begins after 2006, indexed future premium levels to the national average wage index.
2006	**Pension Protection Act of 2006 (PPA)** Selected provisions: Strengthened the minimum funding requirements for DB plans; set certain benefit limitations for underfunded DB plans; enhanced the protections for spouses; amended plan asset diversification requirements; changed provisions concerning the portability of pension plans; allowed the adoption of automatic enrollment and target date funds for DC plans; and increased reporting and disclosure requirements for plan sponsors.
2008	**Worker, Retiree, and Employer Recovery Act of 2008** Selected provision: Modified PPA's funding requirements to grant relief for single-employer DB plans.
2012	**Moving Ahead for Progress in the 21st Century Act (MAP-21)** Selected provisions: Provided funding relief for single-employer DB plans by changing the interest rates used to reflect a 25-year historical average; increased premium rates for sponsors of single-employer and multiemployer DB plans; and included other provisions intended to improve the governance of PBGC.
2012	**American Taxpayer Relief Act of 2012** Selected provisions: Extended the tax-free treatment of distributions from IRAs made for charitable purposes; allowed for certain in-plan transfers to a Roth account.
2014	**Multiemployer Pension Reform Act of 2014 (MPRA)** Selected provisions: Allowed severely underfunded multiemployer plans, under certain conditions and with the approval of federal regulators, the option to reduce the retirement benefits of current retirees to avoid plan insolvency; and expanded PBGC's ability to intervene when plans are in financial distress.
2018	**Bipartisan Budget Act of 2018** Selected provisions: Established a temporary Joint Select Committee on Solvency of Multiemployer Pension Plans. The goal of the Joint Select Committee was to improve the solvency of multiemployer pension plans and PBGC.

Source: GAO I GAO-19-342T.

APPENDIX III: STRUCTURE, SCOPE, AND RECOMMENDATIONS OF THREE PAST FEDERAL COMMISSIONS ON RETIREMENT ISSUES

Table 2. Federal Commissions Addressing Retirement-related Issues since 1974

Commission	President's Commission on Pension Policy	National Commission on Social Security Reform (known as the Greenspan Commission)	President's Commission to Strengthen Social Security
When and how established	In 1978, President Carter signed an executive order authorizing this commission and it was established when committee members were appointed in 1979, 5 years after the enactment of the Employee Retirement Income Security Act of 1974 (ERISA).	Established by the president and appointed by the Congress and President Reagan in 1981.	This bipartisan commission was established in May 2001 by President Bush.
Appointment of members	President Carter appointed all 11 commission members.	The President, the Majority Leader of the Senate and the Speaker of the House of Representatives at the time were each responsible for selecting five members of the commission in a bipartisan way.	President Bush appointed all 16 commission members.
Scope of study	The commission was called upon to conduct a 2-year study of the nation's pension systems and the future course of national retirement-income policies, and issue a series of reports on short-term and long-term issues with respect to retirement, survivor, and disability programs.	The commission was to conduct a study and make recommendations regarding the short-term financing crisis faced by Social Security at the time.	The commission was to study and report, using six guiding principles, specific recommendations to preserve Social Security for seniors while building wealth for younger Americans.

Commission	President's Commission on Pension Policy	National Commission on Social Security Reform (known as the Greenspan Commission)	President's Commission to Strengthen Social Security
Final report	The final report was issued in February 1981.	The final report was issued in 1983 and was the basis for the Social Security Amendments of 1983 which addressed the long-term financing problem by gradually increasing the retirement age from 65 to 67, among other things, and made other significant changes to Social Security such as expanding coverage.	The final report, "Strengthening Social Security and Creating Personal Wealth for All Americans," was issued in December 2001.

Source: GAO. I GAO-19-342T.

Since the enactment of ERISA, there have been three federal commissions on retirement issues: The President's Commission on Pension Policy, the National Commission on Social Security Reform, and the President's Commission to Strengthen Social Security (see Table 2). We examined these commissions to gain insights on possible structures for federal commissions, the scope of work these commissions can take on, and the types of recommendations they can make.

Carter Commission (1979-1981)

In 1978, President Carter signed an executive order authorizing the Carter Commission, which was established when committee members were appointed in 1979. The commission was to conduct a 2-year sturdy of the nation's pension systems and the future course of national retirement income policies. President Carter appointed all 11 commission members. The commission also had an executive director and 37 staffers. Its final report, *Coming of Age: Toward a National Retirement Income Policy*, was released in February 1981.[35]

Charge to the Carter Commission

The commission was ordered to:

- Conduct a comprehensive review of retirement, survivor, and disability programs existing in the United States, including private, federal, state, and local programs.
- Develop national policies for retirement, survivor, and disability programs that can be used as a guide by public and private programs. The policies were to be designed to ensure that the nation had effective and equitable retirement, survivor, and disability programs that took into account available resources and demographic changes expected into the middle of the next century.
- Submit to the President a series of reports including the commission's findings and recommendations on short-term and long-term issues with respect to retirement, survivor, and disability programs. The commission was charged with covering the following issues in its findings and recommendations:
    - overlaps and gaps among the private, state, and local sectors in providing income to retired, surviving, and disabled persons;
    - the financial ability of private, federal, state, and local retirement, survivor, and disability systems to meet their future obligations;
    - appropriate retirement ages, the relationship of annuity levels to past earnings and contributions, and the role of retirement, survivor, and disability programs in private capital formation and economic growth;
    - the implications of the recommended national policies for the financing and benefit structures of the retirement, survivor, and disability programs in the public and private sectors; and

---

[35] President's Commission on Pension Policy, *Coming of Age: Toward a National Retirement Income Policy* (Feb. 26, 1981).

- o specific reforms and organizational changes in the present systems that may be required to meet the goals of the national policies.

Carter Commission's Recommendations

In its final report, the Carter Commission prescribed a goal for retirement income policy and made numerous recommendations. According to the report, a desirable retirement income goal is the replacement of pre-retirement income from all sources. Recommendations focused on strengthening four areas: employer pensions, Social Security, "individual efforts" (personal savings, employment of older workers, and disability), and public assistance. Recommendations were also made regarding the administration of the U.S. retirement system. Examples of ways to strengthen each area follow:

- Strengthening Employer Pensions. The commission recommended establishing a Minimum Universal Pension System (MUPS) for all workers. MUPS was intended to provide a portable benefit that was supplemental to Social Security. It would have built upon existing employer plans and existing plans that did not meet the requirements would have needed to be amended. Another recommendation was to establish a Public Employee Retirement Income Security Act (i.e., a public sector version of ERISA) so that public and private sector employees would receive similar protections.
- Strengthening Social Security. The commission recommended mandatory universal coverage, raising the retirement age for workers who were not approaching retirement, re-examining or making adjustments to the special minimum benefit as well as the spousal benefit and other miscellaneous benefits.
- Strengthening Individual Efforts. The commission recommended that contribution and benefit limitations for all individuals should be treated more consistently for all types of retirement savings. The commission also recommended a refundable tax credit for

low- and moderate-income individuals to encourage saving for retirement. For older workers, recommendations included improving unemployment benefits to provide short-term income maintenance and keep them in the labor force. The commission also recommended further in-depth study of the Disability Insurance program.

- Strengthening Public Assistance. The commission made recommendations to address inflation protection for retirement income and setting Social Security's Supplemental Security Income at the poverty line level and eliminating its assets test.
- Administration. The commission recommended consolidating the administration of all federal retirement systems as well as consolidating ERISA administrative functions under one entity. It also recommended an interdepartmental task force to coordinate executive branch agencies dealing with retirement income.

Greenspan Commission (1981-1983)

In 1981, President Reagan signed an executive order establishing the Greenspan Commission. The President asked the commission to conduct a 1-year study and propose realistic, long-term reforms to put Social Security on sound financial footing and to reach bipartisan consensus so these reforms could be passed into law. The President, the Senate Majority Leader, and the Speaker of the House of Representatives each made five appointments, with no more than three of the five appointments coming from one political party to ensure a bipartisan commission. The President was responsible for appointing the commission's chair. The commission had a staff of 23. The final report, *Report of the National Commission on Social Security Reform*, was issued on January 20, 1983.[36]

---

[36] National Commission on Social Security Reform, *Report of the National Commission on Social Security Reform* (Washington. D.C.: Jan. 20, 1983).

Charge to the Greenspan Commission

The commission was ordered to

- Review relevant analyses of the current and long-term financial condition of the Social Security Trust Funds
- Identify problems that could threaten the long-term solvency of such funds
- Analyze potential solutions to such problems that would both assure the financial integrity of the Social Security system and appropriate benefits
- Provide appropriate recommendations to the Secretary of Health and Human Services, the President, and Congress.

Greenspan Commission's Recommendations

In its final report, the Greenspan Commission found both short and long term financing problems and recommended that action should be taken to strengthen the financial status of the Social Security program. Twelve commission members voted in favor of a consensus package with 13 recommendations to address Social Security's short-term deficit, including, for example:

- Expand Social Security to include coverage for nonprofit and civilian federal employees hired after January 1, 1984, as well as prohibiting the withdrawal of state and local employees.
- Shift cost-of-living adjustments to an annual basis.
- Make the Social Security Administration its own separate, independent agency.
- Make adjustments to spousal and survivor benefits.
- Revise the schedule for Social Security payroll taxes.
- Establish the taxation of benefits for higher-income persons.

In addition, these 12 commission members agreed that the long-range deficit should be reduced to approximately zero, and their recommendations were projected to meet about two-thirds of the long-range financial deficit. Seven of the 12 members agreed that the remaining one-third of the long-range financial deficit should be met by a deferred, gradual increase in the normal retirement age, while the other 5 members agreed that it should be met by an increase in future contribution rates starting in 2010.

After the Greenspan Commission's final report was issued, Congress enacted the Social Security Amendments of 1983. The amendments incorporated many of the Greenspan Commission's recommendations and made comprehensive changes to Social Security coverage, financing, and benefit structure. These changes included addressing Social Security's long-term financing problems by gradually increasing the retirement age from 65 to 67, among other things.

President's Commission to Strengthen Social Security (2001)

In 2001, President Bush signed an executive order establishing the President's Commission to Strengthen Social Security. The President asked the Commission to produce an interim report describing the challenges facing the Social Security system and the criteria by which the Commission would evaluate reform proposals, as well as a final report to set forth the Commission's recommendations regarding how to strengthen Social Security with personal accounts. The commission had a staff of sixteen members appointed by the President, of which no more than eight members were of the same political party. The final report, *Strengthening Social Security and Creating Personal Wealth for All Americans*, was issued in December 2001.[37]

---

[37] President's Commission to Strengthen Social Security, *Strengthening Social Security and Creating Personal Wealth for All Americans* (Washington. D.C.: Dec. 21, 2001).

Charge to the President's Commission to Strengthen Social Security

The commission was asked to submit to the President bipartisan recommendations to modernize and restore fiscal soundness to the Social Security system according to the following principles:

- Modernization must not change Social Security benefits for retirees or near-retirees;
- The entire Social Security surplus must be dedicated to Social Security only;
- Social Security payroll taxes must not be increased;
- Government must not invest Social Security funds in the stock market;
- Modernization must preserve Social Security's disability and survivors components; and
- Modernization must include individually controlled, voluntary personal retirement accounts, which will augment the Social Security safety net.

The President's Commission to Strengthen Social Security Recommendations

In its final report, the Commission offered three models for Social Security reform. All three models shared a common framework whereby voluntary individual accounts were established in exchange for a reduction in the Social Security defined portion of benefit. According to the report:

- Reform Model 1 would have established a voluntary personal account option, but did not specify other changes in Social Security's benefit and revenue structure and was intended to achieve full long-term sustainability.
- Reform Model 2 would have enabled future retirees to receive Social Security benefits that would be at least as great as then current retirees and increased Social Security benefits paid to low-income workers. Model 2 would have established a voluntary

personal account without raising taxes or requiring additional worker contributions. It was intended to achieve solvency and balanced Social Security revenues and costs.

- Reform Model 3 would have established a voluntary personal account option that generally enabled workers to reach or exceed then-current scheduled benefits and wage replacement ratios. It was intended to achieve solvency by adding revenues and by slowing benefit growth less than price indexing.

In: Retirement
Editor: Thomas M. Osborne
ISBN: 978-1-53615-703-1

Chapter 2

THE SOCIAL SECURITY RETIREMENT AGE*

Zhe Li

SUMMARY

The Social Security *full retirement age* (FRA) is the age at which workers can first claim *full* Social Security retired-worker benefits. Among other factors, a worker's monthly benefit amount is affected by the age at which he or she claims benefits relative to the FRA. Benefit adjustments are made based on the number of months before or after the FRA the worker claims benefits. The adjustments are intended to provide the worker with roughly the same total lifetime benefits, regardless of when he or she claims benefits, based on average life expectancy. Claiming benefits before the FRA results in a reduction in monthly benefits (to take into account the longer expected period of benefit receipt); claiming benefits after the FRA results in an increase in monthly benefits (to take into account the shorter expected period of benefit receipt).

The FRA was 65 at the inception of Social Security in the 1930s. Under legislation enacted in 1983, the FRA is increasing gradually from 65 to 67 over a 22-year period (2000-2022). The FRA will reach 67 for

---

* This is an edited, reformatted and augmented version of Congressional Research Service Publication No. R44670, Updated February 28, 2018.

workers born in 1960 or later (i.e., for workers who become eligible for retirement benefits at age 62 in 2022). Currently, the FRA is 66 and 4 months for workers who become eligible for retirement benefits in 2018 (i.e., workers born in 1956).

Workers can claim *reduced* retirement benefits as early as age 62 (the *early eligibility age*). Spouses can also claim reduced retirement benefits starting at age 62. Other dependents, such as widow(er)s, can claim benefits at earlier ages. For workers with an FRA of 66, for example, claiming benefits at age 62 results in a 25% reduction in monthly benefits. For workers with an FRA of 67, claiming benefits at age 62 results in a 30% benefit reduction. A majority of retired-worker beneficiaries claim benefits before the FRA. In 2016, 39% of new retired-worker beneficiaries were age 62; almost two-thirds (66%) were under the age of 66.

Workers who delay claiming benefits until after the FRA receive a *delayed retirement credit*, which applies up to the age of 70. For workers with an FRA of 66, for example, claiming benefits at age 70 results in a 32% increase in monthly benefits. For workers with an FRA of 67, claiming benefits at age 70 results in a 24% benefit increase. In 2016, almost one-fourth (23%) of new retired-worker beneficiaries were age 66; 11% were over the age of 66.

Some lawmakers have called for increasing the Social Security retirement age in response to the system's projected financial imbalance, citing gains in life expectancy for the population overall. Other lawmakers, however, express concern that increasing the retirement age would disproportionately affect certain groups within the population, citing differences in life expectancy by socioeconomic groups. Differential gains in life expectancy are important in the context of Social Security because the actuarial adjustments for claiming benefits before or after the full retirement age are based on *average* life expectancy. Proposals to increase the retirement age are also met with concerns about the resulting hardship for certain workers, such as those in physically demanding occupations, who may be unable to work until older ages and may not qualify for Social Security disability benefits.

INTRODUCTION

The Social Security *full retirement age* (FRA) is the age at which workers can first claim *full* Social Security retired-worker benefits.[1]

[1] The full retirement age is also referred to as the normal retirement age (NRA). In statute, the term "retirement age" is used; see Social Security Act, §216(l) [42 U.S.C. §416(l)].

Among other factors, the age at which an individual begins receiving Social Security benefits has an impact on the size of the monthly benefits. Claiming benefits before the FRA can substantially reduce monthly benefits, whereas claiming benefits after the FRA can lead to a substantial increase in monthly benefits. Benefit adjustments are made based on the number of months before or after the FRA the worker claims benefits. The adjustments are intended to result in roughly the same total lifetime benefits, regardless of when the worker claims benefits, based on average life expectancy.

The FRA was 65 at the inception of Social Security in the 1930s. As part of legislation enacted in 1983, the FRA is increasing gradually from 65 to 67 over a 22-year period that started in 2000. The increase in the FRA will be fully phased-in (the FRA will reach 67) for workers born in 1960 or later (i.e., for workers who become eligible for retirement benefits at age 62 in 2022). For workers who become eligible for retirement benefits in 2018 (i.e., workers born in 1956), the FRA is 66 and 4 months.

Workers can claim Social Security retired-worker benefits as early as age 62, the *early eligibility age*. However, workers who claim benefits before the FRA are subject to a permanent reduction in their benefits. Spouses can also claim reduced retirement benefits as early as age 62. Other types of dependents can claim benefits before the age of 62.[2]

Workers who claim benefits after the FRA receive a delayed retirement credit that results in a permanent increase in their monthly benefits. The credit applies up to the age of 70. Claiming benefits after attainment of age 70 does not result in any further increase in monthly benefits.[3]

---

[2] Widow(er)'s benefits can be claimed as early as age 60; disabled widow(er)'s benefits can be claimed as early as age 50. These benefits are also subject to reduction if claimed before the FRA. There is no minimum eligibility age for dependent child's benefits. For more details, see "Benefits for the Worker's Family Members" in CRS Report R42035, *Social Security Primer*.

[3] The DRC applies to the period that begins with the month the worker attains the FRA and ends with the month before he or she attains the age of 70.

Full Retirement Age (FRA)

The FRA was 65 at the inception of Social Security. According to Robert Myers, who worked on the creation of the Social Security program in 1934 and later served in various senior and appointed capacities at the Social Security Administration (SSA), "[a]ge 65 was picked because 60 was too young and 70 was too old. So we split the difference."[4] On the other hand, SSA suggests that the Committee on Economic Security (CES) made the proposal of 65 as the retirement age due to the prevalence of private and state pensions systems using 65 as the retirement age and the favorable actuarial outcomes for 65 as the retirement age.[5]

In 1983, Congress increased the FRA as part of the Social Security Amendments of 1983[6] which made major changes to Social Security's financing and benefit structure to address the system's financial imbalance at the time.[7] Among other changes, the FRA was increased gradually from 65 to 67 for workers born in 1938 or later. Under the scheduled increases enacted in 1983, the FRA increases to 65 and 2 months for workers born in 1938. The FRA continues to increase by two months every birth year until the FRA reaches 66 for workers born in 1943 to 1954. Starting with workers born in 1955, the FRA increases again in two-month increments until the FRA reaches 67 for workers born in 1960 or later. The increase in the FRA, one of many provisions in the 1983 amendments designed to improve the system's financial outlook, was based on the rationale that it would reflect increases in longevity and improvements in the health status of workers.[8] The 1983 amendments did not change the early eligibility age

---

[4] Robert J. Myers and Richard L. Vernaci, *Within the System: My Half Century in Social Security* (Winsted, CT: ACTEX Publications, 1992), pp. 93-94.

[5] Social Security Administration (SSA), "Age 65 Retirement," at https://www.ssa.gov/history/age65.html.

[6] P.L. 98-21.

[7] An increase in the FRA is a form of benefit reduction. Those who claim benefits at the FRA, for example, receive fewer months of benefits and a reduction in the total amount of lifetime Social Security benefits.

[8] For example, see Rep. Elliott H. Levitas, "Social Security Amendments of 1983," House debate, *Congressional Record*, vol. 129, part 4 (March 9, 1983), p. 4517; Rep. Beryl Anthony, Jr., "Social Security Amendments of 1983," House debate, *Congressional Record*, vol. 129, part 4 (March 9, 1983), p. 4600.

of 62 (discussed below); however, the increase in the FRA results in larger benefit reductions for workers who claim benefits between the age of 62 and the FRA.[9] Table 1 shows the FRA by worker's year of birth under current law.

Table 1. Age to Receive Full Social Security Benefits

Year of Birth	Full Retirement Age (FRA)
1937 or earlier	65
1938	65 and 2 months
1939	65 and 4 months
1940	65 and 6 months
1941	65 and 8 months
1942	65 and 10 months
1943-1954	66
1955	66 and 2 months
1956	66 and 4 months
1957	66 and 6 months
1958	66 and 8 months
1959	66 and 10 months
1960 or later	67

Source: Social Security Administration, https://www.ssa.gov/planners/retire/ retirechart.html.
Notes: Persons born on January 1 of any year should refer to the previous year of birth.

EARLY ELIGIBILITY AGE (EEA)

Currently, the EEA is 62 for workers and spouses; this is the earliest age at which they can claim retirement benefits. Benefits claimed between age 62 and the FRA, however, are subject to a permanent reduction for "early retirement." When the original Social Security Act was enacted in 1935,[10] the earliest age to receive retirement benefits was the FRA (age 65). In 1956, the eligibility age was lowered from 65 to 62 for female

---

[9] For example, retired-worker benefits claimed at age 62 are reduced by 20% if the worker's FRA is 65, by 25% if the worker's FRA is 66, and by 30% if the worker's FRA is 67.
[10] P.L. 74-271, Social Security Act.

workers, wives, widows, and female dependent parents.[11] This was to allow wives, who traditionally were younger than their husbands, to qualify for benefits at the same time as their husbands.[12] Benefits for female workers and wives were subject to reduction if claimed between the ages of 62 and 65; the reduction did not apply to benefits for widows and female dependent parents.

In 1961, the eligibility age was lowered from 65 to 62 for men as well.[13] Benefits for male workers and husbands were subject to reduction if claimed between the ages of 62 and 65; the reduction did not apply to widowers and male dependent parents. Although the eligibility age was made consistent for male and female workers, an inconsistency remained in the calculation of benefits. A man the same age as a woman needed more Social Security credits to qualify for benefits, and, if his earnings were identical to hers, usually received a lower benefit because his earnings were averaged over a longer period. This inconsistency was addressed in legislation enacted in 1972 which provided that retirement benefits would be computed the same way for men and women (the provision was fully effective for men reaching age 62 in 1975 or later).[14]

In subsequent years, further adjustments were made to the eligibility age for surviving spouses.[15] The eligibility age was lowered to age 60 for widows (1965),[16] age 50 for disabled widow(er)s (1967),[17] and age 60 for widowers (1972).[18]

---

[11] P.L. 74-271, Social Security Act.

[12] For example, see Rep. Thomas A. Jenkins, "Social Security Amendments of 1955," House debate, *Congressional Record*, vol. 101, part 8 (July 18, 1955), p. 10778; Rep. Wilbur Mills, "Social Security Amendments of 1955," House debate, *Congressional Record*, vol. 101, part 8 (July 18, 1955), p. 10785.

[13] P.L. 87-64, Social Security Amendments of 1961.

[14] P.L. 92-603, Social Security Amendments of 1972.

[15] Benefits for surviving spouses are subject to reduction if claimed before the FRA (and other factors); see "Benefits for the Worker's Family Members" in CRS Report R42035, *Social Security Primer*.

[16] P.L. 89-97, Social Security Amendments of 1965.

[17] P.L. 90-248, Social Security Amendments of 1967.

[18] P.L. 92-603, Social Security Amendments of 1972.

ACTUARIAL MODIFICATION TO BENEFITS: CLAIMING BEFORE OR AFTER THE FRA

Benefits are adjusted based on the age at which a person claims benefits to provide roughly the same total lifetime benefits regardless of when a person begins receiving benefits, based on average life expectancy. The earlier a worker begins receiving benefits (before the FRA), the lower the monthly benefit will be, to offset the longer expected period of benefit receipt. Conversely, the longer a worker delays claiming benefits (past the FRA), the higher the monthly benefit will be, to take into account the shorter expected period of benefit receipt. The benefit adjustment is based on the number of months between the month the worker attains the FRA and the month he or she claims benefits. The day of birth is ignored for adjustment purposes, except for those born on the first of the month. Workers born on the first of the month base their FRA as if their birthday was in the previous month (e.g., someone born on February 1, 1980, who has an FRA of 67, can apply for full retirement benefits in January 2047). A calculator on SSA's website allows the user to enter his or her date of birth and the expected month of initial benefit receipt to see the effect of early or delayed retirement; the effect is shown as a percentage of the full benefit payable at the FRA.[19]

Actuarial Reduction for Claiming Benefits Before the FRA

When a worker claims benefits before the FRA, there is an *actuarial reduction* in monthly benefits. The reduction for claiming benefits before the FRA can be sizable and it is permanent; all future monthly benefits are payable at the actuarially reduced amount. For each of the 36 months immediately preceding the FRA, the monthly rate of reduction from the full retirement benefit is five-ninths of 1%. This equals a 62/3% reduction each year. For each month earlier than three years (36 months) before the FRA, the monthly rate of reduction is five-twelfths of 1%. This equals a

[19] The calculator is available at https://www.ssa.gov/oact/quickcalc/early_late.html# calculator.

5% reduction each year. The earliest a worker can claim retirement benefits is age 62. For a worker with an FRA of 67, claiming benefits at 62 results in a 30% reduction in their monthly benefit. *Table 2* shows the actuarial reduction applied to retired-worker benefits based on the FRA and the age at which benefits are claimed.[20]

Table 2. Benefit Reduction for Early Retirement by Full Retirement Age

Full Retirement	**Actuarial Reduction to Monthly Amount if Worker Claims at Age...**				
Age	62	63	64	65	66
65	20%	13 1⁄3%	6 2⁄3%	0%	-[a]
66	25%	20%	13 1⁄3%	6 2⁄3%	0%
67	30%	25%	20%	13 1⁄3%	6 2⁄3%

Source: Social Security Administration, https://www.ssa.gov/planners/retire/retire chart.html.

[a] With an FRA of 65, claiming retired-worker benefits at age 66 leads to a delayed retirement credit, resulting in an increase in monthly benefits, as opposed to a reduction.

Delayed Retirement Credit for Claiming Benefits After the FRA

Workers who claim benefits after the FRA receive a *delayed retirement credit* (DRC). As with the actuarial reduction for early retirement, the delayed retirement credit is permanent. The DRC has been modified over the years. Initially, the Social Security Amendments of 1972[21] provided a delayed retirement credit that increased benefits by one-twelfth of 1% for each month between ages 65 and 72 that a worker did not claim benefits (i.e., 1% per year). The credit, which was effective after 1970, applied only to the worker's benefit; it did not apply to a widow(er)'s benefit payable on the worker's record. The Social Security Amendments of 1977[22] increased the credit to 3% per year and included the credit in the computation of a widow(er)'s benefit.

---

[20] Actuarial reductions for spouses and widow(er)s are different; see SSA, "Benefit Reduction for Early Retirement," at https://www.ssa.gov/oact/quickcalc/earlyretire.html.

[21] P.L. 92-603.

[22] P.L. 95-216.

The credit was further increased under the Social Security Amendments of 1983.[23] As shown in *Table 3*, under current law, the amount of the credit varies based on the worker's year of birth (i.e., when the worker becomes eligible for benefits at age 62). The credit increases gradually until it reaches 8% per year (two-thirds of 1% per month) for workers born in 1943 or later (i.e., workers who become eligible for retirement benefits in 2005 or later). In addition, the maximum age at which the DRC applies was lowered from 72 to 70. Any further delay in claiming benefits past age 70 does not result in a higher benefit. The increase in the DRC was intended to ensure that workers who claim benefits after the FRA receive roughly the same total lifetime benefits as if they had claimed benefits earlier (based on average life expectancy). A worker with an FRA of 66, for example, receives a 32% benefit increase if he or she claims benefits at age 70; a worker with an FRA of 67 receives a 24% benefit increase.

Table 3. Benefit Increase for Delayed Retirement by Birth Year

Year of Birth	Monthly Credit	Annual Credit
1 9 1 6 or earlier	1/12 of 1%	1%
1917-1924	1/4 of 1%	3%
1925-1926	7/24 of 1%	3.5%
1927-1928	1/3 of 1%	4%
1929-1930	3/8 of 1%	4.5%
1931-1932	5/12 of 1%	5%
1933-1934	1 1/24 of 1%	5.5%
1935-1936	1/2 of 1%	6%
1937-1938	13/24 of 1%	6.5%
1939-1940	7/12 of 1%	7%
1941-1942	5/8 of 1%	7.5%
1943 or later	2/3 of 1%	8%

Source: Social Security Administration, https://www.ssa.gov/OP_Home/cfr20/404/404-0313.htm.

Note: Persons born on January 1 of any year should refer to the previous year of birth.

[23] P.L. 98-21.

Figure 1 illustrates the effect of claiming age on benefit levels based on an FRA of 66. If the worker claims retirement benefits at age 62, for example, his or her benefit would be equal to 75% of the full benefit amount—a 25% permanent reduction based on claiming retirement benefits four years before attaining the FRA. If the worker delays claiming retirement benefits until age 70, however, his or her benefit would be equal to 132% of the full benefit amount—a 32% permanent increase for claiming benefits four years after the FRA.

RETIREMENT EARNINGS TEST

The decision to claim Social Security benefits before the FRA results in a permanent reduction in monthly benefits for early retirement.

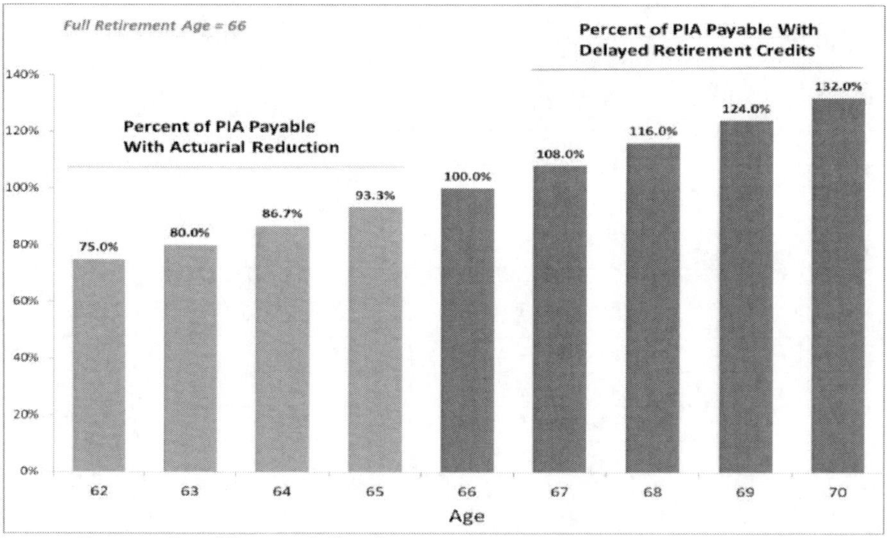

Source: Congressional Research Service.

Notes: PIA = Primary Insurance Amount. The PIA is the benefit payable to the worker at his or her FRA. Workers who become eligible for retirement benefits at age 62 in 2018 have an FRA of 66 and 4 months.

Figure 1. Effect of Claiming Age on Benefit Levels. (Based on an FRA of 66)

In addition, if a Social Security beneficiary is below the FRA and has current earnings, he or she is subject to the retirement earnings test (RET). Stated generally, Social Security benefits are withheld partially or fully, for one or more months, if current earnings exceed specified thresholds. There are two separate earnings thresholds (or *exempt amounts*) under the RET. The first (lower) threshold applies to beneficiaries who are below the FRA and *will not attain* the FRA during the year. In 2018, the lower earnings threshold is $17,040.[24] If a beneficiary has earnings that exceed the lower threshold, SSA withholds $1 of benefits for every $2 of earnings above the threshold.

The second (higher) threshold applies to beneficiaries who are below the FRA and *will attain* the FRA during the year. In 2018, the higher earnings threshold is $45,360. If a beneficiary has earnings that exceed the higher threshold, SSA withholds $1 of benefits for every $3 of earnings above the threshold. The RET no longer applies beginning with the month the beneficiary attains the FRA. Once the beneficiary attains the FRA, his or her benefits are no longer subject to withholding based on earnings.[25]

During the first year of benefit receipt, a special *monthly* earnings test applies.[26] Regardless of the amount of annual earnings in the first year of benefit receipt, benefits are not withheld for any month in which earnings do not exceed a monthly exempt amount (the monthly exempt amount is equal to 1/12 of the annual exempt amount). In 2018, the monthly exempt amounts are $1,420 ($17,040/12) and $3,780 ($45,360/12).

For example, consider a worker who claims benefits at age 62 in January 2018 and has no earnings during the year except for a consulting project that pays $20,000 in July. Although the beneficiary's annual earnings ($20,000) exceed the annual exempt amount ($17,040), benefits are withheld only for the month of July. The beneficiary has $0 earnings in

---

[24] The earnings thresholds generally increase each year based on average wage growth in the economy. See SSA, "Exempt Amounts Under the Earnings Test," at https://www.ssa.gov/OACT/COLA/rtea.html.

[25] The Senior Citizens' Freedom to Work Act of 2000 (P.L. 106-182) eliminated the RET for beneficiaries at the FRA or older.

[26] A person may claim retired-worker benefits in the middle of the year, for example, and have already earned more than the annual earnings limit under the RET.

all other months; July is the only month in which earnings exceed the monthly exempt amount ($1,420).

Benefits withheld under the RET are not "lost" on a permanent basis. When a beneficiary attains the FRA and is no longer subject to the RET, SSA automatically recalculates the benefit, taking into account any months for which benefits were partially or fully withheld under the RET. Stated generally, there is no actuarial reduction for early retirement for any month in which benefits were partially or fully withheld under the RET. The recalculation results in a higher monthly benefit going forward.[27] Starting at the FRA, the beneficiary begins to recoup the value of benefits withheld under the RET; the beneficiary recoups the full value of those benefits if he or she lives to average life expectancy.[28]

AGE DISTRIBUTION OF NEW RETIRED-WORKER BENEFICIARIES

Statistics published by SSA show that a majority of retired-worker beneficiaries claim benefits before the FRA.[29] *Figure 2* shows the age distribution of new retired-worker beneficiaries in 2016.[30] Among 2.4 million new retired-worker beneficiaries that year, 39% claimed benefits at age 62 (the first year of eligibility) and 66% were under the age of 66. About one-fourth (23%) of new retired-worker beneficiaries claimed benefits at age 66, while 11% were age 67 or older. The percentage of retired-worker beneficiaries who claim benefits at earlier ages has declined in recent years. In 2010, for example, more than one-half (52%) of new

---

[27] For more information, see CRS Report R41242, *Social Security Retirement Earnings Test: How Earnings Affect Benefits*.

[28] For more information, see SSA, Office of Retirement Policy, "Retirement Earnings Test," at https://www.ssa.gov/ retirementpolicy/program/retirement-earnings-test.html.

[29] SSA, Annual Statistical Supplement, 2017, Table 6.A4, at https://www.ssa.gov/policy/ docs/statcomps/supplement/ 2017/6a.pdf.

[30] In 2016, there were 2.9 million new retired-worker beneficiaries, including 2.4 million "new entitlements" and 0.5 million "disability conversions" (i.e., disabled-worker beneficiaries who are automatically converted to retired-worker beneficiaries when they attain the FRA). *Figure 1* does not include beneficiaries in the "disability conversion" category.

retired-worker beneficiaries were age 62 and 81% were under the age of 66.[31]

PROPOSALS TO INCREASE THE RETIREMENT AGE

The Social Security full retirement age was 65 when the program was established in the 1930s. It remained 65 until 1983, when Congress included an increase in the FRA among many provisions in the Social Security Amendments of 1983[32] which were designed to address serious near-term and long-range financing problems.

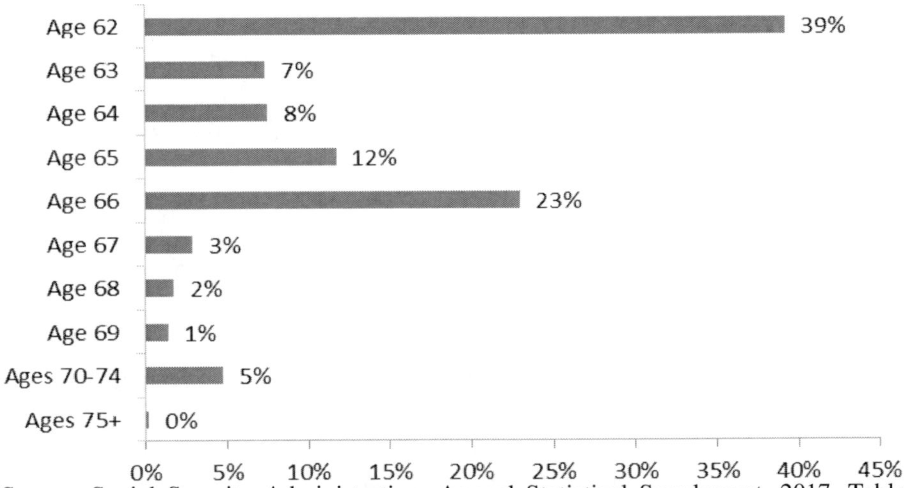

Source: Social Security Administration, Annual Statistical Supplement, 2017, Table 6.A4, https://www.ssa.gov/ policy/docs/statcomps/supplement/2017/6a.pdf.

Notes: Figure does not include disabled-worker beneficiaries who were automatically converted to retired-worker beneficiaries upon attaining the FRA. The Ages 75+ category represents 0.2% of the total.

Figure 2. Age Distribution of New Retired-Worker Beneficiaries in 2016.

[31] SSA, Annual Statistical Supplement, 2011, Table 6.A4, at https://www.ssa.gov/policy/docs/ statcomps/supplement/ 2011/6a.pdf.

[32] P.L. 98-21.

The 1983 Amendments became law on April 20, 1983. Without legislative action, it was anticipated that Social Security benefits could not be paid on time beginning in *July 1983*.[33] The 1983 provision that increased the FRA from 65 to 67 continues to be phased-in; it will be fully phased-in by 2022.[34] The Social Security system once again faces projected long-range funding shortfalls. The Social Security Board of Trustees (the Trustees) projects that full Social Security benefits can be paid on time until 2034 with a combination of annual Social Security tax revenues and asset reserves held by the Social Security trust funds. After the projected depletion of trust fund reserves in 2034, however, annual tax revenues are projected to cover about three-fourths of benefits scheduled under current law.[35]

Over the years, there have been many proposals designed to improve Social Security's financial outlook as well as achieve other policy goals. A common proposal is to increase the early eligibility age and/or further increase the full retirement age. As in the past, lawmakers who support increasing the retirement age point to gains in life expectancy as an indicator that people can work until older ages. Those who oppose this type of policy change, however, point out that gains in life expectancy have not been shared equally across different segments of the population. They cite research showing that life expectancy is lower for individuals with lower socioeconomic status (SES) compared to those with higher SES, and that the gap in life expectancy by SES has been growing over time.[36]

---

[33] *Social Security Amendments of 1983: Legislative History and Summary of Provisions*, Social Security Bulletin, July 1983, Vol. 46, No. 7, at https://www.ssa.gov/policy/docs/ssb/v46n7/v46n7p3.pdf.

[34] The FRA is 67 for workers born in 1960 or later. A worker born in 1960 becomes eligible for reduced retirement benefits at age 62 in 2022 and eligible for full retirement benefits at age 67 in 2027.

[35] The projections are from the 2017 Annual Report of the Board of Trustees of the Federal Old-Age and Survivors Insurance and Federal Disability Insurance Trust Funds, intermediate assumptions, https://www.ssa.gov/OACT/TR/ 2017/tr2017.pdf. For more information, see CRS Report RL33028, Social Security: The Trust Funds, and CRS In Focus IF10522, Social Security's Funding Shortfall.

[36] CRS Report R44846, The Growing Gap in Life Expectancy by Income: Recent Evidence and Implications for the Social Security Retirement Age.

Differential gains in life expectancy are important in the context of Social Security. The actuarial adjustments to benefits for early or delayed retirement (i.e., for claiming benefits before or after the full retirement age) are based on *average* life expectancy. That is, the actuarial adjustments are designed to provide a person with roughly the same total lifetime benefits, regardless of the age at which he or she claims benefits, assuming the person lives to average life expectancy. Research has shown that differential gains in life expectancy have resulted in a widening gap in the value of lifetime Social Security retirement benefits between low earners and high earners.[37]

In recent years, deficit reduction commissions and other policymakers have recommended an increase in the Social Security retirement age. In 2010, for example, the National Commission on Fiscal Responsibility and Reform (also called the *Simpson-Bowles Commission* after co-chairs Alan Simpson and Erskine Bowles) recommended increasing both the early eligibility age (EEA) and the full retirement age (FRA), among other Social Security changes. Under the commission's recommendations, after the FRA reaches 67 in 2027, both the EEA and the FRA would be indexed to increases in life expectancy. The commission estimated that the FRA would reach 68 by about 2050, and 69 by about 2075. The EEA would increase to 63 and 64 in step with increases in the FRA.[38]

In conjunction with proposed increases in the EEA and FRA, the commission recommended policies that would provide people with more flexibility in claiming benefits. Specifically, the commission recommended allowing people to claim up to half of their benefits at age 62 (with an actuarial reduction) and the other half at a later age (with a smaller actuarial reduction). This option was intended to provide a smoother transition for those interested in phased retirement or for households where one member has retired and another continues to work.[39] In general, it could provide a

---

[37] Ibid.

[38] *The Moment of Truth: Report of the National Commission on Fiscal Responsibility and Reform*, December 1, 2010, http://www.fiscalcommission.gov/sites/fiscalcommission.gov/files/documents/TheMomentofTruth12_1_2010.pdf. (Hereinafter cited as *The Moment of Truth*.

[39] The Moment of Truth, p. 51.

stream of income for those with financial difficulties by allowing them to claim a portion of their benefits early and avoid taking a permanent reduction on the full benefit amount.

Recognizing that some workers may be physically unable to work beyond the current EEA (62) and may not qualify for Social Security disability benefits, the commission also recommended a *hardship exemption* for up to 20% of retirees. Under the proposal, as the EEA and FRA increase, certain beneficiaries could continue to claim benefits at age 62 and their benefits would not be subject to additional actuarial reductions. The commission specified that SSA would design the policy taking into consideration factors such as the physical demands of labor and lifetime earnings in developing eligibility criteria.[40] Concerns regarding the effects of increasing the retirement age, especially on certain segments of the population, are not new. The Social Security Amendments of 1983, which increased the retirement age gradually from 65 to 67, mandated a study to examine the effects of increasing the retirement age on workers in physically demanding jobs and/or ill health.[41]

Social Security legislative proposals offered over the years have included changes to the retirement age. SSA's Office of the Chief Actuary (OCACT) provides trust fund solvency projections for selected proposals on their website (see *Proposals Affecting Trust Fund Solvency*).[42] For example, projections for the Social Security changes proposed by the National Commission on Fiscal Responsibility and Reform can be found by scrolling down to *Fiscal Commission* under the column heading *Developer(s) of Proposal*.

In addition, OCACT provides trust fund solvency projections for individual provisions to change the retirement age (see *Individual Changes Modifying Social Security, Category C: Retirement Age*).[43] Under the first

---

[40] Ibid.

[41] The report prepared by the U.S. Department of Health and Human Services, Social Security Administration, is reprinted in the Social Security Bulletin. See *Increasing the Social Security Retirement Age: Older Workers in Physically Demanding Occupations or Ill Health*, Social Security Bulletin, vol. 49, no. 10 (October 1986), at https://www.ssa.gov/policy/docs/ssb/v49n10/v49n10p5.pdf.

[42] SSA, OCACT, https://www.ssa.gov/OACT/solvency/index.html.

[43] SSA, OCACT, https://www.ssa.gov/OACT/solvency/provisions/index.html.

option, for example, the FRA would increase gradually from 67 to 68 (see *Number C1.1 - After the normal retirement age (NRA) reaches 67 for those age 62 in 2022, increase the NRA 1 month every 2 years until the NRA reaches 68*). OCACT projects that this option would improve the Social Security trust fund outlook by eliminating 13% of the system's projected long-range funding shortfall (based on the 2017 Annual Report of the Social Security Board of Trustees, intermediate assumptions).

In: Retirement
Editor: Thomas M. Osborne
ISBN: 978-1-53615-703-1

Chapter 3

SOCIAL SECURITY BENEFIT CLAIMING AGE*

Zhe Li

BACKGROUND

Social Security provides monthly cash benefits to retired or disabled workers and their family members as well as to the family members of deceased workers. The Social Security full retirement age (FRA) is the age at which retired workers can first claim full Social Security retired-worker benefits. The FRA was 65 at the inception of Social Security in 1935. As part of legislation enacted in 1983 (P.L. 98-21), starting with workers born in 1938, the FRA increased by two months every birth year until the FRA reached 66 for workers born in 1943 to 1954, and then increases again in two-month increments until the FRA reaches 67 for workers born in 1960 or later.

Retired workers can claim retirement benefits as early as age 62 (the earliest eligibility age, or EEA). Benefits claimed between age 62 and the FRA, however, are subject to a permanent reduction for early retirement.

* This is an edited, reformatted and augmented version of Congressional Research Service Publication No. IF11115, dated February 26, 2019.

For each of the 36 months immediately preceding the FRA, the monthly rate of reduction from the full retirement benefit is five-ninths of 1%. For each month earlier than three years (36 months) before the FRA, the monthly rate of reduction is five-twelfths of 1%. Therefore, for a worker with an FRA of 65, claiming benefits at 62 results in a 20% permanent reduction in their monthly benefit; the reduction is 25% if the FRA is 66, and 30% if the FRA is 67.

Workers who claim benefits after the FRA may receive a delayed retirement credit (DRC). The maximum age at which the DRC applies is age 70. Any further delay in claiming benefits past age 70 does not result in a higher benefit. Under current law, the amount of the credit varies based on the worker's year of birth. The credit for workers born in 1943 or later is 8% per year.

AGE DISTRIBUTION OF SOCIAL SECURITY BENEFIT CLAIMS FOR RETIRED WORKERS

By Calendar Year

In general, most retired workers claim their retirement benefits at either age 62 (the EEA) or the FRA. In most years after 1985, about three quarters of retired-worker benefits were awarded to workers who claimed benefits at age 62 or the FRA (see *Figure 1*), 20% were awarded to retired workers older than the EEA but younger than the FRA, and the remaining 5% were awarded to retired workers who claimed benefits after the FRA. However, the age distribution of Social Security benefit claims has shifted to later ages in the past two decades. Several factors are likely to have contributed to the change in Social Security benefit claiming ages, including changes in the FRA, the retirement earnings test (RET), the DRC, economic environment, and the population age distribution.

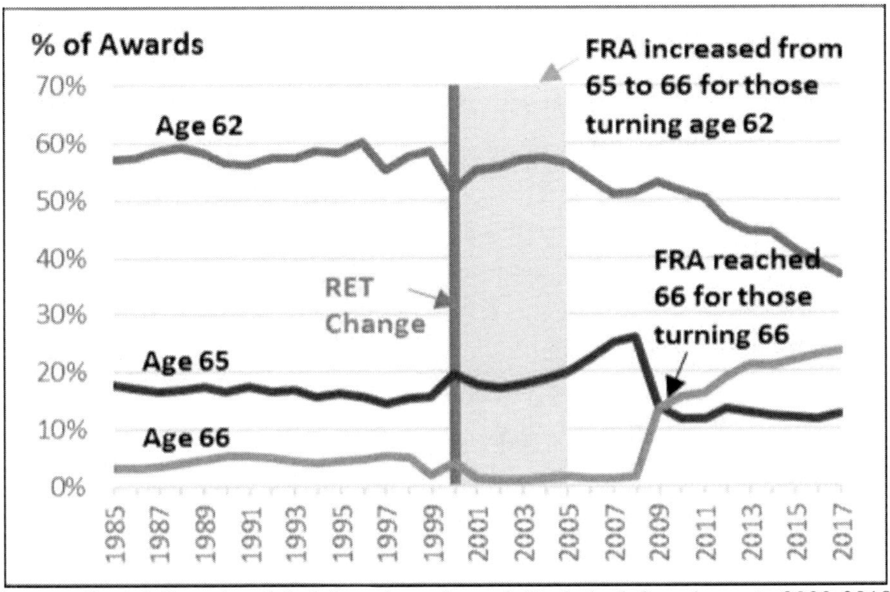

Source: Social Security Administration, Annual Statistical Supplement, 2000-2018, Table 6.A4, and Table 6.B5.

Notes: The RET was repealed for workers who have reached the FRA in 2000 (P.L. 106-182). The proportion of retired workers who claimed Social Security benefits at age 66 includes those between ages 66 and 69 during 1985 to 1998.

Figure 1. Social Security Retired-Worker Benefits, Claiming Age Distribution, 1985-2017.

The majority of retired workers claimed Social Security benefits at age 62 (almost 60%) between 1985 and 1999. In 2000, for those reaching age 62, the FRA began to increase. Under the scheduled increases enacted in 1983 (P.L. 98- 21), starting with workers born in 1938, the FRA increased from age 65 in two-month increments until the FRA reached 66 for workers born in 1943 to 1954. As a higher FRA results in a larger benefit reduction at age 62, the proportion of retired workers who claimed benefits at the FRA has increased and those who claimed benefits at age 62 has declined since 2000. However, the high unemployment during the recent economic recession (2007- 2009) was likely to result in some people claiming early Social Security benefits. When the FRA reached age 66 for those born in 1943, age 66 replaced age 65 as the second peak age at which retired workers claimed Social Security benefits. Since then, there has been a continuing decline in the proportion of retired workers who claimed benefits at age 62, and an increase in the proportion of retired workers who claim benefits at the FRA of 66. The proportion of retired workers who claimed benefits at age 65 dropped, but still remained above 11% after 2009.

The RET results in a withholding of monthly benefits for Social Security beneficiaries whose earnings exceed certain thresholds set in law. In 2000, Congress repealed the RET for workers who have reached the FRA (P.L. 106-182) in order to encourage older people to work. The earnings test now applies only to beneficiaries who are under the FRA. This provision was likely to encourage more workers at and above the FRA to claim Social Security benefits at the FRA, as their benefits would not be reduced for earnings. This among other reasons lead to a larger proportion of retired workers claiming benefits at the FRA, and a smaller proportion at age 62 since 2000.

In addition, the increase in the DRC might have increased the incentive to take up benefits after the FRA, thus shifting the claiming age distribution of Social Security benefits toward later ages. Comparing workers who were born in 1925 with those born in 1943 or later, the DRC increased from 3.5% per year to 8%. The proportion of retired workers who claimed benefits after attaining the FRA increased from about 4% in 2010 (when people born in 1943 attained age 67) to 12% in 2017.

Baby boomers, who were born between 1946 and 1964, started to attain the EEA of 62 in 2008. So the change in the age distribution of Social Security benefit claims among retired workers may also reflect the change in the population age distribution.

BY BIRTH YEAR

To analyze the behavior of each birth cohort, Figure 2 displays the proportion of retired workers between the ages of 62 and 69 who claimed Social Security benefits at age 62, 65, and 66 for workers in the birth cohorts from 1933 to 1948 (people born in 1948 attained age 69 in 2017).

As noted earlier, the FRA gradually increased from age 65 to 66 for workers who were born between 1938 and 1943. Since a higher FRA results in a larger benefit reduction at the EEA of 62, the proportion of workers in the 1938-1943 birth cohorts that claimed benefits at age 62 declined, and the proportion of those workers who claimed benefits at the FRA increased. For workers who were born in 1943, the FRA reached age 66, and the proportion of workers who claimed benefits at the age of 66 increased more than 12 percentage points compared with the prior cohorts.

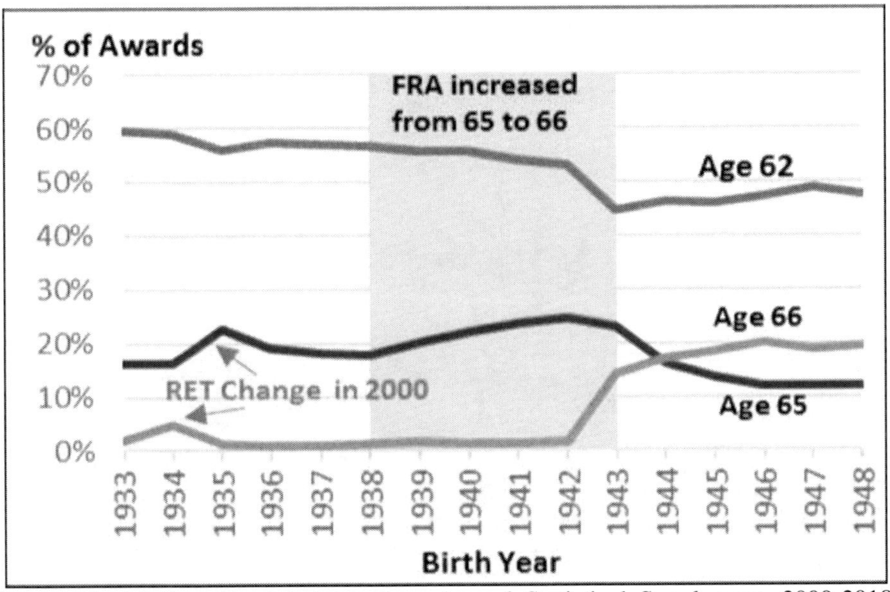

Source: Social Security Administration, Annual Statistical Supplement, 2000-2018, Table 6.A4.

Note: The RET was repealed for workers who have reached the FRA in 2000 (P.L. 106-182).

Figure 2. Social Security Retired-Worker Benefits Claiming Age Distribution, Birth Year 1933-1948.

Workers who were born between 1943 and 1948 have a FRA of 66. The proportion of those workers aged 62 to 69 who claimed Social Security benefits at age 62 remained relatively stable around 47%, the proportion of those who claimed benefits at age 65 declined from 23% to

12%, and the proportion of those who claimed benefits at the FRA increased and stayed around 20%.

The change in the distribution of Social Security benefit claiming age is relatively consistent for both male and female workers. But women were generally more likely than men to claim benefits at age 62, the EEA, and were less likely to claim benefits at the FRA (see Figure 3).

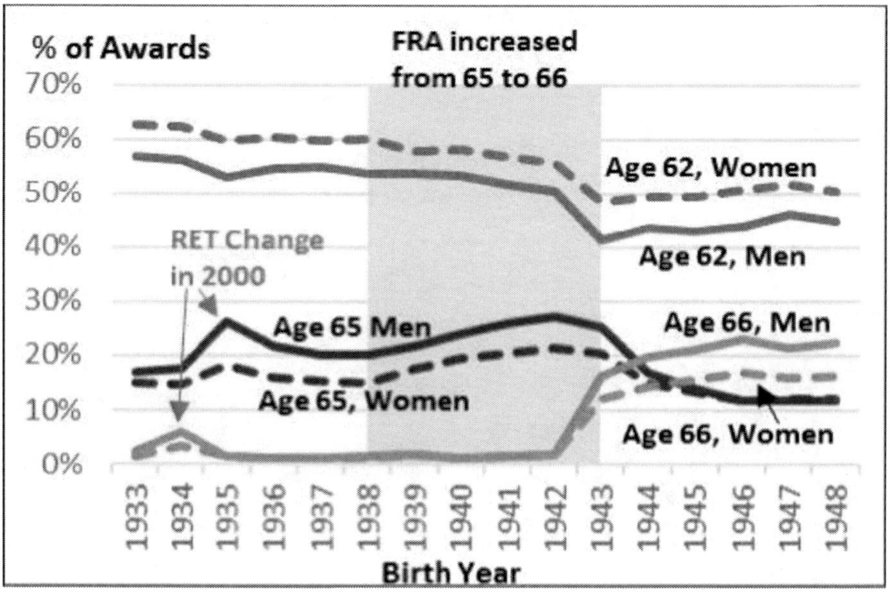

Source: Social Security Administration, Annual Statistical Supplement, 2000-2018, Table 6.A4.

Figure 3. Social Security Retired-Worker Benefits Claiming Age Distribution by Gender, Birth Year 1933-1948.

OTHER FACTORS

In addition to the policy changes discussed above, some other factors may also affect the ages at which retired workers claim Social Security benefits. For example, one study finds that receipt of the Social Security Statement, a benefit estimate statement made available to workers by Social Security Administration since 1995, decreases the likelihood of benefit claiming at earlier ages and increases the likelihood of claiming at later ages such as 65. Some provisions in the Bipartisan Budget Act of 2015 (P.L. 114- 74) changed certain Social Security benefits filing rules and will possibly affect the claiming behavior of some retired workers at the FRA and older.

Further, some studies suggest that couples like to retire together, and because husbands tend to be older than their wives on average, the increased labor force participation of women since the 1960s may lead to later retirement of men. Researchers also have shown that peers at workplace or those closest in age tend to have positive impact on individual retirement decisions, so policies that encourage later retirement spillover to adjacent cohorts and amplify the effect of changes in retirement incentives.

In: Retirement
Editor: Thomas M. Osborne
ISBN: 978-1-53615-703-1

Chapter 4

RETIREMENT SECURITY: ALTERNATE PRICE INDEXES FOR COST-OF-LIVING ADJUSTMENTS PRESENT TRADEOFFS*

United States Government Accountabilty Office

The Honorable Virginia Foxx
Ranking Member, Committee on Education and Labor
House of Representatives

The Honorable Tim Walberg
House of Representatives

Federal benefits programs often include cost-of-living adjustments (COLA) to ensure that benefits keep pace with inflation and to maintain the purchasing power of those benefits. These COLAs are often based on consumer price indexes (CPI), which measure the average change in the prices of goods and services over time. Several federal retirement programs

---

* This is an edited, reformatted and augmented version of the United States Government Accountability Office Publication No. GAO-19-218R, dated January 28, 2019.

adjust benefits using the CPI for Urban Wage Earners and Clerical Workers (CPI-W) after initial benefits have been set, including military pensions, federal employee pensions, and Social Security, one of the largest federal programs that pays benefits to more than 60 million older Americans and workers with disabilities.

The CPI-W was constructed to reflect price increases for urban wage earners and clerical workers, based on the goods and services typically purchased by this population, but some economists have argued that the CPI-W may overestimate the true cost of living in general because individuals can partially offset the effect of relative price increases by purchasing different goods and services. Other economists have argued that it may underestimate the true cost of living for retirees by misrepresenting the goods and services that older Americans consume. Specifically, older Americans devote a substantially larger share of their total budgets to medical care and shelter than others, and costs for medical care and shelter have generally increased more rapidly than costs for most other goods and services.

You asked us to describe the effects of various price indexes on older Americans' retirement security. This chapter provides information on the benefits and disadvantages of alternate price indexes for measuring the cost of living for older Americans. In December 2018, we briefed Representative Walberg and his staff on the results of our review. This chapter publishes the briefing we provided the committee (see enclosure I).

To conduct this work, we interviewed agency officials and reviewed federal publications, which we identified by interviewing agency officials and searching agency websites. These agencies were the Social Security Administration (SSA), Department of Labor, Department of the Treasury, Congressional Budget Office, and Congressional Research Service. We also analyzed CPI data from the Department of Labor's Bureau of Labor Statistics (BLS) as well as other data from SSA to calculate hypothetical COLAs that could have been used if the Social Security COLA were based on an alternate CPI over the 2003–2033 period. To do so, we used third quarter historical CPI data and assumed future CPI data during that time period. For historical data, we used BLS data from 2003 through the most recent year data were available across all indexes, and for future data we used information from SSA's Office of the Chief Actuary based on the intermediate assumptions in the 2018 Trustees Report.

The calculations for these hypothetical beneficiaries are illustrative and may not be representative of actual beneficiaries' experiences. Moreover, the calculations and assumptions reflect the recent low-inflation environment, and results may be different in a high-inflation environment. Further, BLS has modified its methodology over time and may continue to do so in the future. However, we believe these calculations illustrate what the potential effects might have been if an alternate CPI had been used.

For the federal retirement programs within our scope, the COLAs are generally based on the third quarter CPI-W. While we created the hypothetical calculations for Social Security benefits, we believe that the overall trends would hold for other federal retirement programs as well. We also used data from the 2016 Survey of Consumer Finances to understand the average share of total retirement income that Social Security benefits comprise. We assessed the reliability of the data by reviewing relevant documentation and internal controls, interviewing agency officials, and comparing our calculations to published data. We found the data we used to be reliable for our purposes (see enclosure II for a more detailed description of our scope and methodology).

We conducted this performance audit from May 2018 to January 2019 in accordance with generally accepted government auditing standards. Those standards require that we plan and perform the audit to obtain sufficient, appropriate evidence to provide a reasonable basis for our findings and conclusions based on our audit objective. We believe that the evidence obtained provides a reasonable basis for our findings and conclusions based on our audit objective.

BACKGROUND

BLS produces four CPIs, including three official indexes published on its website and an experimental index that is available on request:

- CPI-W: The CPI for Urban Wage Earners and Clerical Workers. First published in 1921, it was the only national CPI when the Social Security Administration began indexing benefits in 1975. It represents the types of expenditures made by about 29 percent of the U.S. population.[1]
- CPI-U: The CPI for All Urban Consumers. First published in 1978, when it became the headline index, it represents the types of expenditures made by about 93 percent of the U.S. population, including retired individuals.
- CPI-E: The CPI for the Elderly. Created in 1988 at the request of Congress, this index addresses spending patterns of those age 62 and older by shifting the weights for certain expenditures such as medical care and shelter. BLS considers this index experimental.[2] It represents the types of expenditures made by about 21 percent of the U.S. population.
- Chained CPI-U: The Chained CPI for All Urban Consumers. It was first published in 2002 to address methodological concerns about more fully capturing consumers' ability to buy different goods and services to adapt to changing prices.[3] It represents the types of expenditures made by about 93 percent of the U.S. population.

BLS regularly reviews and revises the methodologies for producing indexes to improve their accuracy. Several federal retirement programs use COLAs that are generally based on third quarter averages of the CPI-W.

---

[1] From 1978 through 1980, BLS found little difference between data for CPI-W and for those of the newly introduced Consumer Price Index for All Urban Consumers (CPI-U). According to BLS, as a result of this and budgetary issues, BLS stopped collecting separate data for the CPI-W in 1981 and began using CPI-U data to derive the CPI-W.

[2] As with the CPI-W, BLS uses CPI-U data to derive the CPI-E. However, BLS officials told us that unlike for the CPI- W population, BLS does not have data specific to the population of older Americans. As a result, in contrast to the CPI-W, BLS officials said they are unable to determine the extent to which CPI-U data reflect consumption patterns specific to older Americans—where they shop, what they purchase, and how much they pay.

[3] All four indexes to some extent reflect consumers' ability to adapt to changing prices. Specifically, all four indexes reflect consumers' ability to choose among closely-related goods and services as prices change. However, unlike the other three indexes, the Chained CPI-U further reflects consumers' ability to choose among all available goods and services as prices change.

This includes Social Security (the largest of these programs), Military Retirement, Railroad Retirement Board pensions, the Federal Employees Retirement System, the Civil Service Retirement System, and Veterans Affairs pensions. Price indexing also occurs in other federal programs not exclusively focused on older Americans, such as Social Security Disability Insurance, Supplemental Security Income, and the Supplemental Nutrition Assistance Program.

In summary, we found the following:

- Using an alternate index would likely result in changes to benefits and program costs that accumulate over time. A switch to an alternate index for federal retirement programs' COLAs would likely create tradeoffs in regards to individual benefits and program costs.[4] An increase in benefits would also mean an increase in program costs, and a decrease in benefits would mean a decrease in costs. We estimate that a switch to the Chained CPI-U would lower benefits through small annual changes that accumulate over time, relative to using the CPI-W, whereas a switch to the CPI-E would increase benefits in a similar manner. For example, if COLAs had been based on the Chained CPI-U or CPI-E over the 2003–2033 period, our analysis shows that the first year's adjusted monthly benefit in 2004 would change by a few dollars or less, relative to using the CPI-W, but after 30 years we estimate that the monthly difference would be $100 or more for a hypothetical beneficiary with earnings equal to the national average wage index.[5]
- Changing to an alternate index would have the largest relative effect on those who receive benefits the longest and those with

[4] When defining program costs, we are referring to overall costs to federal retirement programs. For example, program costs include outlays that affect the solvency of the Social Security Trust Funds and outlays made by the Federal Employees Retirement System.

[5] These nominal dollar estimates are based on hypothetical calculations of COLAs using historical and assumed CPI data for a beneficiary who retired in 2003 at age 65 with earnings equal to the national average wage index. Income and benefit information is based on SSA's hypothetical retired workers. Using constant 2017 dollars, the difference in monthly benefit in 2033 would be $70 or more relative to the CPI-W.

lower incomes. Beneficiaries who claim benefits over many years and those with lower incomes would most strongly experience the effects of using an alternate index for federal retirement programs' COLAs. This is in part because changes to COLAs accumulate over time and because lower-income beneficiaries rely more heavily on federal retirement programs, such as Social Security. For example, after 30 years of Social Security COLA adjustments using an alternate index, we estimate that the total retirement income for a low-income household would decrease by about[6] percent using the Chained CPI-U or increase by about 4 percent using the CPI-E, relative to the current index.6 In contrast, we estimate that this same change in COLA would affect the total retirement income of a high-income household by only about a 1 percent decrease using the Chained CPI-U or about a 1 percent increase using the CPI-E, relative to the CPI-W.[7]

- Implementing an alternate index could pose issues regarding timeliness of data and cost. The Chained CPI-U data are preliminary and can be subject to significant revisions up to 1 year after they are initially produced. This may require agencies to determine how or whether to address these data lags. BLS considers the CPI-E an experimental index. According to 2017 estimates from BLS, it could cost about $5 million per year over several years to research it and, if BLS finds that the current CPI-E methodology is not sufficient, up to an additional $110 million per year thereafter to produce an official CPI-E. In addition to

---

[6] Percentage change is relative to what the change could have been using the CPI-W. Using historical CPI data from BLS and future inflation assumptions by the SSA, we estimated hypothetical Social Security COLAs that could have been used if the COLA were based on an alternate CPI over the 2003–2033 period. The future inflation information reflects the intermediate assumptions in the 2018 Trustees Report. Retirement income information is from the nationally representative 2016 Survey of Consumer Finances, the most recent available. We use household age 65 and older as a proxy for retirement. Low-income refers to those in the lowest income quintile, and high-income refers to those in the highest income quintile. Total retirement income includes Social Security, defined benefit pension annuities, retirement savings withdrawals, and other sources.

[7] The economy has been in a period of relatively low inflation for the last few decades. If that were to change it is unclear how the hypothetical COLA calculations would be affected.

timeliness and cost issues, switching to an alternate index would require explanations to beneficiaries. Also, SSA officials indicated that any change to how SSA computes COLAs would require a legislative change.[8]

- A change in certain indexes would affect other federal programs. While this chapter focused on federal retirement programs, the information is relevant for other federal programs as well. For example, by law the COLA for Social Security's retirement program applies to some other programs too. The COLA for Social Security retirement benefits is the same as the COLA for Social Security disability benefits, and changes to that COLA trigger changes to the COLA for Supplemental Security Income, Railroad Retirement Board pensions, and Veterans Affairs pensions. The same issues could present themselves if other federal programs changed the CPI used for various program aspects, such as income eligibility levels or benefit amount.

AGENCY COMMENTS

We provided a draft of this chapter to the Department of Labor and the Social Security Administration for review and comment. In its comments, reproduced in enclosure III, the Social Security Administration generally agreed with our findings. The Department of Labor and the Social Security Administration also provided technical comments, which we incorporated as appropriate. In its technical comments, the Department of Labor noted that BLS currently has plans to re-evaluate the methods used to calculate the CPI-W and CPI-E and to identify ways to improve measurement within the current budget.

---

[8] Statutes authorizing selected federal programs refer to the CPI generally, but do not specify which CPI must be used to calculate COLAs, and some link to Social Security's COLA. SSA officials told us that changes in the CPI used for indexation in other instances have historically been the result of statutory changes. Any changes to the CPI for Social Security would need to be reflected in SSA's regulations, which refer specifically to the CPI-W.

* * *

We are sending copies of this chapter to the appropriate congressional committees, the Secretary of Labor, Secretary of the Treasury, and the Acting Commissioner of Social Security, and other interested parties.

Charles A. Jeszeck
Director, Education, Workforce, and Income Security Issues

APPENDIX I. RETIREMENT SECURITY: ALTERNATE PRICE INDEXES FOR COST-OF-LIVING ADJUSTMENTS PRESENT TRADEOFFS, BRIEFING FOR THE HONORABLE TIM WALBERG, HOUSE OF REPRESENTATIVES

Introduction

Consumer Price Indexes Are Used for Cost-of-Living Adjustments

- Federal benefits programs often include cost-of-living adjustments (COLA) to ensure that benefits keep pace with inflation and to maintain the purchasing power of those benefits.
- Several federal retirement programs adjust benefits using the Consumer Price Index for Urban Wage Earners and Clerical Workers (CPI-W), in whole or in part, after initial benefits have been set. These benefits include military pensions, federal employee pensions, and Social Security, one of the largest

federal programs that pays benefits to more than 60 million older Americans and workers with disabilities.

- The CPI-W is constructed to reflect price increases for urban wage earners and clerical workers, based on the goods and services typically purchased by this population.

CPI-W

- Some economists have argued that the CPI-W may overestimate the true cost of living in general because individuals can partially offset the effect of relative price increases by purchasing different goods and services.
- Other economists have argued that the CPI-W may underestimate the true cost of living for retirees by misrepresenting the goods and services that older Americans consume.
- Specifically, according to the Bureau of Labor Statistics, older Americans devote a much larger share of their total budgets to medical care and shelter[9] than other groups, and the costs of these items have generally increase more rapidly than for most other goods and services.

Objective, Scope, and Methodology

- You asked us to describe the effects of various price indexes on older Americans' retirement security.
- This briefing provides information on the benefits and disadvantages of alternate price indexes for measuring the cost of living for older Americans.
    - o To do this we:

---

[9] Some debate exists over the methods used to calculate owner-occupied housing costs for consumer price indexes. In the U.S., the "owner's equivalent rent" is used to capture what a homeowner would pay in rent for a similar property.

- o Interviewed agency officials from the Congressional Budget Office, Congressional Research Service, Department of Labor, Department of me Treasury, and Social Security Administration (SSA).
- o Reviewed federal publications, which we identified through interviews with agency officials and by reviewing agency websites.
- o Used third quarter historical and assumed future consumer Price index (CPI) data to calculate Social Securi1Y. COLAs and retirement benefits that would have been received had different CP is been used instead of the CPI-W over a 30 year period (2003 through 2033).[10]
- o Assumed future CPI data came from SSA and were based on the intermediate assumptions in the 2018 Trustees Report.
- o We assessed the reliability of the data by reviewing relevant documentation and internal controls interviewing agency officials, and comparing our calculations to published data. We found the data we used to be reliable for our purposes.

Summary of Observations

- Alternate price indexes for calculating federal retirement program COLAs would likely present tradeoffs in benefit levels, program costs, and implementation.
- Using an alternate index would likely result in changes to benefits and program costs that accumulate over time.
- Changing to an alternate index would have the largest relative effect on those who receive benefits the longest and those with lower incomes.

---

[10] While other inflation indexes exist, such as wage indexes, we examined four CPis produced by the Bureau of Labor Statistics, including the CPI-W.

- Implementing an alternate index could pose issues regarding timeliness of data and cost.
- There would be effects on other federal programs.

Background

The Department of Labor's Bureau of Labor Statistics (BLS) Produces Four CPIs

- The CPI for Urban Wage Earners and Clerical Workers (CPI-W) was first published in 1921 to measure the average cost of living for Americans who lived in urban areas and were considered wage earners or clerical workers. For a simplified depiction of the process to create a CPI, see figure 1. When SSA began indexing benefits in 1975, the CPI-W was the only national CPI that BLS produced. The CPI-W represents the types of expenditures made by about 29 percent of the U.S. population.
- The CPI for All Urban Consumers (CPI-U) was first published in 1978 and CPI-U data linked to the CPI-W go back to 1913. On average the CPI-U tracks closely to the CPI-W but represents a larger population that includes retired individuals. The CPI-U represents the types of expenditures made by about 93 percent of the U.S. population.
- The CPI for the Elderly (CPI-E) was created in 1988 to address spending patterns of those age 62 and older by shifting the weights for certain expenditures.[11] For example, medical care and shelter account for about 12 and 37 percent of the expenditure weights in the CPI-E, compared to 8 and 31 percent in the CPI-W. BLS considers the CPI-E an experimental index. The CPI-E represents the types of expenditures made by about 21 percent of the U.S. population.

---

[11] BLS created the CPI-E pursuant to a provision in the Older Americans Act Amendments of 1987. See Pub. L. No. 100-175, § 191, 101 Stat. 926, 967.

- The Chained CPI for All Urban Consumers (Chained CPI-U) was first published in 2002 to address methodological concerns about more fully capturing consumers' ability to buy different goods and services to adapt to changing prices. For example, if the price of steak were to rise more than the price of chicken, the Chained CPI-U takes into account consumers' ability to switch from buying steak to buying chicken instead.[12] The Chained CPI-U represents the types of expenditures made by about 93 percent of the U.S. population.

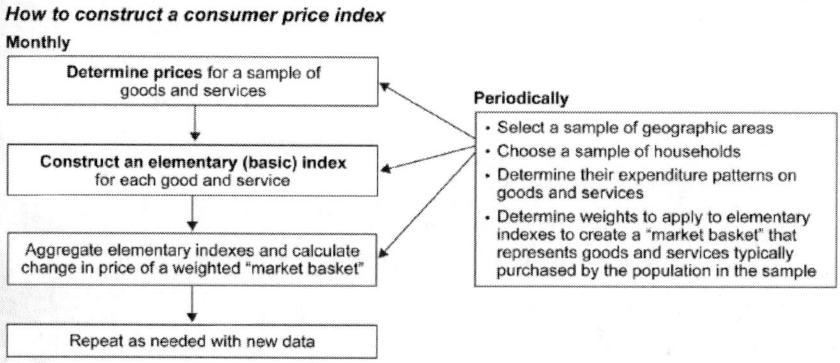

Source: GAO analysis of information from the Department of Labor. | GA0-19-218R.

Figure 1. Simplified Depiction of the Process to Create a Consumer Price Index.

Major Retirement Programs That Use Price Indexing

- Several federal retirement programs use COLAs that are generally based on third quarter averages from the CPI-W to adjust benefits:
- Military Retirement; Railroad Retirement Board pensions; the Federal Emloyees Retirement System; the Civil Service Retirement System; Veterans Affairs pensions; and one of the

[12] All four indexes to some extent reflect consumers' ability to adapt to changing prices. Specifically, all four indexes reflect consumers' ability to choose among closely-related goods and services as prices change. However, unlike the other three indexes, the Chained CPI-U further reflects consumers' ability to choose among all available goods and services as prices change.

largest federal programs that covers older Americans and workers with disabilities, Social Security.13

- CPI-W is also used to increase regular and catch-up contribution limits for retirement savings plans such as:
- 401(k), 403(b), 457, and the federal Thrift Savings Plan.

Other Federal Programs That Use Price Indexing

- Price indexing is also used to adjust benefit amounts for other programs not exclusively focused on older Americans (e.g., Supplemental Security Income, Social Security Disability Insurance, Federal Employees' Compensation Act, and the Supplemental Nutrition Assistance Program).
- The tax code provides for indexation in certain instances, such as for income tax brackets and standard deductions.
- Price indexing is also used for the federal poverty level and to measure income eligibility amounts for some federal programs.

Benefits

Using an Alternate Index Would Likely Result in Changes to Benefits That Accumulate Over Time

- Based on our calculation of hypothetical COLAs over a 30 year period (2003-2033), using historical and assumed future inflation data, switching to an alternate index would create relatively small annual benefit changes that compound over time.[14] For example:

---

[13] The Federal Employees Retirement System sets the COLA to be equal to or less than the change in the CPI-W, and one part of Railroad Retirement Board pensions sets the COLA at 32.5 percent of the Social Security COLA. The Pension Benefit Guaranty Corporation uses wage indexing to increase premiums and to adjust maximum benefits.

[14] We analyzed historical CPI data and used SSA assumptions about future CPI growth based on the intermediate assumptions in the 2018 Trustees Report.

- o We estimate that using the Chained CPI-U would decrease the COLA by an average of about a quarter of 1 percent per year, relative to the CPI-W; however, this decrease would accumulate to more than 7 percent by 2033.
- o We estimate that using the CPI-E would increase the COLA by an average of about 1/7 of 1 percent per year, relative to the CPI-W. By the end of the 30 year time span, that 1ncrease would accumulate to more than 4 percent.

- The CPI-U has historically tracked closely to the CPI-W and SSA expects this trend to continue. Based on that, we estimate that a switch to the CPI- U would show little change from the CPI-W (see figs. 2 and 3).

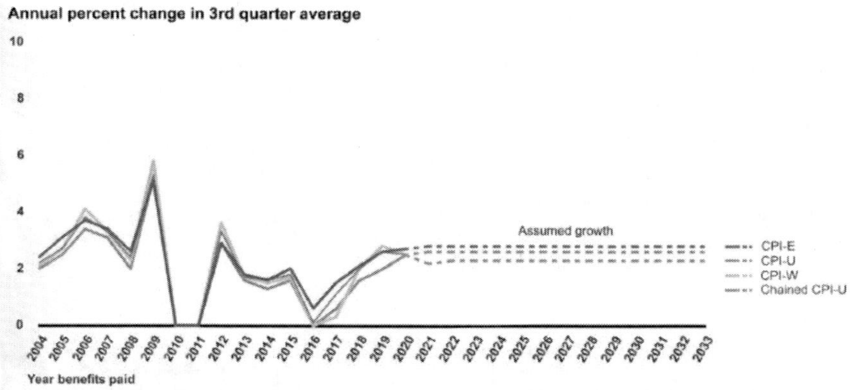

Source: GAO analysis of Social Security Administration and Bureau of Labor Statistics information. | GA0-19-218R

Note: Assumed growth data are based on the intermediate assumptions in the 2018 Trustees Report. All historical CPI data are based on final data. For some years, separate lines do not appear for CPI-W and CPI-U because the data points are the same.

Figure 2. Annual Differences in COLAs Using Alternate CP is Are Relatively Small.

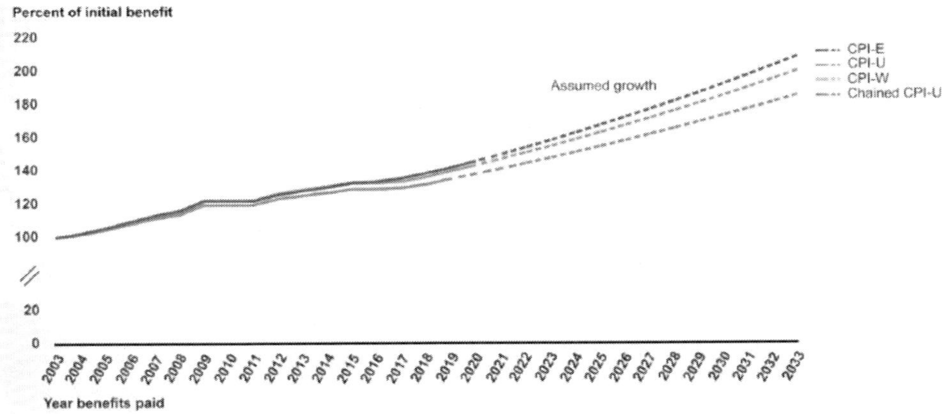

Source: GAO analysis of Social Security Administration and Bureau of Labor Statistics information. | GA0-19-218R.

Note: assumed growth data are based on the intermediate assumptions in the 2018 Trustees Report. All historical CPI data are based on final data. For some years, separate lines do not appear for CPI-W and CPI-U because the data points are the same.

Figure 3. Differences in COLAs Using Alternate CP is Accumulate Over Time.

Examples of Effect on Individual Benefits for Hypothetical COLAs over Period 2003-2033[15]

- Example 1: Under the Chained CPI-U, for a hypothetical individual who retired in 2003 at age 65 with earnings equal to the national average wage index, we estimate that the 2004 annual adjusted benefit would have decreased by about $12 (about $1 a month), compared to if the CPI-W had been used to index benefits.
- But over 30 years (2033) the differences would compound so that the final year's annual benefit would decrease by about $2,000 (more than $165 a month), relative to the CPI-W.

[15] Hypothetical individual income and benefit amounts are based on SSA's hypothetical retired workers with scaled earnings equal to the national average wage index. In 2003, the national average wage index was $33,256 per year and the hypothetical annual benefit amount was $13,896. Dollar amounts above are nominal, though using constant 2017 dollars the annual benefit in 2033 would be about $1,300 less (about $100 per month) using the Chained CPI-U and $840 more (about $70 per month) using the CPI-E.

- Example 2: Under the CPI-E, we estimate that the same hypothetical retiree's 2004 annual adjusted benefit would have increased by about \$36 (about \$3 a month), compared to if the CPI-W had been used.
- But over 30 years, that amount would grow so that the final year's annual benefit would increase by about \$1,300 (more than \$100 a month), relative to the CPI-W.

Low Inflation Adds Uncertainty to Future Effects

- The U.S. experienced high inflation rates in the 1970s and early 1980s (see fig. 4).
- Since then, the U.S. has experienced lower inflation rates (often less than 3 percent), which are reflected in our assumptions of the alternate indexes moving forward.
- However, the Chained CPI-U was first published in 2002 and the CPI-E in 1988, and they have only been documented in a relatively low inflation environment.
- It is uncertain how high inflation would affect our hypothetical COLA calculations.

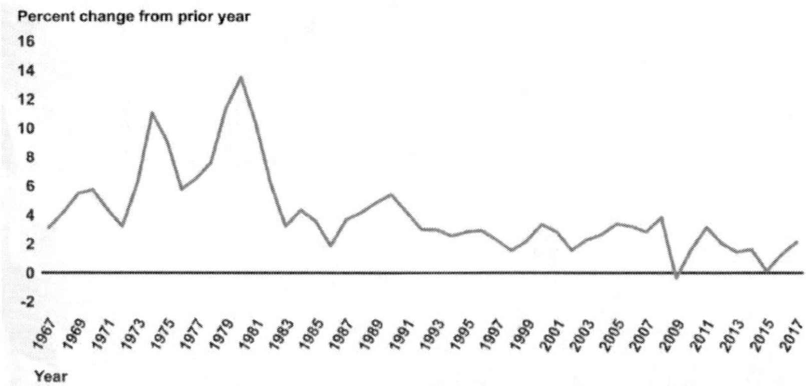

Source: GAO analysis of Consumer Price Index for All Urban Consumers (CPI-U).| GA0-19-218R.

Figure 4. Changes in Inflation for the U.S. 1967-2017.

Costs

Tradeoffs between Individual Benefits and Program Cost

- Absent other changes, an increase in individual benefits would lead to an increase in program costs (such as projected using the CPI-E). Similarly, lowering benefits would lead to a decrease in program costs (such as projected using the Chained CPI-U).[16]
- Like benefits, the effect on annual program outlays may be relatively modest in the first years, but they would accumulate over time.

Alternate Indexes Projected to Affect Social Security's Finances

- Using an alternate index for COLA would have less absolute effect on Social Security's long-range finances than many of the other specific policy options that SSA and the Congressional Budget Office (CBO) evaluated.[17] For example, both SSA and CBO project that switching to the Chained CPI-U or CPI-E would affect

---

[16] When defining program costs, we are referring to overall costs to federal retirement programs. For example, program costs include outlays that affect the solvency of the Social Security Trust Funds, and outlays made by the Federal Employees Retirement System. Moreover, while the CPI-E is not always higher and the Chained CPI-U is not always lower than the CPI-W, this has been the overall trend, and this trend is expected to continue in the future, according to information by the SSA Office of the Chief Actuary.

[17] See Social Security Administration, Summary of Provisions That Would Change the Social Security Program (September 13, 2018) and Congressional Budget Office, Social Security Policy Options, 2015 (Washington, D.C.: December 2015). To put the effects of using the CPI-E or Chained CPI-U into context, we compared these effects to the effects of all policy options evaluated in the aforementioned publications. We further compared these effects to the effects of some commonly discussed categories of policy options, namely changing the taxation of earnings and raising the retirement age. Using the Chained CPI-U would have less of an effect than 27 of 35 options SSA examined and 9 of 10 options CBO examined to change the taxation of earnings. For the CPI-E the figures were 28 of 35 and 10 of 10, respectively. Regarding raising the retirement age, using the Chained CPI-U would have less of an effect than 10 of 15 options SSA examined and 3 of 4 options CBO examined. For the CPI-E the figures were 13 of 15 and 4 of 4, respectively. The degree of the effect depends on the scale of the specific policy option, such as how much the retirement age would be raised.

program finances less than the vast majority of other recent policy options they examined to:

- o change the taxation of earnings, and
- o raise the retirement age.

- Social Security is a large program that is currently on a fiscally unsustainable path, and changing the CPI used to calculate COLA would affect program finances to differing degrees based on the option selected.[18]
- According to SSA projections, switching to the CPI-E would worsen Social Security's finances.
- Switching to the CPI-E in 2020 for both retirement and disability benefits is estimated to decrease Social Security's long-range actuarial balance by 0.39 percent of taxable payroll, which is estimated to increase the shortfall in the balance by 14 percent. However, it is not projected to change the calendar year in which Social Security's Old-Age, Survivors, and Disability Insurance Trust Funds will be unable to pay full benefits.
- In contrast, SSA projects that switching to the Chained CPI-U would improve Social Security's finances. A switch to the Chained CPI-U in 2019 for retirement benefits only is estimated to increase Social Security's long-range actuarial balance by 0.49 percent of taxable payroll, which is estimated to reduce the shortfall by 17 percent. This would extend the projected date in which the combined Trust Funds will be unable to pay full benefits by about 2 years (to 2036).

[18] Based on 2018 estimates by the SSA Office of the Chief Actuary. The effect on the long-range actuarial balance is relative to the current payroll tax rate of 12.4 percent of taxable payroll. Comparisons are based on the closest available policy options that SSA examined to change to the CPI-E or Chained CPI-U. The Social Security Trust Funds are distinct legal entities, and on a hypothetical combined basis they are projected to be unable to pay full benefits in 2034. Note that changing to the CPI-E does not change the year in which the combined Trust Funds are unable to pay full benefits, but it would still affect program finances. SSA assumes that the CPI-E will increase by 0.2 percentage points more than the CPI-W and that the Chained CPI-U will increase by 0.3 percentage points less than the CPI-W.

Equity

Alternate Indexes Would Have Larger Effect on Those Who Receive Benefits Longest

- Because the changes to COLA accumulate over time, effects of using an alternate index would be more pronounced for those who receive benefits over the longest periods. This includes:
  - o beneficiaries of retirement programs who live longer, such as those with a college educat1on and women; and
  - o those who start receiving benefits earlier than others, such as recipients of disability and survivor's benefits.
- For example, early claimers of Social Security retirement benefits are more likely to be widowed, have worked in physically-demanding blue collar jobs, or be veterans, as we reported in 2014.19

Alternate Indexes Would Have Larger Effect on Lower-Income Beneficiaries

- Lower-income beneficiaries tend to be more sensitive to changes in income, so changes in COLAs would affect them more so than others.
- For example, Social Security benefits make up a larger share of the1r ret1rement 1ncome, on average.
- Among households age 65 and older, Social Security makes up about 81 percent or the retirement income for those in the lowest income quintile. For those in the highest income quintile, Social Security makes up about 5 percent of their retirement income.[20]
- In 2015, SSA projected that changing Social Security's COLA to be based on the Chained CPI-U would move about 456,000 people

---

[19] GAO, Retirement Security: Challenges for Those Claiming Social Security Benefits Early and New Health Coverage Options, GA0-14-311 (Washington, D.C.: April 23, 2014).

[20] We analyzed 2016 Survey of Consumer Finances data using age as a proxy for retirement.

into poverty by 2050, and that changing it to be based on the CPI-E would move 238,000 people out of poverty by 2050.[21]

Effect of Alternate CP is over 30 Years on Households with High and Low Incomes

An illustrative example:[22]

- As described previously, if the Chained CPI-U had been used to calculate COLAs for retirees starting in 2003, we estimate that aggregate Social Security benefits would have decreased in 2033 relative to the CPI-W, based on our analysis using historical and assumed future inflation.
- For a low-income household, this represents about a 6 percent decrease in retirement income. For a high-income household, this represents about a 1 percent decrease 1n retirement income.
- If the CPI-E had been used, we estimate that Social Security benefits would have increased in 2033 relative to the CPI-W, based on our analysis using historical and assumed future inflation.
- For a low-income household, this represents about a 4 Percent increase in retirement income. For a high-income household, this represents about a 1 percent increase 1n retirement income.

---

[21] SSA projections are based on the microsimulation "Modeling Income in the Near Term 7" and incorporate intermediate assumptions from the 2012 Trustees Report. For context, in 2017 there were about 45.5 million recipients of Social Security retirement benefits and the Census Bureau estimated that 39.7 million Americans lived in poverty.

[22] Using historical CPI data from BLS and future inflation assumptions by SSA, we estimated hypothetical Social Security COLAs that could have been used if the COLA were based on an alternate CPI over the 2003-2033 period. The inflation assumptions reflect the intermediate assumptions in the 2018 Trustees Report. Income amount and composition information is from the nationally representative 2016 Survey of Consumer Finances, the most recent available. We use household age 65 and older as a proxy for retirement. As discussed in the prior slide, Social Security benefits make up 81 percent of retirement income for those in the lowest income quintile and 15 percent for those in the highest income quintile.

Implementation

Alternate Indexes for Calculating COLAs Would Likely Present Tradeoffs

- If an alternate CPI were adopted, the following steps could potentially be needed in addition to a potential legislative change:

Potential Steps Needed:	CPI-U	Chained CPI-U	CPI-E
Explain change to beneficiaries	X	X	X
Consider lack of timely data		X	
Research and develop new official index			X

Source: GAO analysis of agency information and interviews with agency officials.

Potential Legislative and Regulatory Changes to Switch to an Alternate Index

- Statutes authorizing selected federal programs refer to the CPI generally, but do not specify which CPI must be used to calculate COLAs, and some link to Social Security's COLA.
- However, SSA officials told us that changes in CPI have historically been the result of legislation.
- For example, the December 2017 tax law changed which CPI
- is used to adjust taxable income brackets.23
- SSA officials also indicated that any changes to how it computes
- COLAs would require a legislative change.
- Any changes to the CPI for Social Security would need to be reflected in SSA's regulations, which refer specifically to the CPI- W.

---

[23] Prior to this law, CPI-U data were used. Initial Chained CPI-U data are now used. See later slides for further discussion of initial and final Chained CPI-U.

Switching Indexes Would Necessitate Communication to Beneficiaries

- Agencies would need to explain the change and why it is being made.
- This would likely come at a cost, though the amount is unknown.
- Changes could be more difficult to explain if they involve complex methodological issues or a decrease in benefits.

Issues with Timeliness of Chained CPI-U Data

- A switch to the Chained CPI-U may require SSA and other agencies to determine how or whether to address data lags of up to 1 year.
- BLS produces the Chained CPI-U in stages:
- Initial Chained CPI-U (monthly, subject to revision)
- Interim revised data (quarterly, subject to revision)
- Final Chained CPI-U (10-12 months after initial data)
- According to BLS, this is necessary because expenditure data used to calculate weights become available after a significant lag, so as to allow the Chained CPI-U to reflect consumers' ability to buy different goods and services in response to price changes. Experts generally agree that including that type of substitution makes the Chained CPI-U more
- reflective of consumer behavior, according to Congressional Budget Office and Congressional Research Service documents.
- This data lag is not an issue for other CP is because they do not require current period expenditure weights and are final once released.

Some Options to Address Timeliness of Chained CPI-U

- Wait until final data are released to calculate COLA.
  - Pro: Data would be final and most accurate.
  - Con: COLA would be based on price changes from 1 to 2 years ago.
- Use cohort-specific COLAs that rely on initial, interim, and final data.[24]

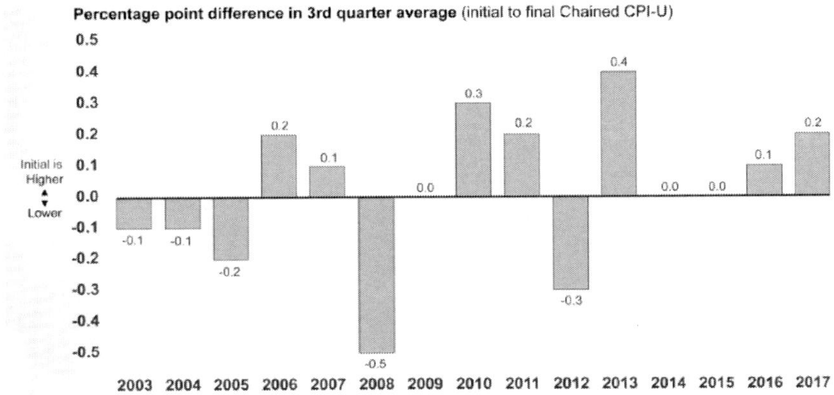

Source: GAO analysis of Bureau of Labor Statistics information. I GA0-19-218R

Note: There was no cost-of-living adjustment based on CPI-W data for 2009, 2010, and 2015.In 2009 and 2015 there would not have been one using the initial or final Chained CPI-U. However, in 2010 there would have been a cost-of-living adjustment using the initial Chained CPI-U but not using the final Chained CPI-U.

Figure 5. Differences between Initial and Final Chained CPI-U Can Be Substantial.

  - Pro: Unusual errors in the initial index would be corrected in a subsequent year using this method, according to the Congressional Budget Office.

---

[24] This method would require calculating a separate COLA each year for the group of people that claim for the first time that year. See Congressional Budget Office, Testimony before the Subcommittee on Social Security, Committee on Ways and Means, U.S. House of Representatives: Using the Chained CPI to Index Social Security, Other Federal Programs, and the Tax Code for Inflation (Washington, D.C.: April 18, 2013).

    - Con: It could be complicated to administer different COLAs for different cohorts; if the difference between initial and final data is not zero on average, this would lead to permanent change in benefits.
- Use initial data without later adjusting them.
    - Pro: No delay.
    - Con: Initial data are subject to larger measurement error compared to the final data, and errors would lead to permanent differentials in benefits (see figure 5).

Additional Information on the Difference between Initial and Final Chained CPI-U

- As we discussed earlier, even small annual changes to COLA accumulate over time and could have significant effects on an individual's benefits.
- In 2015, BLS changed the methodology to calculate the initial Chained CPI-U.[25]
- Agency officials said this change decreased the difference between initial and final data.
- BLS has also made improvements to the timeliness of the final Chained CPI-U data, as prior to 2015 it took up to 2 years for the final Chained CPI-U to be available.

Making the CPI-E Official Could Be Costly

- BLS considers the CPI-E an experimental index and does not consider it as accurate as the official indexes.
- BLS officials said they would need to conduct research to assess whether the current CPI-E methodology is sufficient and, if not, develop an official CPI-E.

---

[25] J. Klick, "Improving Initial Estimates of the Chained Consumer Price Index," Monthly Labor Review, Bureau of Labor Statistics (Washington, D.C.: February 2018).

- According to 2017 BLS estimates, it could cost about $5 million annually over several years to research the issue.
- If the official CPI-E required additional surveys, BLS said it could cost up to $110 million per year thereafter.[26]
- Other CP is are based off of the same set of surveys, so they do not require this additional cost.

Other Considerations for the CPI-E

- If BLS determined the current methodology is sufficient, BLS could change the status of the CPI-E from an experimental index to an official index without additional costs for more surveys.
- None of the agency officials we spoke with were aware of retirement programs (federal or otherwise) that indexed benefits to the CPI-E.
- However, several legislative proposals have been introduced to index various federal retirement benefits to the CPI-E.

Effects on Other Federal Programs

Ripple Effects

- Using an alternate CPI for federal retirement programs would have ripple effects for other federal programs.
- For example, by law, the COLA for Social Security retirement benefits is the same as the COLA for Social Security Disability Insurance (DI) benefits. Changes to that COLA would trig er changes to Supplemental Security Income (SSI) benefits.[27]

---

[26] These BLS estimates include an at least 80 percent increase in the number of households surveyed to produce the expenditure weights, and they also include additional price collection for items purchased by the elderly at outlets frequented by the elderly, among other things.

[27] Further, a change in the Social Security COLA triggers a change in Railroad Retirement Board pensions and Veterans Affairs pensions.

- Dl and SSI beneficiaries have different characteristics than Social Security retirement beneficiaries. It is uncertain whether using a different CPI would accurately represent the market basket: of goods and services consumed oy beneficiaries in air of these programs.
- Dl and SSI beneficiaries tend to be younger, so they could experience compounded effects for a longer period of benefit receipt.

Cost Shifting

- A "hold-harmless" provision prevents Medicare Part 8 premiums from increasing by more than the Social Security COLA for some participants in both Medicare Part 8 and Social Security.
- Thus, a lower COLA could lead to smaller premium increases for these participants.
- These costs may be borne by:
    - other participants not subject to this provision, or
    - the Medicaid programs that cover their premiums, in the case of some low-income participants.

Other Effects

- While this work focused on federal retirement programs, the same dynamics would be at play for other programs that use COLAs based on price indexes.
- If income eligibility for the Supplemental Nutrition Assistance Program (SNAP) were indexed to the Chained CPI-U, the number of program participants and costs would have likely decreased. In contrast, using the CPI-E would have likely resulted in an increase. In fiscal year 2017, about 42 million people received SNAP benefits.
- There are cases in which the effect on program cost would be reversed, such as with refundable tax credits or cost- sharing with

non-federal parties. For example, if Medicare Rarticipants' cost-sharing amounts were indexed to the Chained CPI-U, program costs would likely increase, whereas under the CPI-E they would likely decrease.

Appendix II: Objective, Scope, and Methodology

In this chapter, we examined the benefits and disadvantages of alternate price indexes for measuring the cost of living for older Americans. To conduct this work, we interviewed agency officials and reviewed relevant federal publications, which we identified by interviewing agency officials and searching agency websites. Relevant agencies were the Social Security Administration (SSA), Department of Labor, Department of the Treasury, Congressional Budget Office, and Congressional Research Service.

Using historical and assumed future consumer price index (CPI) data for hypothetical beneficiaries, we calculated Social Security cost-of-living adjustments (COLA) that could have been used if the COLA were based on various CPIs over the 2003–2033 period. To calculate these COLAs, we analyzed CPI data from the Department of Labor's Bureau of Labor Statistics (BLS) as well as other information from SSA. We calculated COLAs based on the third quarter average of the CPI for Urban Wage Earners and Clerical Workers (CPI-W, on which Social Security COLAs are currently based) as well as three alternate CPIs: CPI for All Urban Consumers (CPI-U), Chained CPI for All Urban Consumers (Chained CPI-U, both initial and final data), and the CPI for the Elderly (CPI-E).[28] To analyze the effect of using alternate CPIs over time, we assumed the hypothetical beneficiaries retired in 2003 and received adjusted benefits for

[28] Chained CPI-U data are produced in stages: the initial data are produced monthly, updates are produced quarterly, and the final data are published as the fourth quarterly revision, available up to a year after initial data are produced. For example, the most recent final Chained CPI-U data available in October 2018 were from September 2017.

30 years.[29] We used the most recent historical CPI data that were available for all indexes.[30] For future CPI data, we used inflation information from SSA's Office of the Chief Actuary that was based on the intermediate assumptions from the 2018 Trustees Report.[31]

To calculate hypothetical benefit amounts based on these alternate COLAs, we used information from SSA's Office of the Chief Actuary on hypothetical benefit and earnings amounts. Specifically, we selected hypothetical beneficiary characteristics based on SSA's hypothetical retired workers with earnings equal to the national average wage index. These workers were assumed to have scaled-earnings patterns, which are earnings patterns derived from the earnings experienced by actual workers covered by Social Security. For example, for a hypothetical worker retiring in 2003, the national average wage index was $33,256. We calculated hypothetical benefits for workers retiring at age 65, which is the full retirement age for that birth cohort.

We described benefit amounts in nominal rather than inflation-adjusted dollars, partly because the subject of this chapter is the effect of whichever inflation adjuster is used. However, to provide a fuller picture, we also calculated constant dollar amounts adjusted using the CPI-U.

Consistent with other analyses in this chapter, we used historical CPI data and future inflation information from SSA's Office of the Chief Actuary that was based on the intermediate assumptions from the 2018 Trustees Report.

---

[29] We do not presume that 30 years is a typical length of retirement; rather we wanted to examine the cumulative effects that could have occurred over time.

[30] The most recent final Chained CPI-U data were from 2017, and for all other indexes the most recent data were from 2018.

[31] *The 2018 Annual Report of the Board of Trustees of the Federal Old-Age and Survivors Insurance and Federal Disability Insurance Trust Funds* (Washington, D.C.: June 5, 2018). The Trustees Report describes assumed future inflation for the CPI-W, and we confirmed the assumptions for other CPIs with the Office of the Chief Actuary. Specifically, the CPI-W and CPI-U are assumed to increase by 2.5 percent in 2019 (for benefits payable in 2020), and 2.6 percent in 2020 and later. When scoring legislative proposals to change the CPI, the Office of the Chief Actuary assumes that the CPI-E will increase by 0.2 percentage points more than the CPI-W in the future and that the Chained CPI-U will increase by 0.3 percentage points less than the CPI-W in the future. Because final Chained CPI-U data were not available for the third quarter of 2018, we based the 2018 data on the aforementioned assumed difference from the historical CPI-W.

We also used data from the 2016 Survey of Consumer Finances (SCF) to understand the average share of total retirement income that Social Security benefits comprise. The SCF is a triennial, nationally representative household survey sponsored by the Board of Governors of the Federal Reserve System. The SCF captures detailed information about household income by source. It also captures information on the age of each household head, which it defines as a male within a mixed-sex couple or the older individual within a single-sex couple, for purposes of data organization. We used age 65 and older as a proxy for retirement, though we recognize that some members of this group may not be retired. As with all surveys based on self-reported data, SCF is subject to nonsampling error. It is also subject to sampling error since it is one of a large number of random samples that might have been drawn. Because of this, we express our confidence in the precision of the sample results as 95 percent confidence intervals. All percentage estimates in our report based on the SCF have 95 percent confidence intervals that are within 3 percentage points of the estimate itself.

The calculations for these hypothetical beneficiaries are illustrative and may not be representative of actual beneficiaries' experiences. Moreover, the calculations and assumptions reflect the recent relatively low-inflation environment, and results may be different in a high- inflation environment.[32] Further, BLS has modified its methodology over time and may continue to do so in the future. However, we believe these calculations illustrate what the potential effects might have been if an alternate CPI had been used. For the federal retirement programs within our scope, the COLAs are generally based on the third quarter CPI-W. While we created the hypothetical calculations for Social Security benefits, we believe that the overall trends would hold for other federal retirement programs as well.

---

[32] While the Chained CPI-U was first published in 2002, if we had chosen another timeframe prior to 2003 for other CPIs, our results could have been different. For example, over the 2003–2018 time period, the hypothetical COLA based on the CPI-E was on average 0.09 percentage points higher than the COLA based on the CPI-W. In the 15 years prior to 2003, the hypothetical COLA based on the CPI-E was on average 0.33 percentage points higher than the COLA based on the CPI-W.

Some SSA publications we reviewed used a microsimulation model, Modeling Income in the Near Term (MINT). SSA developed MINT with others to analyze how proposed changes to Social Security benefits could affect different groups of beneficiaries. This model includes calculations using numerous data sources, such as the Survey of Income and Program Participation and the Health and Retirement Study. The projections were built using economic assumptions, such as anticipated inflation, as well as demographic and programmatic assumptions from the 2012 Trustees Report. We reported on MINT projections through 2050 because SSA officials told us the effects of a change in index would be fully realized over this period. While MINT provides very rough estimates of future incomes, they may be useful for comparing future incomes across alternative policy scenarios and over time.

Further SSA publications we reviewed projected the effects of using the Chained CPI-U and the CPI-E to calculate Social Security's COLA, and there are differences in the parameters of these policy options.[33] Specifically, the option to use the CPI-E would begin in December 2020 and apply to both recipients of disability and retirement benefits. In contrast, the option to use the Chained CPI-U would begin in December 2019 for recipients of retirement benefits, while disability recipients would only be affected when their benefit converts to retirement benefit at the full retirement age. We used these projections because, although there are differences, they were the closest available policy options that SSA examined to replace the CPI-W with the CPI- E or Chained CPI-U. While these differences do not affect the direction of the option's effect on Social Security's finances, they do affect the magnitude of that effect.

We assessed the reliability of the data we used by reviewing relevant documentation, interviewing knowledgeable agency officials, reviewing internal controls, and comparing our calculations to published data. We found the data to be reliable for our purposes.

---

[33] According to SSA officials, the policy options SSA examined are ones that have been proposed by policymakers and other interested parties, so it is not surprising that there are differences.

Appendix III: Comments from the Social Security Administration

SOCIAL SECURITY

Office of the Commissioner

January 7, 2019

Mr. Charles Jeszeck
Director, Education, Workforce, and Income Security Issues
United States Government Accountability Office
441 G Street, NW
Washington, DC 20548

Dear Mr. Jeszeck:

Thank you for the opportunity to review the draft report, "Retirement Security: Alternate Price Indexes for Cost-of-Living Adjustments Present Tradeoffs" (GAO-19-218R). As noted in the report, we currently rely on the Consumer Price Index for Urban Wage Earners and Clerical Workers to compute cost-of-living adjustments (COLA). Over the years, our Chief Actuary has scored various COLA computation options proposed by policymakers. Each option would have varying effects on Social Security program costs, individual benefit levels, and administrative costs, as acknowledged by the report. We also acknowledge that any change to how we compute COLAs would require a legislative change.

Sincerely,

Stephanie Hall

Stephanie Hall
Acting Deputy Chief of Staff

In: Retirement
Editor: Thomas M. Osborne
ISBN: 978-1-53615-703-1

Chapter 5

RETIREMENT ACCOUNTS: FEDERAL ACTION NEEDED TO CLARIFY TAX TREATMENT OF UNCLAIMED 401(K) PLAN SAVINGS TRANSFERRED TO STATES*

United States Government Accountability Office

ABBREVIATIONS

DC	defined contribution
DOL	Department of Labor
ERISA	Employee Retirement Income Security Act of 1974
ICI	Investment Company Institute
IRA	individual retirement account
IRS	Internal Revenue Service
NAUPA	National Association of Unclaimed Property Administrators

* This is an edited, reformatted and augmented version of United States Government Accountability Office, Report to the Ranking Member, Committee on Finance, U.S. Senate, Publication No. GAO-19-88, dated January 2019.

PBGC	Pension Benefit Guaranty Corporation
RMD	Required Minimum Distribution
UUPA	Uniform Unclaimed Property Act

WHY GAO DID THIS STUDY

Over the course of individuals' careers, their retirement savings can be spread across multiple retirement accounts and they can change jobs, both of which can cause their savings to become unclaimed and even lost. Prior GAO work has found that unclaimed retirement savings are sometimes transferred to the states. GAO was asked to review such transfers.

This chapter examines (1) how much in retirement savings is transferred to states as unclaimed property and what happens to those savings once transferred and (2) the steps IRS and DOL have taken to oversee these transfers and what improvements are needed. GAO interviewed federal and state officials, industry representatives, and other stakeholders, and surveyed all 50 states and the District of Columbia (and received 22 responses). GAO also surveyed 401(k) plan service providers and IRA trustees regarding the volume of retirement savings transferred to states and their federal tax reporting and withholding practices for those transfers.

WHAT GAO RECOMMENDS

GAO is making three recommendations, including that IRS should consider clarifying whether transfers from employer-based plans (such as 401(k) plans) to states constitute reportable and taxable distributions and consider modifying its list of permitted reasons for rolling over savings after the 60-day rollover deadline. IRS agreed with our recommendations and noted that it will work with the Department of the Treasury to address them.

WHAT GAO FOUND

Millions of dollars in retirement savings are transferred to states as unclaimed property, only some of which is later claimed by owners. Of the 22 states responding to GAO's survey, 17 states provided data indicating that $35 million in unclaimed retirement savings was transferred to them from employer plans and individual retirement accounts (IRAs) in 2016. When account owners do not claim money from retirement savings accounts or cash checks from their plans, the funds may be transferred to state unclaimed property offices (see Figure). Assets and uncashed checks from employer plans (such as 401(k) plans), were the most common form of retirement savings transferred to states. After funds are transferred, owners can claim their savings from the state. According to the 15 states providing data on this, owners claimed about $25 million in retirement savings in 2016: $601, on average, from 401(k) plan checks, and $5,817, on average, from traditional IRAs. States reported using a range of strategies to maintain the value of retirement savings while holding these funds, such as applying interest. States also reported various efforts to locate owners. However, not all savings will be claimed because, among other reasons, owner information is not always associated with transferred savings when the amount is small, which complicates state efforts to locate some owners.

The Internal Revenue Service (IRS) and the Department of Labor (DOL) have issued guidance on transferring retirement savings to states; however, IRS has not clarified certain responsibilities or ensured that the retirement savings that owners claim from states can be rolled over into other tax-deferred retirement accounts. IRS is responsible for communicating and enforcing tax responsibilities, but has not specified whether 401(k) plan providers should report state transfers to IRS as distributions and withhold federal income taxes. IRS officials said the agency has not issued guidance to clarify this issue because of competing priorities. As a result, 401(k) plan provider practices vary—some providers withhold taxes when transferring savings to states while others do not. This makes the IRS less likely to collect federal income taxes that may be due if transfers are taxable events. IRS also has not taken action to ensure that individuals who claim 401(k) savings from a state can roll over these savings to other tax-deferred retirement accounts after IRS's 60-day deadline. IRS allows individuals to roll over savings after 60 days for several reasons, none of which include claiming 401(k) savings from a state. Federal law seeks to protect the interests of participants in retirement plans. Account owners who are unable to roll over their reclaimed savings forgo the opportunity to continue investing the funds on a tax-deferred basis.

January 18, 2019

The Honorable Ron Wyden
Ranking Member
Committee on Finance United States Senate

Dear Senator Wyden:

In 2017, U.S. workers held about $17 trillion in retirement savings accounts, specifically employer-based defined contribution accounts, like 401(k) plans, and individual retirement accounts (IRAs).[1] An individual's retirement savings can be spread across multiple accounts of the same type, such as multiple 401(k) plans, as well as across 401(k) plans and IRAs. In addition, during the course of their careers, individuals can change jobs multiple times and retirement plans can terminate. Each event can cause an individual to lose their connection to some or all of their retirement

---

[1] Investment Company Institute (ICI), 2018 Investment Company Fact Book (Washington, D.C.: 2018). Data are year-end 2017. Defined contribution (DC) plans, such as 401(k) plans, provide retirement benefits that are based on contributions and the performance of the investments in participants' individual accounts. Retirement savings in DC accounts totaled $7.7 trillion in 2017, according to ICI's 2018 Factbook. ICI specifies that the DC plan data include private employer-sponsored DC plans (including 401(k) plans), 403(b) plans, 457 plans, and the Federal Employees Retirement System's Thrift Savings Plan. Two common types of IRAs are Traditional and Roth IRAs, for which contributions are tax-deferred and after-tax, respectively. IRA assets nationwide totaled about $9.2 trillion in 2017, according to ICI's 2018 Factbook. ICI's data for IRAs include traditional IRAs, Roth IRAs, and employer-sponsored IRAs (SEP IRAs, SAR-SEP IRAs, and SIMPLE IRAs) and are estimated.

savings, in some cases permanently. As U.S. workers continue to change jobs and leave behind retirement savings accounts, retirement savings are more likely to be unclaimed.[2]

While an exact figure is not known, the amount of unclaimed retirement savings in the United States has been estimated to exceed $100 billion.[3]

Retirement savings can be classified as unclaimed property when an account owner has forgotten about an account or when owner-associated activity on a retirement account—such as logging in online to check an account balance—has ceased for a certain amount of time generally specified under state laws. In certain circumstances, unclaimed retirement savings may end up transferred to a state.[4] Although estimates exist for the amount of unclaimed retirement benefits in the United States, little is known about the amount of unclaimed retirement savings ultimately transferred to states as unclaimed property.

You asked us to review issues related to the transfer of retirement savings to the states as unclaimed property. This chapter examines (1) how much in retirement savings is transferred to states as unclaimed property and what happens to those savings once transferred, and (2) the steps the Internal Revenue Service (IRS) and the Department of Labor (DOL) have taken to oversee the transfer of unclaimed retirement savings to the states and what improvements, if any, are needed.

To identify the amount of retirement savings transferred to states and what happens to those savings once transferred, we sent surveys to the unclaimed property offices of all 50 states and the District of Columbia

---

[2] E.A. Bruce & J. Turner, *Lost Pension Money: Who is Responsible? Who Benefits?*, 3 J. Marshall L. Rev. 695 (2004).

[3] Bruce and Turner, *Lost Pension Money*. The authors of this article specifically used the term "lost pension", defined as "money held by a qualified pension plan that the party entitled to it has not claimed." The article states that lost pension money may be from a defined benefit plan or a DC plan, may be owed to either a retiree or retiree's beneficiary, and may include employer or employee contributions. *Id.* at 697-98.

[4] Although some states may refer to some unclaimed property as abandoned property, in this chapter we refer to retirement savings that, as a result of a lack of owner-associated activity for a certain period of time, have been designated as unclaimed property under state laws as "unclaimed retirement savings" or "unclaimed savings." For ease of reference, we use these terms to describe property both before and after it has been transferred to a state.

(our state survey). We focused our analysis on employer-based defined contribution (DC) plans, such as 401(k) plans, and IRAs.[5] Our analysis includes responses from 22 states (including the District of Columbia) with populations that together comprise 57 percent of the U.S. population; 17 of the 22 states provided data on retirement savings transferred to their states in 2016, which was the most recently completed year at the time of our review; and 15 of the 22 states also provided data on the amount owners claimed that year. We assessed the quality of the data we collected by including questions in the survey to help us determine data completeness and accuracy. Although we identified some limitations in the quality of the data, we determined that the data were sufficient for the purposes of our reporting objectives. See appendix I for more information about our methodology and data quality.

To gain further insight into the amount of savings transferred to states, we surveyed companies that belong to two industry associations. For the first industry association, we conducted a nongeneralizable survey of all 129 transfer agent companies that are members of the Investment Company Institute to obtain IRA transfer data (our IRA transfer agent survey).[6] Of the 129 companies surveyed, we received and analyzed survey responses from 21 companies that collectively managed $299 billion in IRA assets in 2016, or about 4 percent of total assets managed in the IRA

---

[5] 401(k) plans are the predominant type of employer-based plan in the United States, according to Department of Labor data. See Employee Benefits Security Administration, United States Department of Labor, *Private Pension Plan Bulletin: Abstract of 2015 Form 5500 Annual Reports Data Extracted on 7/7/2017* (Feb. 2018). IRAs are key retirement savings vehicles for workers not covered by an employer-based plan.

[6] ICI is an association that represents mutual fund companies. Transfer agents are companies that maintain records of mutual fund shareholder accounts. According to its website, ICI members manage total assets of $22 trillion in the United States, serving more than 100 million U.S. shareholders. Most IRA assets are invested in mutual funds. In 2015, the largest portion (48 percent) of IRA assets was invested in mutual funds, according to industry data. See Cerulli Associates, *The Cerulli Report: U.S. Evolution of the Retirement Investor 2016: Regulation and Investor Addressability*. Our survey results are not generalizable because the transfer agents that completed the surveys are voluntary members of ICI. Therefore, they may differ from companies that are not ICI members in terms of their knowledge of or concern about the issues addressed in the surveys, which has implications on their survey responses.

market, based on industry data.[7] For the second industry association, we conducted a nongeneralizable survey of all 32 401(k) plan service provider companies that are members of the SPARK Institute to obtain 401(k) plan transfer data (our 401(k) plan service provider survey).[8] We received and analyzed responses from seven companies that collectively managed more than $580 billion in 401(k) assets in 2016 (one survey respondent did not report the amount of assets managed), or more than 13 percent of total 401(k) assets nationwide, based on DOL data.[9] To assess the quality of the data we obtained through these surveys, we included questions in the surveys that asked respondents to identify the data sources they consulted and any data limitations. An overview of our three surveys is provided in Table 1.

In addition, we obtained IRA transfer data from four large companies that collectively managed over $1.4 trillion in IRA assets in 2016, or about 20 percent of the IRA market, based on industry data.[10] These data collection efforts together provided us with insight on transfer activity from the perspectives of the stakeholders that are involved in the transfer process.

To determine the steps that IRS and DOL have taken to oversee the transfer of unclaimed retirement savings to the states and whether any improvements are needed, we reviewed relevant documentation from IRS and DOL, including guidance issued on topics such as the permissibility of

---

[7] Cerulli Associates, *The Cerulli Report: U.S. Evolution of the Retirement Investor 2016: Regulation and Investor Addressability*.

[8] The SPARK Institute is an association that represents DC plan service providers. SPARK members include 401(k) record keepers as well as representatives from mutual fund companies and investment brokerage firms, and serve approximately 85 million participants in 401(k) and other DC plans. Our survey results are not generalizable because the plan service providers that completed the surveys are voluntary members of the SPARK Institute. Therefore, they may differ from companies that are not SPARK Institute members in terms of their knowledge of or concern about the issues addressed in the surveys, which has implications on their survey responses.

[9] Employee Benefits Security Administration, United States Department of Labor, *Private Pension Plan Bulletin: Abstract of 2015 Form 5500 Annual Reports Data Extracted on 7/7/2017* (Feb. 2018).

[10] Cerulli Associates, *The Cerulli Report: U.S. Evolution of the Retirement Investor 2016: Regulation and Investor Addressability*.

certain transfers of savings to states and the tax related requirements that apply to those transfers.

Table 1. Overview of GAO Surveys Used to Obtain Data on Transfers of Unclaimed Retirement Savings to States

GAO Survey	Entities surveyed	Responses
State survey	50 states and D.C.	• 22 states responded, whose populations amount to 57% of the total U.S. population. • 17 provided data on retirement savings transferred.
IRA transfer agent survey	129 IRA transfer agent companies that are members of industry group Investment Company Institute.	• 21 transfer agents, holding about 4% of total IRA assets nationwide.
401(k) plan service provider survey	32 401(k) plan service providers, such as record keeping companies, that are members of industry group SPARK Institute.	• 7 companies responded, covering more than 13% of total 401(k) assets nationwide. • 5 reported that they made transfers and 2 reported they did not make such transfers

Source: GAO description of research methodology. | GAO-19-88.

We also included questions in all of our surveys that asked respondents to provide their perspectives on whether additional federal guidance is needed on the transfer of retirement savings to the states, such as guidance on the tax related requirements that apply to transfers. In addition, our surveys of IRA transfer agents and 401(k) plan service providers included questions that asked respondents to identify whether federal income taxes were withheld from the amounts they transferred to the states in 2016. We also reviewed relevant federal laws and regulations and interviewed IRS and DOL officials as well as relevant industry groups.

We conducted this performance audit from October 2016 to January 2019 in accordance with generally accepted government auditing standards. Those standards require that we plan and perform the audit to obtain sufficient, appropriate evidence to provide a reasonable basis for our findings and conclusions based on our audit objectives. We believe that the evidence obtained provides a reasonable basis for our findings and conclusions based on our audit objectives.

BACKGROUND

Unclaimed Retirement Savings

Unclaimed retirement savings are savings that individuals are entitled to receive, but have not claimed because employers or other entities that maintain their retirement accounts cannot locate the individuals or because the individuals have forgotten about the savings. Individuals can lose track of retirement savings held in multiple accounts across different employers. As we have previously reported, when employees change jobs some leave their savings in their former employers' 401(k) plans.[11] This may be a prudent choice under some circumstances, but it opens up the person to the risk of forgetting the account. Unclaimed retirement savings often come in the form of uncashed distribution checks—checks made out to individuals to comply with required minimum distribution (RMD) requirements,[12] or for other reasons, that go uncashed. Plan terminations can also result in unclaimed retirement savings if a terminating plan, which must distribute savings to complete the termination process, cannot obtain instruction from the account owner on what to do with the savings. According to the Department of Labor, 19,155 401(k) plans terminated in 2016.

State Laws Generally Govern the Transfer of Unclaimed Retirement Savings to the States

According to literature and unclaimed property experts, all 50 states and the District of Columbia have laws that generally govern the transfer of unclaimed retirement savings to the state once certain requirements are

---

[11] GAO, *401(K) Plans: Greater Protections Needed for Forced Transfers and Inactive Accounts*, GAO-15-73 (Washington, D.C.: Nov. 21, 2014).

[12] Under the Internal Revenue Code, individuals age 701/2 or older who are participants in qualified DC plans or who have an IRA generally must receive minimum annual payments from their plan account or IRA based on their account balance and remaining life expectancy. RMDs apply to employer plans and traditional IRAs. RMDs do not apply to Roth IRAs while the owner is alive.

met.[13] According to the National Association of Unclaimed Property Administrators (NAUPA),[14] the vast majority of state unclaimed property law provisions relating to retirement savings come from one of the versions of the Uniform Unclaimed Property Act, which the states and the financial services industry jointly drafted. State laws generally identify an event that triggers the start of a dormancy period for retirement savings, or the amount of time in which no activity has occurred on the account before it can be transferred as unclaimed savings to a state and, according to NAUPA officials, during which time the entities in possession of the accounts are not able to locate the owners.[15] Retirement savings may come to satisfy a state's dormancy period after an event that results in a payment being due, such as an owner's death or owners reaching the age when they must begin taking required minimum distributions of their savings, as shown in Figure 1.[16]

---

[13] Throughout this chapter, our statements about state unclaimed property laws and the process for transferring unclaimed retirement savings to the states are solely based on our review of available literature, including state unclaimed property guidance, as well as information from unclaimed property experts. GAO did not independently review states' unclaimed property laws. When unclaimed savings are transferred to a state, they are transferred to the state where the account owner last resided or, if unknown, the state where the holder—such as a plan administrator or IRA trustee—is located. State unclaimed property laws address various types of property and are not specific to retirement savings. However, for purposes of this chapter, our discussion of state laws is limited to how they affect retirement savings. In addition, under certain circumstances, federal requirements may apply to transfers of retirement savings to states. For example, as discussed later, a DOL advisory opinion expresses DOL's view that the Employee Retirement Income Security Act of 1974 (ERISA) preempted a state's law as it related to requiring a plan to transfer unclaimed amounts held in plan accounts to the state- meaning the plan was not required to transfer the funds to the state. ERISA provides the legal framework for most private sector workplace retirement plans. See 29 U.S.C. § 1001 et seq.

[14] NAUPA is a non-profit organization affiliated with the National Association of State Treasurers. NAUPA's members are unclaimed property officers from all states and the District of Columbia as well as other jurisdictions. NAUPA holds meetings and seminars to provide professional education opportunities to holders, and maintains an informational website. According to NAUPA officials, the organization created and periodically updates a common electronic reporting format for use by all the states.

[15] For example, according to one state's unclaimed property guidance, an owner can demonstrate activity by logging into their account online to check their balance. In the context of unclaimed retirement savings, owners are those individuals with a legal right to claim the retirement savings, such as 401(k) plan participants, owners of IRAs, and the heirs of deceased participants or owners.

[16] The term "plan participant" describes the owner before their savings are transferred to the state, while "owner" describes them even after their savings are no longer in the plan.

Table 2. Examples of Circumstances under Which Unclaimed Retirement Savings Are Transferred to States, According to a Variety of Sources GAO Reviewed

Type of account	What is transferred to the states?	Under what conditions?
Active 401(k) plan	Account balances	If, after a participant turns age 70 ½, there is no activity in an account, mail is returned, and the state dormancy period is met.
Uncashed checks	Once a check has remained uncashed for 6 months, there has been no contact with the owner, and the state dormancy period has been met.	
Terminating 401(k) plan	Account balances	If a plan terminates and has made certain efforts to locate owners, funds can be transferred before the expiration of the state dormancy period.
Individual Retirement Account (IRA)	Account balances	If there is no account activity or contact for three years after the account owner dies or turns age 70 ½ and the funds are not claimed during this period.
Uncashed checks	Once a check has remained uncashed for 6 months, there has been no contact with the owner, and the state dormancy period has been met.	

Source: Information from 401(k) plan service providers, an unclaimed property expert, state documentation, and an IRA provider. | GAO-19-88.

Note: For the purposes of this chapter, when we refer to the transfer of uncashed checks to the states, we are not referring to the physical checks themselves, but rather the funds underlying the checks.

From a state's perspective, savings are unclaimed and must be transferred to the state after the dormancy period has expired. Holders—those entities in possession of unclaimed savings and responsible for the maintenance of those savings accounts, such as plan administrators or IRA trustees—transfer the savings to the state.[17]

[17] According to literature, this process is commonly referred to as "escheatment". However, DOL officials indicated that their understanding was that "escheatment" as a technical matter occurs if the state assumes ownership of the retirement savings. Because states act as custodians for transferred retirement savings and owners generally maintain the right to claim their savings indefinitely, according to literature, the savings are not technically escheated. However, true escheatment of unclaimed property to states may start to occur.

According to NAUPA, holders are responsible for making a reasonable effort to locate the owners of otherwise unclaimed accounts before transferring them to state custody. States may also accept transfers of retirement savings in other specific circumstances. For example, according to NAUPA officials, a terminating 401(k) plan sponsor may transfer retirement savings to the state if the owners remain missing after the plan takes certain steps to contact them, as outlined in federal guidance.[18] See Table 2 below for examples of when savings are transferred from 401(k) plans and IRAs.

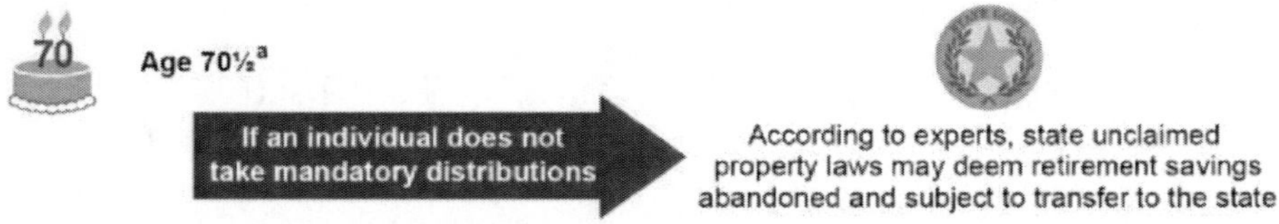

Source: GAO analysis of information from state unclaimed property experts and federal law. | GAO-19-88.

Note: This figure does not address all potential consequences of failing to take required minimum distributions.

[a] Under the Internal Revenue Code, individuals age 70 1/2 or older who have savings in certain retirement accounts generally must receive minimum annual payments from their accounts.

Figure 1. According to Stakeholders, Required Minimum Distribution Rules Sometimes Lead to the Transfer of Unclaimed Retirement Savings to a State.

Federal Laws, Regulations, and Oversight

The Internal Revenue Service (IRS) and the Department of Labor (DOL) share enforcement responsibility for the Employee Retirement

---

According to NAUPA officials, until recently all state laws had provided for owners' indefinite eligibility to claim their property. However, in March 2018, Arizona passed a law capping at 35 years (from the time the state receives the property) the length of time in which an owner can claim property—including retirement savings—from the state. Similar legislation proposed in Louisiana would have set a 30-year cap on claims.

[18] An unclaimed property expert and representatives from an industry association told us that terminating plans can transfer unclaimed savings to states prior to the end of the dormancy period typically required to designate savings as unclaimed property.

Income Security Act of 1974 (ERISA). The IRS's mission is to help U.S. taxpayers understand and meet their tax responsibilities under the Internal Revenue Code. To help achieve its mission, IRS issues tax regulations and other guidance. The IRS is responsible for helping to ensure that individuals pay income taxes on distributions from tax-deferred retirement accounts and any additional tax for distributions before age 591/2.[19] IRS also establishes guidelines regarding the calculation of RMDs from qualified plans as well as the federal tax reporting and withholding requirements that apply to RMDs and other plan distributions.[20] Additionally, IRS enforces the requirements within the Internal Revenue Code, including requirements related to the potential transfer of unclaimed retirement savings to states:

- When distributions from 401(k) plans and IRAs occur, plan sponsors and IRA administrators are generally required to withhold and remit to the IRS a percentage of the amount distributed from a qualified retirement account to cover anticipated federal income taxes. The amount withheld varies from generally 10 percent for certain traditional IRA and 401(k) plan distributions to 20 percent for eligible rollover distributions.[21] Qualifying Roth IRA and Roth plan account distributions are not subject to federal income taxes.[22]

---

[19] Distributions of amounts attributable to employee elective contributions prior to age 59- 1/2 generally require a distribution event—such as death or hardship—to occur. See 26 C.F.R. §1.401(k)-1(d).

[20] Distributions of retirement savings are reported to IRS and individuals on Form 1099-R. Form 1099-R shows the amount of funds distributed from a retirement account and the amount of taxes withheld from the distribution.

[21] See 26 U.S.C. § 3405(b)(1) & (c)(1)(B). In some instances, individuals can choose to have no taxes withheld from distributions. For example, recipients of periodic distributions from plans and IRAs can choose to forgo tax withholding.

[22] Roth distributions that are not qualified distributions may be subject to withholding. Enacted as part of the Taxpayer Relief Act of 1997, Roth IRAs allow eligible individuals to make nondeductible contributions to these accounts but generally receive tax-free distributions. According to IRS guidance, a designated Roth plan account is a separate account in a 401(k) plan that holds designated Roth contributions. The amount contributed to a designated Roth account is includible in gross income in the year of the contribution, but eligible distributions from the account (including earnings) are generally tax-free.

- If, within 60 days of receipt, an individual deposits eligible rollover distributions into another qualified account—an indirect rollover—the distribution is not treated as income for federal income tax purposes.[23] However, the amount deposited must be the full amount distributed, including the amount of any income tax withheld. Otherwise, the distribution amount not rolled over is taxable and may be subject to additional tax for early distribution if the individual is younger than age 591/2.
- Individuals must take RMDs from their qualified retirement accounts— both 401(k) plan accounts and traditional IRAs—according to a schedule set by the IRS.[24] These distributions, which cannot be rolled over to another qualified account, generally must begin by April 1st of the calendar year following the calendar year in which an individual turns age 701/2 or retires.[25]

Prior to the later of age 62 or normal retirement age, plans are restricted in their ability to take actions with respect to savings left behind by inactive[26] participants if the individuals did not provide distribution instructions. An inactive account owner's vested balance up to $5,000 can be forced out of an active plan.[27] Without the account owner's instructions for where to transfer the account, balances greater than $1,000 and less

---

[23] See 26 U.S.C. §§ 402(c) and 408(d)(3). Certain distributions are not eligible rollover distributions and therefore cannot be rolled over. Distributions that are not eligible to be rolled over include required minimum distributions, hardship distributions, and life annuities.

[24] See 26 U.S.C. §§ 401(a)(9) and 408(a)(6). RMDs also apply to individuals who inherit Roth IRAs from deceased account owners.

[25] In 2016, 2.5 million people were age 70 and by 2050 about 4 million are projected to be 70 each year, according to U.S. Census data. See https://www.census.gov/data/datasets/2017/demo/popproj/2017-popproj.html.

[26] We use the term "inactive" to refer to individuals who have changed jobs and are no longer making contributions.

[27] Vesting policies are plan policies that require employees to work for a minimum length of time before their employer's contributions become fully nonforfeitable or "vested," meaning employees have an unconditional and legally enforceable right to keep their employer contributions if they separate from their job. An employee's own contributions and any returns on those contributions always belong to the employee and are not forfeitable to the plan if they leave their employer. For more information on force-outs from plans, see GAO, *401(K) Plans: Greater Protections Needed for Forced Transfers and Inactive Accounts*, GAO-15-73 (Washington, D.C.: Nov. 21, 2014).

than or equal to $5,000 may only be transferred to an IRA, while smaller balances may be "cashed out" meaning a check is issued to the owner.[28] Generally, balances in excess of $5,000 may not be distributed without the consent of the owners. However, federal law permits plans to exclude rollover contributions from the account balance that they use to determine if the account is small enough to force out.[29]

DOL's Employee Benefits Security Administration is generally responsible for issuing guidance to plan sponsors and other plan fiduciaries on compliance with Title I of ERISA. A plan's decision regarding what to do with unclaimed retirement savings, which can include transferring these savings to the states,[30] is a decision that is subject to ERISA's fiduciary standards.[31] In Advisory Opinion 1994-41A, DOL expressed its view that ERISA preempted a state unclaimed property law as it related to requiring a plan to transfer amounts held in plan accounts to the state. This means that, in DOL's view, the state law could not compel the plan to transfer unclaimed retirement savings to the state.[32] DOL has issued guidance for terminating DC plans that specifically permits them to transfer certain participant accounts to state unclaimed property funds, generally small accounts of $1,000 or less, when the participant is missing or fails to respond to notices requesting an election of a form of distribution if certain conditions are met.[33]

---

[28] See 26 U.S.C. §§ 401(a)(31)(B) and 411(a)(11).

[29] See 26 U.S.C. § 411(a)(11)(D). Rollover contributions are amounts transferred into a new plan from another workplace plan or an IRA.

[30] Other potential options for handling unclaimed savings include rolling them into an IRA or transferring them to a federally insured bank account. For more information on this topic, see our prior report: GAO, *401(K) Plans: Greater Protections Needed for Forced Transfers and Inactive Accounts*, GAO-15-73 (Washington, D.C.: Nov. 21, 2014).

[31] DOL, *Field Assistance Bulletin 2014-01* (Washington, D.C.: 2014). ERISA contains various provisions intended to protect the interests of plan participants and beneficiaries in workplace retirement plans. These provisions include fiduciary standards to which plans must adhere to ensure that workplace retirement plan funds are handled prudently and in the sole interest of participants.

[32] See DOL Advisory Opinion 1994-41A, Dec. 7, 1994. According to NAUPA officials, some states have expressed disagreement with DOL's advisory opinions on this matter.

[33] See 29 C.F.R. § 2550.404a-3, 29 C.F.R. § 2578.1, and Field Assistance Bulletin 2014- 01.

AVAILABLE STATE SURVEY DATA SHOW THAT SEVENTEEN STATES RECEIVED $35 MILLION IN UNCLAIMED RETIREMENT SAVINGS IN 2016, AND TOOK STEPS TO LOCATE THE OWNERS

Seventeen States' Survey Data Show They Received $35 Million in Unclaimed Retirement Savings

Survey data provided by 17 states show that, in 2016, they collectively received approximately 54,000 transfers of retirement savings worth about $35 million.[34] Because transfers occur every year, the cumulative dollar value of savings held by states is larger than the amount transferred during the one year covered by our state survey. In the context of about $17 trillion in retirement savings accounts nationwide in 2017,[35] $35 million may seem relatively small. However, for individuals, losing track of savings can negatively affect their retirement security.

Transfers of Unclaimed Retirement Savings from Employer-Sponsored Plans

Assets and uncashed checks from employer-based DC plans (employer plans) were the most common form of retirement savings transferred to

[34] We surveyed all 50 states and the District of Columbia. Twenty-two states responded to our survey, and 17 provided aggregate transfer data for specific retirement-related property-type codes. As described in appendix I, the accuracy of states' data depends largely on the accuracy of information provided by holders when they send savings to states. Most states reported that they did not know how accurately holders may have applied the property-type codes used to report transfers to the states, while four states indicated that they thought holders applied the codes somewhat accurately. Because holders using an incorrect property-type code could result in both over and underreporting of retirement savings, we cannot determine whether such errors, if they exist, have resulted in the reported transfer totals being high or low. Also, the dollar value of transfers is underreported because retirement savings transferred in the form of securities often have no associated value recorded, according to several state survey responses. Given these data quality concerns, our state survey is not generalizable, but the values reported by states provide a sense of the scale for such activity.

[35] Investment Company Institute, 2018 Investment Company Fact Book (Washington, D.C.: 2018). This amount includes assets held in both IRAs and DC plans like 401(k) plan. ICI estimated the value of IRA assets.

states, accounting for 84 percent of accounts transferred to the 17 states that provided retirement savings-related transfer data in responding to our state survey.[36] In 2016, $22.4 million was transferred from employer plans to those states. The average dollar value of transfers was generally small—$628 from plans and $301 from retirement plan checks.[37]

Federal law restricts the amount of retirement savings that can be forced out of a plan and outlines rules for how to calculate the amount of savings that can be forced out, both of which affect the size of transfers from plans to states. Forced distributions from employer plans were generally small, based on our state survey data, likely because federal law restricts the size of accounts that can be forced out of a plan.[38] According to a 401(k) plan service provider that we interviewed, when individuals do not cash forced distribution checks, those checks can be transferred to states as unclaimed property. However, forced distributions can also be large, which can mean that significant amounts of retirement savings potentially lose the protections afforded by ERISA. Large account balances can be forced out of a plan because federal law permits plans to exclude rollover contributions when calculating whether the balance is small enough to force out.[39] Therefore, if plans exclude rollover balances,

---

[36] 401(k) plans are the predominant type of employer-based DC plan in the U.S. See Employee Benefits Security Administration, United States Department of Labor, *Private Pension Plan Bulletin: Abstract of 2015 Form 5500 Annual Reports Data Extracted on 7/7/2017* (Feb. 2018).

[37] We calculated this average based on the total dollar value of accounts transferred divided by the number of transfers reported by states. While state data only identify unclaimed retirement savings as savings from "pension or profit sharing plans" and as "pension checks", interviews with industry experts indicate these savings typically exclude defined benefit plans and reflect transfers from DC plans that occur under the varying circumstances described in the background of this chapter. According to experts we interviewed, "pension checks" can actually be distribution checks from (a) active DC plans, made to former employees, which remained uncashed for a lengthy dormancy period and (b) terminating DC plans, which were uncashed and may be transferred to states prior to the end of the dormancy period typically required to designate savings as unclaimed.

[38] A former employee's vested balance of up to $5,000 can be forced out of an active plan. Without the former employee's instructions for where to transfer the account, balances greater than $1,000 and less than or equal to $5,000 may only be transferred to forced-transfer IRAs, while smaller balances may be "cashed out," meaning a check is issued to the owner. See 26 U.S.C. §§ 401(a)(31)(B) and 411(a)(11).

[39] See 26 U.S.C. § 411(a)(11)(D) and 29 U.S.C. § 1053(e)(4). Large account balances could also be forced out as a result of death and other circumstances.

accounts larger than $1,000 can be cashed-out and might end up being transferred to a state after the forced-distribution check goes uncashed.

Recognizing the significance of forced distributions of large balances that include rollover savings, we previously recommended that Congress consider repealing the provision that allows plans to disregard amounts attributable to rollovers when determining if a participant's plan balance is small enough to forcibly transfer it.[40] In a prior report, we concluded that requiring plans to include rollover balances would ensure that larger balances receive the extra protection of remaining in an ERISA-covered plan. Remaining in the plan would also give missing participants more time to reconnect with their plans before savings are potentially transferred to a state.

According to our 401(k) plan service provider survey data, transfers from employer retirement plans often include savings from terminating plans and can affect individuals of all ages. Survey data from the seven service providers responding to our survey—whose plan assets under management make up more than 13 percent of the 401(k) marketplace (one survey respondent did not report the amount of assets managed)— show that the majority of savings these providers transferred to states in 2016 included savings from terminating 401(k) plans. Specifically, survey data from the three providers that could supply such detail show that, of $2.25 million transferred to states, $2.19 million involved savings from terminated plans.[41] Since transfers of savings from employer plans to states can occur as a result of plan terminations, they can affect individuals of all ages. The one 401(k) plan service provider that supplied age-specific data in responding to our survey indicated that transfers it made in 2016 often affected individuals who were younger than 701/2, the age at which individuals generally must begin taking required minimum distributions

---

[40] GAO, *401(K) Plans: Greater Protections Needed for Forced Transfers and Inactive Accounts*, GAO-15-73 (Washington, D.C.: Nov. 21, 2014). At the time of our review, Congress had not taken action on this recommendation.

[41] Five survey respondents reported that they transfer unclaimed savings to states. However, only three of these respondents were able to provide the amount of savings transferred to states in 2016 *and* describe the circumstances under which savings were transferred, with two specifying that they transfer savings from terminating plans. These data reflect the responses of these two respondents.

(RMD) of their savings. In fact, the data showed that very few of the participants who had savings transferred to states in 2016 (4 out of253) were older than 701/2.[42] The same provider reported that they only transfer savings to states when plans terminate.

Transfers of Unclaimed Retirement Savings from IRAs

According to our state survey data, in 2016, transfers from IRAs accounted for 16 percent of the retirement savings accounts transferred to the 17 states that could provide retirement savings-related transfer data.[43] During this year, a total of $12.6 million was transferred from IRAs to the 17 states responding to our survey and the average amount transferred from traditional IRAs was $1,610.[44] The state survey data only reflect aggregate amounts transferred; therefore, we did not capture data on the size of individual account balances transferred. However, it is possible for large IRA balances to be transferred to states because IRAs, unlike employer plans, are subject to neither forced distributions nor limits on the size of distributions.

Our IRA transfer agent survey found that most of the unclaimed savings from IRAs transferred to states by the 16 transfer agents that responded to our survey was for individuals older than 70%.[45]

---

[42] This 401(k) plan service provider reported that it was the trustee/custodian for more than $46 billion in 401(k) assets in 2016. This was the only provider that reported age-specific transfer data.

[43] According to unclaimed property experts we interviewed and state survey responses, states are uncertain about the accuracy of the property-type codes used by holders when reporting and transferring property, including retirement savings, to the states. Therefore, if property codes were applied inaccurately, this percentage could be more or less than what we found. See appendix I for more information about data quality issues for the state survey.

[44] We calculated this average based on the total dollar value of traditional IRA accounts transferred divided by the number of such transfers reported by states. Transfers from Roth IRAs, which consist of post-tax contributions, were uncommon and accounted for just 568 transfers worth $277,258, a relatively small portion of the retirement-related assets transferred. Some states reported additional IRA transfers that did not istinguish between traditional and Roth IRAs, so more Roth transfers may be included in these data. Most of the IRA assets transferred were in the form of cash (72 percent) compared to mutual funds (11 percent) and securities (2 percent). No asset type was identified for the remaining 15 percent of IRA savings transferred.

[45] We received survey responses from 21 transfer agents, but only 16 provided data on the age of individuals who had IRA savings transferred to states.

Dormancy period

According to our analysis of the sources noted below, a dormancy period is the period of time that typically must pass before unclaimed savings can be transferred to a state and during which time owners do not demonstrate activity on or acknowledge their accounts and the holder of the savings is unable to locate the owner. According to these sources, dormancy periods are governed by state laws and are typically triggered by an event that results in a payment being due, such as an individual retirement account (IRA) owner reaching the age when the Internal Revenue Code requires that they begin taking required minimum distributions of their savings, generally age 70%. For example, if an IRA account holder cannot locate an account owner for several years after the owner has turned 70%, the state where the owner is last known to have lived may consider the savings to be unclaimed and require the IRA holder to transfer the savings to the state.

Source: GAO analysis of interviews and information from the National Association of Unclaimed Property Administrators, retirement industry officials, and unclaimed property experts; and Reid, Tracey L., *Unclaimed Property: A Reporting Process and Audit Survival Guide* (Hoboken, New Jersey: 2008). | GAO-19-88.

Specifically, these survey data show that, out of 667 IRA owners who had savings transferred to states in 2016 and for whom respondents provided age information, 583 were older than 70%.[46] This suggests that these IRA savings were transferred in accordance with state unclaimed property laws for retirement savings, as described by unclaimed property experts we interviewed. (See the sidebar for additional information on dormancy periods).

---

[46] This analysis is based on just the IRA savings reported along with age data and excludes additional savings reported for which no age data were provided. We collected data on whether individuals with savings transferred were younger or older than 70% because turning 70% is a common dormancy period trigger for retirement savings. The actual age of individuals with savings transferred because of dormancy would be 70% plus the number of years required by a state's dormancy period.

With the Help of States, Owners Claimed About $25 Million in Retirement Savings from 15 States in 2016, According to GAO Survey Results

In 2016, owners claimed about $25 million in retirement savings, according to the 15 states that responded to our survey and could provide retirement savings-related claims data.[47] After they learn that the states have their savings and satisfy the states' requirements for proving ownership, owners or their beneficiaries can, according to information provided by the National Association of Unclaimed Property Administrators, claim retirement savings from the state.[48]

Table 3. Retirement Savings Claimed by Owners from 15 States in 2016, According to GAO's State Survey

Type of savings claimed from states	Number of retirement savings properties claimed	Dollar value (rounded)
All retirement savings	15,406	$25 million
Employer-based plans	13,941	$17 million
IRAs	1,465	$8 million

Source: GAO analysis of responses from a survey of states and DC, based on 2016 data. | GAO-19-88.

Note: As with retirement savings transferred to states, the savings in a single individual retirement account (IRA) could be split up by asset type and result in multiple, separate properties that may be claimed by an owner. An owner might also have several different retirement accounts that were transferred to the states. For these reasons the number of retirement-savings properties claimed is not equivalent to the number of people who claimed retirement savings.

Most retirement savings claimed from states are originally from employer plans, which is not surprising because most of the retirement savings transferred to the 17 states that responded to our survey were from employer plans. According to our state survey data, about two-thirds of

---

[47] These claims were of savings transferred in all years, including but not limited to 2016. We asked for claims data in this way because property may be reported to states as infrequently as once per year, so the property reported in 2016 could not, in many cases, also be claimed in that same year. One state reported only claims of property also transferred in 2016, which results in an underreporting of claims in that state for the year. Other states that responded to our state survey did not provide claims data.

[48] This process can often be accomplished by mail, but state unclaimed property offices also typically provide assistance by telephone and online claims can also be an option.

retirement savings dollars claimed were from employer plans, while the remaining third was from IRAs.[49] (See Table 3). As shown in Figure 2, states' unclaimed property offices receive retirement savings transfers in the form of cash or securities, including mutual fund shares.[50] The form of the retirement savings claimed from the state—a payment made from the state to the owner for the cash value of their savings or a transfer of securities—is based on the states' policies. For example, the form could depend on whether and for how long a state will hold securities or whether a state will sell the securities immediately and reimburse the owner for the sale price.[51] No matter how the states receive the funds, owners may not necessarily be able to claim their savings in the same form if the state has converted it to cash. This can affect the amount of an individual's savings depending on market conditions. If, for example, a state receives retirement savings in the form of securities and sells them before they are claimed, owners could lose the opportunity to sell their securities at a profit when they claim their savings if the market value of the securities increased after the state sold them.[52] Of 22 states responding to our survey, 10 states always or sometimes sell securities, including mutual fund shares, immediately after such properties are transferred to them.

---

[49] We do not know whether data from all the states would also reflect that a majority of retirement savings transfers were from employer-based plans.

[50] About 59 percent of the $7.7 trillion held in DC plans, which include 401(k) plans, was invested in mutual funds according to ICI data. Investment Company Institute, 2018 Investment Company Fact Book (Washington, D.C.: 2018).

[51] The Revised Uniform Unclaimed Property Act (RUUPA) states that a state unclaimed property administrator may not sell securities until 3 years after the administrator receives the securities and gives the apparent owner notice and that if the apparent owner claims the securities within 6 years of the delivery of the securities to the state administrator, the apparent owner may request a replacement of their securities or the market value of those securities at the time of their claim, and not at the time of the securities' sale, plus dividends, interest, and other increments on the security up to the time the claim is paid. See Rev. Unif. Unclaimed Prop. Act §§ 702-703 (2016). States are not required to follow the RUUPA. However, all states have their own unclaimed property laws and, according to materials provided by NAUPA, most have adopted language similar to the model law. For instance, a Florida statute requires that, generally, the state administrator will sell securities upon receipt and, if the owner claims their property, the owner is entitled to the value at the time of the securities' sale, not the value at the time of the claim.

[52] Securities refer to certificates or records that prove ownership of stocks or bonds. There is no guarantee that investments will increase in value over time; their value could also decrease.

Source: GAO analysis of state survey data and information from unclaimed property experts. | GAO-19-88.

a Until recently owners could indefinitely claim their property from each state, but at least two states have taken steps to cap the claims period at 30 and 35 years, according to unclaimed property experts.

Figure 2. States Receive Retirement Savings in Cash, Securities, and Mutual Fund Shares but Owners May Not Necessarily Be Able to Claim Savings in the Same Form.

The amount of claimed retirement savings from the state can end up being less than the amount owners left behind in their employer-based retirement plans or IRAs if owners use third-party "heir-finders." Although it is unnecessary for owners to use heir-finders to claim their retirement savings, according to state officials we interviewed, these heir-finders offer to help owners locate and collect their unclaimed retirement savings and typically charge owners a percentage of their recovered savings as a fee. One state official said she had seen a finder fee as high as 40 percent of the claimed property's value. Seventeen of 22 states responding to our survey reported that they always or sometimes limit finder fees; those limits ranged from 10 to 25 percent of property value. Nevertheless, one state official we interviewed emphasized that owners who work directly with the state to claim their retirement savings can do so at no cost and keep all of their savings.

Although no data exist on the number of heir-finders operating nationwide, state efforts to regulate them indicate that they are prevalent enough to warrant states' attention. Of states responding to our survey, 19 limit heir-finder or related services after property is transferred to the states, and 11 said they require that heir-finders or related persons are licensed in the state. An unclaimed property official from one state surveyed said that she was concerned about heir-finders who contact owners before savings have even been transferred to the state, adding that these locators are not regulated by anyone. See Figure 3 for an example of one state's approach to restricting these fees after property is transferred to the state, which asserts that a finder's fee is "unenforceable" if property claimed has been with the state less than 2 years. An unclaimed property expert we interviewed said that owners can claim their savings at no cost in almost every state, although he noted two states that do charge a fee—one does so based on a percentage of the property claimed while the other can reduce property values to reflect any costs in connection with the sale of the property, efforts to locate the owner, and a "reasonable" service charge.

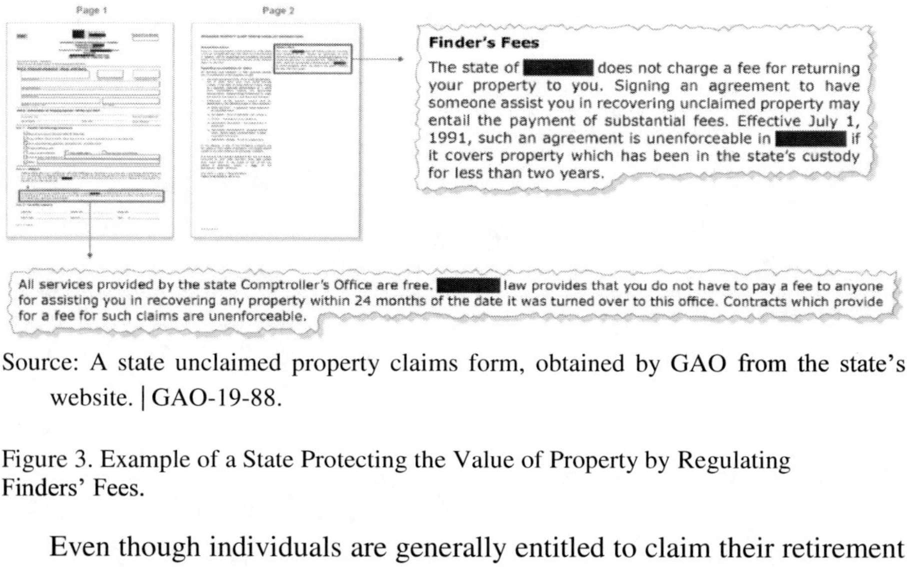

Source: A state unclaimed property claims form, obtained by GAO from the state's website. | GAO-19-88.

Figure 3. Example of a State Protecting the Value of Property by Regulating Finders' Fees.

Even though individuals are generally entitled to claim their retirement savings, according to information from unclaimed property experts, not all owners will be able to do so because savings are sometimes transferred with no owner information, making it difficult for the state to search for the owner. An unclaimed property expert we interviewed said that each year states receive a large amount of unclaimed property without owners' names or addresses. One official responding to our state survey explained that property without owner information is difficult to advertise to potential owners. Another factor that reduces the likelihood of individuals claiming their savings is that some states accept aggregate transfers of multiple relatively small accounts bundled together without information about individual owners.[53] States would have no way to link these transfers back to their owners, so they would remain unclaimed unless owners obtain their own records of the transfers from their retirement plans or IRA providers.[54] Even with a name and address, returning retirement savings can be challenging because, as one state unclaimed property official noted, in his state, it is presumed that holders have already done their due diligence to locate owners when savings are transferred to the state—so owners who were easy to locate typically would not have their savings transferred to the state.

When owners are able to claim their savings from states and avoid heir-finder fees, their retirement income security may still be reduced. That is because the savings claimed from states are no longer in tax-qualified retirement accounts, which permit invested savings to grow tax-deferred over time. That feature is important for individuals to achieve better financial security in retirement.

States responding to our survey use a range of strategies to maintain the value of unclaimed retirement savings. State strategies to maintain the value of savings are consistent with their assertion that the property does not belong to the holder of the savings but to the individual owner.[55] The most commonly reported strategy used to maintain the value of unclaimed savings is the delayed liquidation of savings received in the form of securities (used by 16 of 22 states responding to our state survey). Some states (7 of 22) apply interest to savings held for owners. (See appendix III

---

[53] According to NAUPA, such aggregate transfers are made up of properties valued at less than $50 in most states and are not mandatory but are made at the election of the holder.

[54] An IRS advisory group has twice recommended that the agency add a code to the form used to report transfers out of a retirement plan (the 1099-R), which would convey that savings were transferred to a state as unclaimed property. Such IRS records could potentially help an individual to track down their retirement savings after it is transferred to a state, even if their name was not associated with it—as in the case of these aggregate transfers. IRS officials told us that they are considering adding such a code, but have no timeframe for when that might occur.

[55] See Rev. Unif. Unclaimed Prop. Act § 503 (2016) ("Property received by the administrator under this [act] is held in custody for the benefit of the owner and is not owned by the state.") States are not required to follow the Uniform Unclaimed Property Act but, according to materials provided by NAUPA, most have adopted language similar to the model law.

for full survey results concerning state treatment of unclaimed property, which includes retirement savings).

States responding to our survey also use a combination of strategies to locate owners of unclaimed savings. Some of these strategies are required by states' own unclaimed property laws which, according to materials provided by NAUPA, are typically based on some version of the uniform laws on unclaimed property.[56] For example, the Revised Uniform Unclaimed Property Act from 2016 would require a conforming state to, among other things, publish information about specific unclaimed properties in the newspaper, post property information on a database, and send notification letters. These are indeed among the most commonly reported strategies[57] for locating owners that were reported by the 22 states that responded to our state survey: 17 publish information in the newspaper; 19 post information to a national database (21 post to their state's own website); and 19 use direct mailings to contact owners.[58] One state responding to our survey described a tiered-approach whereby owner names for new transfers are uploaded to a web-based information services company nightly for a search of its databases for up-to-date contact information, which is downloaded to the state each morning. For retirement savings of any amount, the state unclaimed property office then sends a letter to any contacts for which it has a new address. For amounts that are $25,000 or higher, an individual staff person is assigned to track down the owner, according to a state official.

Our own search of a database of U.S. newspapers identified relevant articles published in 2017 that corroborate some states' use of news media to educate the public and alert potential owners to the existence of unclaimed property. Nineteen of 22 states responding to our survey reported that they always or sometimes publicize the unclaimed property office on television, which may include newscasts, and also through a

[56] GAO did not independently review states' unclaimed property laws.

[57] Response tallies are for states which indicated that a certain strategy was always or sometimes used.

[58] According to an unclaimed property expert, several states have recently taken action to leverage address records maintained by state and local government agencies—such as those that administer taxes—to improve their ability to locate owners and return property.

state's own educational videos posted to the internet.[59] Through our own internet search, we found that more than half of all states have produced educational video content to inform the public about unclaimed property and the opportunity to search for and claim property. See our related video.

Watch a related video describing the issue of unclaimed retirement savings transferred to states that shows two examples of state outreach efforts at **https://www.gao.gov/products/GAO-19-88**

IRS AND DOL HAVE ISSUED SOME GUIDANCE ABOUT TRANSFERRING RETIREMENT SAVINGS TO STATES, BUT HAVE NOT CLARIFIED CERTAIN STAKEHOLDER RESPONSIBILITIES OR ENSURED CLAIMED SAVINGS CAN BE RETURNED TO RETIREMENT ACCOUNTS

The Internal Revenue Service (IRS) and the Department of Labor (DOL) have issued some guidance related to the transfer of unclaimed retirement savings to the states, but have not addressed certain issues. For example, IRS guidance provides information about the tax withholding

---

[59] One of the 22 states did not provide any response to the survey question regarding the use of television.

requirements applicable to the transfer of IRA savings, and DOL issued regulations that outline certain circumstances under which savings in qualified plans can be transferred to states. However, IRS and DOL have not taken action on key issues that could have implications for the collection of federal tax revenue, as well as individuals' retirement security, respectively. Specifically, IRS has not (1) clarified the tax requirements that apply to transfers of 401(k) savings to states or (2) ensured that individuals from terminated plans can return savings they claim from a state to a retirement account. DOL has not specified whether uncashed distribution checks from active plans may be transferred to states.

IRS Has Not Clarified if Transfers of Certain Unclaimed Retirement Savings are Taxable Distributions and What, If Any, Tax Reporting and Withholding Requirements Apply

IRS has issued regulations and other guidance pertinent to transfers of unclaimed retirement savings to states from IRAs, but has not clarified if transfers of unclaimed retirement savings from employer-based plans such as 401(k) plans are distributions and what, if any, reporting and withholding requirements apply. This in turn could have implications for the collection of federal income taxes that may be due.[60] IRS regulations

[60] Department of Labor Field Assistance Bulletin (FAB) 2014-01 and its predecessor, FAB 2004-02, discuss fiduciary duties with respect to missing participants in terminated defined contribution plans, including transfers of retirement savings to state unclaimed property funds. IRS officials said that they and the Department of the Treasury provided input to the Department of Labor on both FABs with respect to tax issues. For example, DOL FAB 2014-01 states that fiduciaries should be aware that transferring a participant's benefits to either a bank account or state unclaimed property fund will subject the deposited amounts to "income taxation, mandatory income tax withholding and a possible additional tax for premature distributions." Although such tax information was included in both the 2004 and 2014 FABs (in the context of terminated DC plans), IRS has not published its own separate guidance stating such tax information with respect to transfers of DC plan assets to state unclaimed property funds. Current federal law allows individuals with account based plans, like 401(k)s, to have the income taxes on their contributions and any market gains on their accounts deferred *until* the funds are distributed. Withholding helps the federal government collect taxes and prevents some individual taxpayers from owing large amounts when they

specify federal tax reporting and withholding requirements that apply to distributions from 401(k) plans and IRAs,[61] and IRS recently issued guidance that clarifies tax reporting and withholding requirements that specifically apply to the transfer of unclaimed IRA savings to the states.[62]

Table 4. Federal Tax Withholding Requirements on Distributions from Retirement Accounts

Source of distribution	Tax Withholding Rate
401(k) plan non-periodic distributions	Generally 10%
Eligible rollover distributions	20%
401(k) plan periodic distributions	Varies, based on the withholding amount individuals select when completing IRS Form W-4Pa
Traditional IRA non-periodic distributions	Generally 10%
Traditional IRA periodic distributions	Varies, based on the withholding amount individuals select when completing IRS Form W-4P
Roth IRA[b]	Generally 0%

Source: GAO review of relevant IRS guidance. | GAO-19-88.

Note: Periodic distributions are those made in installments at regular intervals (such as annually, quarterly, or monthly) over a period of more than 1 year. In some instances, individuals have the option to choose no withholding. Distributions from 401(k) plans that are transferred to a traditional IRA or another eligible retirement plan are generally not subject to tax withholding.

a Form W-4P, Withholding Certificate for Pension or Annuity Payments, is a form that individuals provide to payers of pensions and annuities to specify the amount of federal income tax to withhold from payments. Form W-4P generally may be used to elect out of withholding on periodic and nonperiodic payments under sections 3405(a) and (b). Also, with respect to periodic payments, if an individual fails to furnish a Form W-4P, a default withholding rate applies under section 3405(a)(4) (for 2018, a rate that assumes the individual is married, with three allowances).

b Roth IRAs allow eligible individuals to make nondeductible contributions to retirement accounts but generally receive tax-free distributions.

---

file their tax returns. For more information on federal tax withholding, see GAO, *Federal Tax Withholding: Treasury and IRS Should Document the Roles and Responsibilities for Updating Annual Withholding Tables*, GAO-18-548 (Washington, D.C.: July 2018).Tax reporting also helps to ensure that the federal government collects taxes that are due, as it has been shown to improve the accuracy of income reporting by taxpayers and allows IRS to use automated processes to address noncompliance. See GAO, *Tax Gap: IRS Needs Specific Goals and Strategies for Improving Compliance,* GAO-18-39 (Washington, D.C.: Oct. 2017).

[61] 26 C.F.R. §§ 31.3405(c)-1 Q-1, Q-15, & Q-16 and 35.3405-1T a-12, a-13, & e-1.

[62] Internal Revenue Service, *Rev. Rul. 2018-17 Withholding and Reporting With Respect to Payments From IRAs to State Unclaimed Property Funds.* IRS officials said that this guidance does not apply to transfers from employer-based plans.

(See Table 4 for more information about IRS tax withholding requirements and see the sidebar for details on the logistics for withholding taxes from distributions). According to May 2018 IRS guidance, certain transfers of unclaimed IRA savings to the states are distributions for tax reporting and withholding purposes, and IRA trustees should apply a 10 percent tax withholding rate to transfers and report them to IRS on Form 1099-R—as they would for other types of non-periodic IRA distributions.[63] IRS also issued regulations specifying that in certain instances transfers of retirement plan savings to states do not violate the nonforfeitability requirements, which pertain to employees' rights to keep their employer contributions in their retirement accounts.[64] However, IRS has not clarified if transfers of unclaimed savings from employer-based plans such as 401(k) plans are taxable distributions and what, if any, tax reporting and withholding requirements apply to those transfers.[65] IRS officials said they have not issued guidance specific to transfers from 401(k)-type plans because the agency is still prioritizing the areas where guidance is needed in light of other priorities.[66] IRS's mission is to help U.S. taxpayers understand and meet their tax responsibilities and to enforce the law with integrity and fairness.[67] Officials indicated that they are considering

---

[63] Under the guidance, an IRA trustee will not be treated as failing to comply with these withholding and reporting requirements for transfers made before the earlier of 1) January 1, 2019 or 2) the date it becomes reasonably practicable for the trustee to comply with the requirements. Notice 2018-90, issued November 20, 2018, extends the January 1, 2019 date to January 1, 2020.

[64] See 26 C.F.R. § 1.411(a)-4(b)(6). IRS officials told us they plan to update these regulations, but did not specify the changes they are making. Plans are permitted to establish vesting policies that require employees to work for a minimum length of time before their employer's contributions become fully nonforfeitable, meaning employees have an unconditional and legally enforceable right to keep their employer contributions if they separate from their job. See 26 U.S.C. § 411(a).

[65] See the previous sections of the report for details on the circumstances under which unclaimed savings from plans are transferred to the states, such as when plans terminate, and the amount of savings plans transferred to the states in 2016.

[66] The Department of Treasury's (Treasury) 2017-2018 Priority Guidance Plan released on August 17, 2018, which outlines guidance priorities for Treasury and IRS, mentions "Guidance on missing participants" and cites the recently issued guidance on IRA transfers, but provides no further details on any other types of guidance in this area. Individuals whose retirement savings are transferred to the states because they fail to claim them prior to the expiration of the relevant dormancy period are sometimes referred to as "missing."

[67] Federal agencies are responsible for establishing and maintaining internal controls to achieve their mission-related and other objectives. Internal control principle 15.03 highlights the

guidance in this area, but did not provide any details on what the guidance might cover or when it might be issued.

Logistics for withholding taxes from distributions

Under Internal Revenue Service (IRS) regulations, plan administrators are generally responsible for reporting distributions from plans to the IRS and withholding federal income taxes from the amounts distributed. Distributions of retirement savings are reported to IRS on Form 1099-R and a 10 percent tax rate is generally applied to non-periodic distributions from plans. For example, to calculate the amount of federal income tax to withhold and remit to IRS for a one-time distribution of 401(k) funds, the amount of the distribution is generally multiplied by 10 percent. Form 1099-R shows the amount of funds distributed from a retirement account and the amount of taxes withheld from the distribution. In addition to submitting form 1099-R to IRS, plans are required to send it to participants.

Source: GAO analysis of federal law and regulations, relevant IRS guidance, and Form 1099-R. | GAO-19-88.

Our 401(k) plan service provider survey indicated that, in the absence of specific guidance, some providers are handling transfers of unclaimed retirement savings from plans, including the tax reporting and withholding activities associated with the transfers, in various ways.[68] Five out of seven service providers reported that they transferred unclaimed savings from 401(k) plans to the states in 2016. Of these five service providers, two indicated that they "never or rarely" reported these transfers to IRS using Form 1099-R or withheld federal income taxes from transferred savings, while two others indicated that they "always or almost always" reported

need for agencies to communicate quality information externally so that external parties can help them achieve their objectives. Therefore, the issuance of guidance or other information to ensure that external parties, such as 401(k) service providers, are clear on their tax reporting and withholding responsibilities can improve IRS's ability to achieve its mission and is consistent with this internal control principle. For more information on internal control standards, see GAO, *Standards for Internal Control in the Federal Government,* GAO-14-704G (Washington, D.C.: Sept. 2014).

[68] We surveyed 32 401(k) plan service providers that are members of the SPARK Institute, an association that represents DC plan service providers.

transfers and withheld federal income taxes. The remaining provider indicated that it reported transfers and withheld taxes "about 50 percent of the time."[69]

Most of the 401(k) plan service providers in our survey also indicated that current federal guidance on the tax reporting and withholding requirements related to the transfer of unclaimed savings from 401(k) plans to the states is not clear and many also indicated that additional guidance is needed. Specifically, most of the providers that rated the clarity of federal guidance on tax reporting and withholding (5 out of 7) said that guidance is "not clear at all"; two indicated that guidance in these areas is "very clear." Four out of seven 401(k) plan service providers responding to our survey indicated that additional federal tax guidance is needed. For example, one service provider who reported that it "never or rarely" reported to the IRS or withheld taxes from 401(k) savings transferred to the states in 2016 explained that it made assumptions regarding the appropriate tax reporting and withholding requirements and would like clear guidance.

Another service provider who reported that it "always or almost always" reported to IRS and withheld taxes indicated that it would like guidance that clarifies whether it should ask IRS for refunds of taxes withheld from unclaimed savings from 401(k) plans before transferring them to the states. This service provider explained that when plans terminate, it issues distribution checks to all participants for their entire account balance and withholds federal income taxes from these checks. This same service provider pointed out that if these savings are transferred to states as unclaimed property because the checks are not cashed, there is uncertainty as to whether a taxable event occurred since individuals do not actually receive their savings.

Stakeholder groups that we interviewed corroborated the views of the plan service providers that responded to our survey and identified the need for additional guidance on tax reporting and withholding requirements for 401(k) savings transferred to states. SPARK Institute officials explained that, because IRS has not issued relevant guidance, it is not clear whether a

---

[69] For the purposes of this chapter, we did not assess plan compliance with the Internal Revenue Code.

Form 1099-R should be issued and federal income taxes withheld, and that practices vary. SPARK officials indicated that some providers issue a Form 1099-R and that taxes are typically withheld, but pointed out that federal guidance could rectify disagreement within the industry. Similarly, officials from the Investment Company Institute (ICI)[70] told us that additional federal guidance is needed to clarify whether the transfer of unclaimed 401(k) savings to the states is a taxable event and to identify the relevant tax reporting requirements. ICI also highlighted the need for additional guidance in a letter it submitted to Treasury and IRS officials, which outlined items it believes should be included in Treasury's Priority Guidance Plan.[71]

The lack of guidance on whether transfers of unclaimed retirement savings from 401(k) plans to states are taxable distributions that are subject to tax reporting and withholding, and the varying tax reporting and withholding practices that plan providers use as a result, could have implications for the collection of federal income taxes that may be due in light of IRS's recent guidance on transfers from IRAs. If transfers of unclaimed retirement savings from 401(k) plans to the states were considered distributions, just as IRS guidance treats transfers of unclaimed IRA savings to the states as distributions, 401(k) plan service providers would be responsible for issuing a 1099-R and remitting tax withholding on tax-deferred amounts to IRS when transferring savings. However, if this withholding doesn't occur, IRS may be less likely to collect federal income taxes that may be due as a result of these tax-deferred funds being distributed from plans to the states.[72] Figure 4 illustrates the amount of

---

[70] ICI is an association that represents mutual fund companies. According to its website, ICI members manage total assets of $22 trillion in the United States, serving more than 100 million U.S. shareholders. According to ICI data, in 2017, about 59 percent of the $7.7 trillion held in DC plans was invested in mutual funds. Investment Company Institute, 2018 Investment Company Fact Book (Washington, D.C.: 2018).

[71] Investment Company Institute, *Priority Guidance Plan Recommendations on Retirement Security Issues* (May 16, 2016).

[72] As previously noted, current federal law allows individuals with account based plans, like 401(k)s, to have the income taxes on their contributions and any market gains on their accounts deferred *until* the funds are distributed. Withholding helps the federal government collect taxes and prevents some individual taxpayers from owing large amounts when they file their tax returns. For more information on federal tax withholding, see GAO, *Federal*

federal income tax withholding IRS may not collect, assuming this transaction is a taxable event, based on the amount of 401(k) savings transferred to the states in 2016 by a survey respondent who reported that it "never or rarely" withheld taxes from transferred savings.[73]

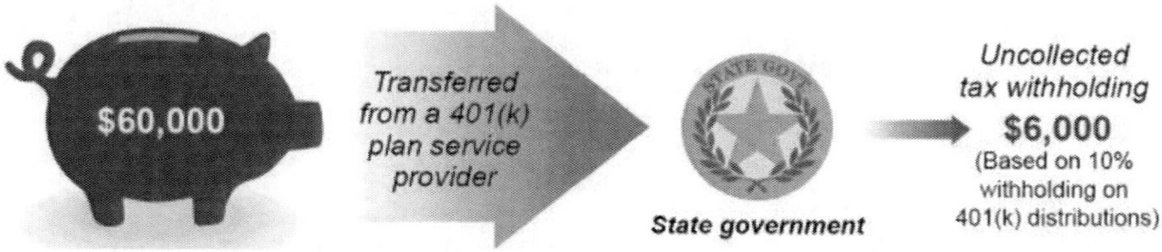

Source: GAO analysis of 401(k) plan service provider survey data and federal regulations. | GAO-19-88.

Note: For the purpose of illustrating tax withholding that could potentially not be collected, this hypothetical illustration assumes that the transfer of 401(k) savings to the states is a taxable event in light of recent IRS guidance indicating that transfers of IRA savings to the states are distributions for tax withholding purposes. This illustration also assumes that individuals do not become aware of their transferred savings and take action to pay any taxes due. If, within 60 days of receipt, an individual deposits distributed funds into another qualified account—via an indirect rollover—the distribution is not treated as income for federal income tax purposes. Tax liability for a given year is ultimately based on individuals' particular tax situations, and can be determined when they complete their tax returns. If the transfer of 401(k) savings to the states were not considered a taxable event and taxes were withheld from transferred savings nonetheless, the $6,000 figure shown above would represent the amount by which retirement savings were reduced when they should not have been.

Figure 4. Hypothetical Illustration of the Amount of Federal Income Tax Withholding Potentially Not Collected by IRS When $60,000 in Unclaimed 401(k) Savings Transferred to the States is Not Subject to Tax Withholding.

Tax Withholding: Treasury and IRS Should Document the Roles and Responsibilities for Updating Annual Withholding Tables, GAO-18-548 (Washington, D.C.: July 2018).

[73] We did not assess taxpayer compliance with the Internal Revenue Code. Individuals are ultimately responsible for paying any taxes that are due. Therefore, if individuals were to become aware of their transferred savings and take action to pay any taxes that are due, IRS would not fail to collect taxes.

IRS Has Not Taken Action to Ensure That Savings from Terminated Plans Claimed From States Can Be Transferred Back into Retirement Accounts to Benefit from Favorable Tax Treatment

IRS has not taken steps to ensure that individuals from terminated plans can transfer savings claimed from states back into a retirement account. Our 401(k) plan service provider survey data showed that transfers of retirement savings to the states from 401(k) plans typically included savings from terminated plans.[74] Furthermore, our state survey data show that retirement savings from employer-based plans represent about two-thirds of savings claimed from the states that responded to our survey. When individuals whose plans are terminated claim their savings from the states, they must decide what to do with these savings. One option could be to roll over the savings into a qualified retirement account so the savings continue to be considered tax-deferred; however, IRS's current procedures do not allow this option for savings distributed from a plan unless it occurs within 60 days of when the funds were received.[75] Under IRS's "self-certification" procedures, individuals may prepare and submit a letter to a plan administrator or IRA trustee—by using a model IRS letter or their own similar letter—to roll over savings into a retirement account after the 60-day rollover deadline, provided they missed the deadline for certain reasons and meet other conditions.[76] The pre-approved reasons for

---

[74] Of $2.25 million transferred to states in 2016, $2.19 million included savings from terminated plans, according to our 401(k) plan service provider survey data.

[75] Under the Internal Revenue Code, if an individual's retirement savings are distributed from a qualified plan or IRA and transferred to an eligible account within 60 days of receipt, they are excluded from the individual's income for federal income tax purposes.

[76] Rev. Proc. 2016-47, 2016-2 C.B. 346. IRS officials said that the pre-approved reasons are based on requests the agency has approved on numerous occasions through the private letter ruling process, which allows individuals to apply to IRS for a waiver of the 60- day rollover requirement. IRS officials decide on whether to approve these requests based on an evaluation of the facts and circumstances, and ultimately provide individuals with a letter outlining the agency's decision. However, under the self-certification procedures, individuals do not have to wait to receive a private letter ruling from IRS before making a rollover contribution after the 60-day deadline nor do they have to pay a fee to IRS, as they would under the private letter ruling process. According to IRS guidance, a fee of $10,000

missing the 60-day deadline include financial institution error, post office error, and the death of a family member, among other reasons, but do not include claiming retirement savings transferred to a state. IRS officials said they have not considered adding this reason to the list of pre-approved reasons because the agency has never received a request to waive the 60-day deadline based solely on the fact that savings were transferred to a state. Since retirement savings become unclaimed as a result of employers being unable to locate individuals and individuals forgetting about their savings, it is not surprising that IRS has not received such a request.

Some individuals from terminated plans whose savings are distributed and later transferred to states may not be able to complete a rollover prior to the end of the 60-day rollover period. An unclaimed property expert and representatives from an industry association told us that terminating plans can transfer unclaimed savings to states prior to the end of the 3- year dormancy period typically required to designate savings as unclaimed property, according to our state survey results.[77] However, one of seven 401(k) service providers that responded to our survey indicated that it typically waits until the end of a dormancy period before transferring savings to the states after plans terminate.[78] The provider explained that since it distributes assets from terminating plans through the issuance of checks, it follows state dormancy period rules for uncashed checks and typically waits for the full dormancy period to expire before transferring unclaimed savings to the state. Therefore, since this provider distributes funds by issuing checks to individuals and then waits for the full dormancy period to expire before transferring funds to the states—which can take 3 years according to our state survey data—individuals who claim their savings from a state may be unable to complete a rollover prior to the 60-

must accompany every request for a private letter ruling related to the 60-day rollover requirement.

[77] According to an industry association, even though terminating plans can transfer unclaimed savings to states prior to the end of the dormancy period, they must comply with all other state law requirements before transferring funds.

[78] The provider reported that, as of December 31, 2016, it served 939,105 participants in 401(k) plans and that 254 participants had some or all of their 401(k) savings transferred to the states in 2016. In addition, this provider indicated that it "always or almost always" reported these transfers to IRS using Form 1099-R and withheld federal income taxes from transferred savings.

day deadline, depending on when they are considered to have received the funds. If they are considered to have received the funds during the year in which their distribution checks are issued, or otherwise well in advance of the completion of the dormancy period that would precede the transfer of funds to a state, they may be unable to complete a timely rollover after claiming the funds from the state.

Some individuals from terminated plans could benefit from rolling their claimed savings back into a retirement account. Our 401(k) plan service provider survey data show that plan terminations affect participants of all ages. One service provider out of seven survey respondents reported that nearly all of the retirement savings it transferred to the states due to plan terminations was associated with participants younger than RMD age, generally age 701/2.[79] Federal law seeks to protect the interests of participants in retirement plans.[80] However, without including savings claimed from states among the reasons to allow a rollover after more than 60 days, IRS may be missing an opportunity to allow individuals an avenue to retain their retirement savings in a tax-deferred vehicle after a plan termination. Our prior work has shown that even small amounts of retirement savings can grow substantially over time as a result of compound interest. For example, based on a hypothetical scenario we found that, with reasonable interest rate and other assumptions, $2,643 in retirement savings for a younger worker can grow to $85,857 by the time they reach retirement age due to compound interest.[81] In addition, individuals who roll over their savings may be able to get a refund for any federal income taxes withheld before their savings were transferred to a state, provided they roll over their savings and seek a refund prior to the

---

[79] This respondent reported that it transferred $194,288 in unclaimed 401(k) savings to the states in 2016, all of which was attributed to plan terminations; $190,941 of the amount transferred was associated with participants younger than RMD age. Our survey did not ask respondents to provide the specific ages of participants.

[80] The Employee Retirement Income Security Act of 1974 (ERISA), the primary statute governing most private sector pension plans, seeks to protect the interests of employee benefit plan participants and their beneficiaries. See 29 U.S.C. § 1001. et seq..

[81] The dollar values above are nominal. We considered individuals between the ages of 18 and 20 to be younger workers. For more information, see GAO, *401(K) Plans: Effects of Eligibility and Vesting Policies on Workers' Retirement Savings*, GAO-17-69 (Washington, D.C.: Oct. 21, 2016).

expiration of IRS's statute of limitations.[82] (See sidebar for more information about IRS's statute of limitations and obtaining a refund for taxes withheld before savings are transferred).

Statute of limitations

Under federal law, IRS' statute of limitations generally ranges from 2 to 3 years, based on the particular circumstances. 26 U.S.C. § 6511(a). Before the expiration of the statute of limitations, individuals who complete a rollover can obtain a refund for taxes withheld before their retirement savings were distributed when they file their return for a given tax year, or they can file an amended return to obtain a refund for a tax year for which they have already filed a return. According to an unclaimed property expert and industry association representatives we interviewed, distributed savings from terminated plans can be transferred to the states prior to the expiration of the 3-year dormancy period typically applied to retirement savings. Therefore, individuals from terminated plans may be unaffected by IRS's statute of limitations.
Note: For the purpose of illustrating the potential to receive a tax refund after a rollover, transfers of retirement savings to the states are considered distributions in the discussion above since, by definition, a distribution must precede a rollover.

Source: GAO analysis of federal laws, IRS documentation, responses from a state survey and industry documentation. | GAO-19-88.

DOL Has Not Specified Whether Active Plans May Transfer Uncashed Distribution Checks to States

DOL has issued regulations and guidance focused on the transfer of unclaimed retirement savings from terminating plans to the states, but it has not clarified issues related to active plans. Under ERISA, DOL is responsible for issuing regulations and guidance to assist plan sponsors and

[82] To complete an indirect rollover, an individual must roll the remaining 80 percent into a tax-qualified account and will have to contribute funds from other sources to replace the 20 percent withheld or the withholding will count as income subject to federal income tax.

plan fiduciaries with managing qualified retirement plans.[83] Current DOL regulations and guidance include the following:

- DOL regulations permit the qualified termination administrator of an abandoned defined contribution plan[84] to transfer small amounts of retirement savings, $1,000 or less, to a state unclaimed property fund with the assurance that doing so will not violate ERISA's fiduciary standards, provided plans comply with applicable notice provisions and the participants and beneficiaries fail to elect a form of distribution within 30 days of the furnishing of the notice.[85]
- DOL guidance related to a state's unclaimed property law expresses DOL's view that ERISA preempted the state's law as it related to requiring a plan to transfer unclaimed amounts held in

---

[83] Under GAO's internal control standards, federal agencies are responsible for establishing and maintaining internal controls to achieve their mission-related and other objectives. Internal control principle 15.03 highlights the need for agencies to communicate quality information externally so that external parties can help them achieve their objectives. Therefore, the issuance of guidance or other information to ensure that external parties, such as plan sponsors and fiduciaries, are clear on their responsibilities can improve DOL's ability to fulfill its responsibilities under ERISA and is consistent with this internal control principle.

[84] According to information on DOL's website, an abandoned plan is generally a plan without a responsible plan sponsor or plan administrator and a qualified termination administrator is the asset custodian (such as a bank, insurance company, or other similar financial institution) that terminates the plan. See Employee Benefits Security Administration, United States Department of Labor, *FAQs About the Abandoned Plan Program*, available at https://www.dol.gov/sites/default/files/ebsa/about-ebsa/ouractivities/resource-center/faqs/abandoned-plan-program.pdf.

[85] See 29 C.F.R. § 2550.404a-3(d)(1)(iii) and 29 C.F.R. 2578.1. Under ERISA, a fiduciary is any person, to the extent they (1) exercise any discretionary authority or control over plan management or any authority or control over the management or disposition of plan assets, (2) render, or have the authority or responsibility to render, investment advice for a fee or other compensation with respect to plan money or property, or (3) have any discretionary authority or responsibility for plan administration. See 29 U.S.C. § 1002(21)(A). Plan fiduciaries are required to act prudently, solely in the interest of plan participants and beneficiaries, and for the exclusive purpose of providing benefits and defraying reasonable expenses of administering the plan. Fiduciaries are also required to diversify the investments and act in accordance with plan documents governing the plan, insofar as such documents are consistent with ERISA. See 29 U.S.C. § 1104(a). According to DOL, a plan's decision regarding what to do with unclaimed retirement savings—which can include transferring these savings to the states—is a decision that is subject to ERISA's fiduciary standards.

plan accounts to the state—meaning the plan was not required to transfer the funds to the state.[86]

- DOL guidance, however, explains when such transfers of any amount from terminating plans are allowed, if other distribution options (such as a rollover to an IRA) are not available, provided plans properly search for participants prior to transferring their savings.[87]

DOL, however, has not clarified whether active plans may transfer uncashed distribution checks to the states under ERISA.[88] Federal law provides some guidelines for the actions that active plans may take when account owners leave behind retirement savings, but these guidelines do not cover all scenarios that involve uncashed checks. For instance, federal law permits active plans to cash out balances of $1,000 or less that are left behind, but it does not specify whether these funds can be transferred to the states if account owners never claim them.[89] As noted earlier, many uncashed checks could fall within this dollar threshold, as our state survey shows that the average dollar value of savings transferred to 17 states in 2016 from "retirement plan checks" (which is comprised of uncashed checks) was $301. DOL officials said that they have not provided specific fiduciary guidance on when uncashed checks can be transferred from active plans to state unclaimed property funds, but are considering the appropriate prioritization of such guidance within the context of a broader range of missing participant issues being raised by various stakeholder groups, such as search requirements and updating plan records, among other things.

---

[86] See DOL Advisory Opinion 1994-41A, Dec. 7, 1994. DOL reached this conclusion based on its belief that plan compliance with state unclaimed property laws would directly affect the core plan functions by reducing, through the transfer of savings to the states, the amount of plan assets held in trust for the benefit of all participants and beneficiaries of the plan. In general, DOL advisory opinions apply the law to a specific set of facts.

[87] DOL, *Field Assistance Bulletin 2014-01* (Washington, D.C.: 2014).

[88] For the purposes of this chapter, when we refer to the transfer of uncashed checks to the states, we are not referring to the physical checks themselves, but rather the funds underlying the checks.

[89] See 26 U.S.C. § 401(a)(31)(B).

Recent state actions suggest that states are not clear on whether uncashed checks from active plans can be transferred to the states, which could affect whether participants claim their savings. For example, California, the largest state in the United States based on population, submitted a letter to DOL that requests an advisory opinion on whether active plans may transfer uncashed checks to the states as unclaimed property without violating ERISA. According to DOL officials, between 20 and 30 other states wrote letters to DOL in support of California's request. In its letter to DOL, California's Controller indicated that the uncertainty over whether states can receive uncashed checks as unclaimed property is partly due to a lack of clarity regarding whether the funds underlying uncashed checks remain plan assets.[90] The letter states that neither ERISA nor its regulations explicitly address whether uncashed checks issued to DC plan participants are plan assets, and, according to the letter, if DOL does not clarify these issues, plans do not have a way to definitively terminate their fiduciary responsibilities as long as the checks remain uncashed.

In addition, according to California's letter, if plans do not transfer uncashed checks to the states, key information such as the name of the participant to whom the check was issued can be lost.[91] If this type of information is lost, individuals may be less likely to ever claim their savings, which would reduce the amount of money they have for

[90] According to California's letter, the federal courts have held that ERISA preemption does not preclude the application of state unclaimed property laws to participant distributions unless those disbursements are considered "plan assets." In other words, the California letter argues that, to the extent distributions are not plan assets, they may not be covered by the ERISA preemption clause, which would ordinarily give plans the option to forgo transferring retirement savings to the states as unclaimed property. Controller of the State of California, *Re: Request for Advisory Opinion Pursuant to ERISA Procedure 76-1* (June, 7, 2017).

[91] For example, according to California's letter, when some plans issue checks to participants, the underlying funds are retained in an account outside of the plan that is maintained by a service provider. The letter indicates that if checks are not cashed, the underlying funds are retained in this outside account and, in many cases, never returned to the plan. Over time, and as a result of systems conversions, the letter argues that critical data elements (such as participant names and addresses and the name of the plan that issued the checks) may become compromised or purged altogether.

retirement.[92] In light of these issues, California's letter indicated that transferring uncashed checks to the states is a prudent option for reuniting individuals with their retirement savings. DOL officials said they plan to respond to California's request and that their response will be made public, but did not specify what would be included in their response or when they will issue it. Regarding the scope of advisory opinions, DOL officials said that they are not precedent for others—meaning they only apply to the entities that requested them.

Through our 401(k) plan service provider survey and review of documents from relevant industry associations, we also found that 401(k) plan service providers, who are responsible for deciding an appropriate action if checks are not cashed, are not certain whether uncashed checks from active plans can be transferred to the states. For instance, four of seven 401(k) plan service providers responding to our survey indicated that additional federal guidance on transferring unclaimed 401(k) savings to the states is needed, with one reporting specifically that guidance on whether the transfer of uncashed checks to the states is acceptable under ERISA is needed.[93] In addition, ICI highlighted the need for DOL guidance on uncashed checks, saying that DOL issued guidance for terminating plans that permits 401(k) providers to transfer uncashed checks to states, but it has not done so for active plans.[94]

According to these officials, in the absence of guidance, some plans transfer uncashed checks to the plan's forfeiture account. They said that this is not ideal because plans are required to deplete the funds in a forfeiture account, rather than allow them to accumulate, but would also have to use the funds to pay participants if they are eventually located. Transferring uncashed checks to a forfeiture account—rather than transferring them to a state—could also affect the likelihood of individuals claiming their savings. According to one large 401(k) service provider that

---

[92] As noted in the background section of this chapter, uncashed checks can include checks that are issued when individuals reach RMD age, which is generally age 701/2.

[93] As of December 31, 2016, this provider managed $250 billion in 401(k) savings for 2 million participants.

[94] Investment Company Institute, *Re: Proposed Rules on Missing Participants RIN 1212- AB13* (Nov.21, 2016). For DOL's guidance for terminating plans, see United States Department of Labor, *Field Assistance Bulletin 2014-01* (Washington, D.C.: 2014).

typically transfers uncashed checks to a forfeiture account, it is not clear whether a plan sponsor, in its role as a fiduciary, has an obligation to search for individuals to whom checks are owed.[95] To the extent that plans do not search for these individuals, they may be less likely to ever claim their savings.[96] ICI recommended that DOL either clarify that the current guidance for terminating plans applies to active plans or issue parallel guidance for active plans. In addition, officials from the SPARK Institute, an association that represents 401(k) plan service providers, told us the same thing, that additional DOL guidance is needed because the agency has not clarified whether uncashed distribution checks are plan assets and therefore whether they can be transferred to the states.

CONCLUSION

Retirement savings may go unclaimed by account owners who are unaware of or unable to locate their savings as they change jobs, move, and age. Since unclaimed retirement savings may be transferred to states, this issue affects not only the account owners, but also the retirement industry and states. GAO has previously recommended that Congress make it easier for individuals to keep their savings in an employer's plan by requiring plans to include rollover balances when determining what balances are small enough to force out of the plan. Such an action would make fewer retirement savings accounts subject to transfer to the state. Action on the part of IRS and DOL could help ensure that federal taxes are properly applied to transfers and better protect the retirement security of the many individuals affected by these transfers every year.

IRS has provided guidance on the tax reporting and withholding requirements for transfers from IRAs, but it has not done so for 401(k) plans. Without IRS clarification on whether transfers should be reported to

---

[95] This service provider was among the 10 largest providers in the nation based on total DC assets, according to 2016 industry data.

[96] As noted in the first section of this chapter, states use a variety of strategies to locate owners of unclaimed savings.

IRS as distributions and when they should be subject to federal income tax withholding, not all plan service providers can be certain about the appropriate actions to take. The action providers take not only may affect the collection of federal income tax withholding, it can directly affect individuals' retirement security. If transfers of savings to the states from tax-deferred 401(k) accounts constitute distributions and federal income tax withholding is not applied, IRS is less likely to collect federal income taxes that may be due.

Individuals from terminating plans may have their retirement savings transferred to states, but may not always be able to return their savings to a qualified retirement account after they claim them from a state. IRS can help protect account owners' retirement security by permitting them to roll over savings that they have claimed from states. However, IRS should modify its procedures that allow individuals to rollover savings after the 60-day deadline to ensure that individuals who claim their savings from a state can complete a rollover. Without the ability to roll over savings, individuals miss out on the opportunity to grow their savings tax-deferred.

Further, DOL has not specified whether uncashed 401(k) plan distribution checks can be transferred to the states as unclaimed property under ERISA. This clarification would help both states and retirement plan service providers better navigate the available options for managing these checks. Clear options could result in better outcomes for the account owners, since the options may increase the likelihood of the owners receiving their retirement savings.

RECOMMENDATIONS FOR EXECUTIVE ACTION

We are making a total of three recommendations, including two to IRS and one to DOL.

The IRS Commissioner should work with the Department of the Treasury to consider clarifying if transfers of unclaimed savings from employer-based plans (such as 401(k) plans) to states are distributions, what, if any, tax reporting and withholding requirements apply, and when they apply. (Recommendation 1)

The IRS Commissioner should work with the Department of the Treasury to consider adding retirement savings transferred to states from terminating DC plans to the list of permitted reasons for rolling over savings after the 60-day rollover period, in a form consistent with the rules adopted on the taxation of transfers of unclaimed retirement savings. (Recommendation 2)

The Secretary of Labor should specify the circumstances, if any, under which uncashed distribution checks from active plans can be transferred to the states. (Recommendation 3)

AGENCY COMMENTS AND OUR EVALUATION

We provided a draft of this chapter to the Department of the Treasury (Treasury), the Internal Revenue Service (IRS), and the Department of Labor (DOL). Treasury, IRS, and DOL provided technical comments, which we have incorporated where appropriate. IRS and DOL provided formal comments, which are reproduced in appendixes IV through V.

IRS agreed with our recommendations. In its formal comments, IRS stated that it will work with Treasury to consider clarifying the issues raised by our first recommendation and addressing the issues outlined in our second recommendation. We are pleased that IRS has agreed to take the actions we have recommended. As noted in our report, there is confusion in the industry regarding the applicability of tax reporting and withholding to transfers of unclaimed savings from active plans to the states. Further, some individuals who claim their savings from a state may not be able to return them to a qualified retirement account where they can continue to be invested on a tax-deferred basis.

In its formal comments, DOL neither agreed nor disagreed with our recommendation. However, DOL stated it plans to continue to evaluate whether there are circumstances in which the transfer of uncashed distribution checks from an ongoing plan to the states advances the goal of reuniting missing participants with their savings, which is consistent with our recommendation. We commend DOL for recognizing the importance of this issue and continue to believe our recommendation is valid. As we noted in our report, assets and uncashed checks from employer-based DC plans were the most common form of retirement savings transferred to states according to our survey of state unclaimed property offices.

As arranged with your office, unless you publicly announce its contents earlier, we plan no further distribution of this chapter until 30 days from the date of this letter. At that time, we will send copies to the Secretaries of Labor and Treasury and the Commissioner of the Internal Revenue Service.

Sincerely yours,

Charles Jeszeck, Director
Education, Workforce, and Income Security Issues

APPENDIX I: OBJECTIVES, SCOPE, AND METHODOLOGY

This chapter examines (1) how much retirement savings is transferred to states as unclaimed property and what happens to those savings once transferred; and (2) the steps that the Internal Revenue Service (IRS) and the Department of Labor (DOL) have taken to oversee the transfer of unclaimed retirement savings to the states and what improvements, if any, are needed.

To determine how much retirement savings is transferred to the states as unclaimed property, we focused our analysis on the transfer of savings from 401(k) plans and individual retirement accounts (IRAs)[97] and

---

[97] Several experts we interviewed said they do not believe that defined benefit pension plans typically transfer unclaimed retirement benefits to states. An official from the National Association of State Retirement Administrators told us that, based on his experience, public state and local government retirement plans do not transfer unclaimed benefits to other states' unclaimed property offices. An unclaimed property expert that we interviewed also told us that such transfers do not occur.

conducted three surveys as well as obtained data from four large IRA providers.

- First, we surveyed the unclaimed property offices in all 50 states as well as the District of Columbia (our state survey) to obtain the number and dollar value of unclaimed savings from retirement accounts both transferred to states and claimed by owners in 2016, the most recent year for which complete data were available at the time of our review. We received survey responses from 22 states, representing 57 percent of the nation's total population. Of those 22 states, 17 provided transfer data. These 17 states represent 46 percent of the total population. Responses from states we surveyed are not generalizable across all states.
- Second, to supplement the data we obtained from responses to our state survey and to corroborate those findings, we surveyed members of two private industry associations—the Investment Company Institute (ICI) and the SPARK Institute—to collect data on the number of individuals who had some or all of their retirement savings transferred to the states in 2016 from IRAs and 401(k) plans, and the dollar value of those transfers.[98] Throughout the report, we refer to these surveys as our IRA transfer agent survey and 401(k) plan service provider survey, respectively.
- We selected ICI and SPARK primarily based on the large amount of assets their members manage and their knowledge of the retirement industry. Based on our discussions with ICI and SPARK officials, we conducted the surveys anonymously, meaning we did not require survey respondents to provide their name or contact information. To further ensure anonymity, ICI and SPARK distributed our survey to their members and respondents

[98] ICI is an association that represents mutual fund companies. According to ICI officials, the amount of IRA assets managed by their mutual fund company members accounts for most of the assets under management in the IRA industry. The SPARK Institute is an association that represents DC plan service providers. SPARK members include 401(k) record keepers as well as representatives from mutual fund companies and investment brokerage firms, and serve approximately 85 million participants in 401(k) and other DC plans.

submitted their surveys via a portal, which prevented us from seeing the identity of the survey respondent. To collect IRA transfer data, we provided a web-based survey to 129 transfer agent members of ICI.[99] In total, we received responses from 21 companies that collectively managed $299 billion in IRA assets in 2016, which is about 4 percent of the total IRA market, based on 2016 industry data.[100] Responses from these 21 companies are not generalizable across all transfer agent companies. To collect data specific to 401(k) plan transfers, we provided a web-based survey to all 32 of SPARK's member companies that serve 401(k) plans. We received responses from 7 companies that collectively managed more than $580 billion in 401(k) assets in 2016 (one survey respondent did not report the amount of assets managed), which is more than 13 percent of total 401(k) assets nationwide, based on DOL data.[101] Responses from these 401(k) plan service providers are not generalizable across all 401(k) plan service providers.

- To obtain further insight into the amount of retirement savings transferred to the states, we collected nongeneralizable 2016 IRA transfer data from four companies that are large IRA providers, based on the amount of IRA assets managed.[102] In recent years, these companies collectively managed over $1.4 trillion in IRA assets,[103] which is about 18 percent of total IRA assets, based on 2016 industry data.[104] Specifically, we collected data on the number of IRA accounts transferred to the states in 2016 and the

---

[99] The IRA transfer agent survey was also sent to some mutual fund companies, but ICI officials told us that these companies' transfer agents would respond on their behalf. Therefore, for reporting purposes, we are referring to the 129 survey recipients as transfer agents.

[100] Cerulli Associates, *The Cerulli Report: U.S. Evolution of the Retirement Investor 2016: Regulation and Investor Addressability*.

[101] DOL, *Private Pension Plan Bulletin: Abstract of 2015 Form 5500 Annual Reports (data extracted on 7/7/17)* February 2018. These were the most recent DOL data available at the time of our review.

[102] We requested data from a fifth company, but they declined our request.

[103] One company actually provided 2017 data on the amount of IRA assets managed, another provided 2015 data, while the remaining two companies provided 2016 data.

[104] Cerulli Associates, The Cerulli Report: U.S. Evolution of the Retirement Investor 2016: Regulation and Investor Addressability.

> dollar value of those transfers. Since these companies are also large defined contribution (DC) plan service providers, based on the amount of assets they manage and the number of plan participants they serve, we also collected data from them on the number of 401(k) plan participants who had some or all of their retirement savings transferred to the states in 2016 and the total dollar value of those transfers.

To determine what happens to unclaimed retirement savings after they are transferred to the states, we collected relevant data through our state survey, reviewed online state media outreach efforts, and interviewed industry and state officials. Through our state survey, we collected information on the steps states take to preserve the value of unclaimed retirement savings in their custody (e.g., applying interest) as well as the steps they take to locate the owners of retirement savings, such as posting information online and in newspapers as well as conducting outreach at public events. We interviewed officials from the National Association of Unclaimed Property Administrators (NAUPA),[105] officials from a large state, and unclaimed property experts to gain further insight on how unclaimed retirement savings are handled after states receive them, such as how quickly they liquidate securities in instances where retirement savings are transferred in the form of securities rather than cash. To corroborate state survey responses related to the steps taken to locate owners, we searched a database of U.S. newspapers and used an internet search engine to identify related articles published in 2017 and analyzed them to determine whether they represented examples of outreach activities related to unclaimed property. We also verified the existence and general content of each state's unclaimed property office website. We did not do a comprehensive review of state laws. Therefore, our statements about state unclaimed property laws are based on our review of available literature and information from unclaimed property experts.

---

[105] NAUPA's hundreds of members are unclaimed property officers from D.C. and all 50 states.

To determine the steps that IRS and DOL have taken to oversee the transfer of unclaimed retirement savings to the states and identify potential areas for improvement, we reviewed relevant federal laws and regulations and documentation from IRS and DOL, including guidance pertinent to the transfer of unclaimed retirement savings to the states. In addition, we included questions in our state, ICI, and SPARK surveys that asked for perspectives on issues pertinent to IRS and DOL oversight. Specifically, we included questions in our state survey that asked states to indicate whether additional federal guidance on tax reporting and withholding for unclaimed retirement savings would be useful. In addition, we included questions in our ICI and SPARK surveys that asked respondents to (1) evaluate the clarity of federal guidance regarding whether transfers of retirement savings to the states should be reported to the IRS as distributions and subject to tax withholding, and (2) identify areas where additional federal guidance is needed. To supplement our review of agency documentation and survey data, we interviewed officials from IRS and DOL to gain further insight on the steps they have taken to oversee transfers of retirement savings to the states. We also interviewed private sector officials from three retirement industry associations –ICI, the Securities Industry and Financial Markets Association (SIFMA),[106] and SPARK –as well as state officials to obtain industry and state perspectives on IRS and DOL oversight of the process for transferring unclaimed retirement savings to the states.

Survey Analysis and Limitations

State survey. To minimize errors and assure the validity of our questions, we conducted pretests with four states' unclaimed property officers as well as with the two largest providers of unclaimed property tracking software, which is used by more than 40 states. We made

[106] SIFMA is an association that represents broker-dealers, banks, and asset managers. According to SIFMA's website, the association's members manage more than $67 trillion in assets for individual and institutional clients including mutual funds and retirement plans.

adjustments to the survey questions based on feedback from these pretests. To assess the quality of the survey data, we included questions in the survey that asked state officials to identify the source of their data, assess the accuracy of holder's use of property codes (which are used to identify the specific type of property—in this case, retirement savings—that holders transfer to a state) as well as the completeness of the data on the number and value of properties transferred, and to explain any other data concerns.

To analyze the state survey responses, we conducted standard calculations and reviewed written responses. We excluded data from our calculations, as needed, based on data limitations that we observed. For example, one state provided the value of all retirement savings transferred to the state irrespective of the year in which it was transferred, so we excluded their data from our quantitative analysis since we focused on fiscal year 2016. We did not conduct an independent review of the quality of the data states provided. Nonetheless, we determined that the data are of sufficient quality for our purposes, which are to aggregate state transfer data and provide a sense for the volume of such transfers.

The state survey data are not generalizable and must be considered in light of a few data limitations:

- Our state survey was voluntary, so we did not receive survey responses from every state. Therefore, the aggregate data we report is not the national total for the amount of unclaimed retirement savings transferred to states.
- Holders (e.g., retirement plans and IRAs) may not use accurate property-type codes when transferring unclaimed retirement savings to the states and the states' knowledge of what types of property they have is limited to the codes holders use. Because of the lack of controls in place, some property is likely miscoded and neither the states responding to our survey nor we were able to determine the prevalence of these errors or if they are likely to overstate or understate the amount of savings reported with specific codes. Additionally, holders may apply property-type

codes differently because, as NAUPA officials told us, there is no single, common explanation for how each code should be used.

- For certain property-type codes, states cannot identify the type of retirement plan from which savings were transferred. For example, if a property has a "pension check" property-type code, the state does not know if the property was from a defined benefit or a DC plan. The states' data do not specifically identify DC plans and uncashed distribution checks from these plans as the sources of the unclaimed property they received from employer retirement plans, but based on our interviews with state officials as well as unclaimed property experts we determined that these are the most likely and common sources.

IRA Transfer Agent and 401(k) Plan Service Provider Surveys. In line with the approach taken for our state survey, we conducted pretests for both surveys to minimize errors arising from differences in how questions might be interpreted and to reduce variability in responses that should be qualitatively the same. For the IRA transfer agent survey, we conducted pretests with two different types of transfer agents: one affiliated with a large mutual fund company and another that is affiliated with a mutual fund company, but outsources certain functions to a third party, unaffiliated transfer agent. For the 401(k) plan service provider survey, we conducted pretests with a 401(k) plan record keeper that primarily serves larger plans and another that primarily serves smaller plans. Our pre-test approach allowed us to obtain varying perspectives on both surveys. GAO staff with expertise in survey design also reviewed both surveys for content and consistency. Based on feedback from these pretests, we revised the surveys to improve question clarity and content.

To analyze the survey data, we used standard descriptive statistics. Because this was not a sample survey, there were no sampling errors. To minimize other types of errors, commonly referred to as non-sampling errors, and to enhance data quality, we employed recognized survey design practices in the development of the survey and in the collection, processing, and analysis of the survey data.

For instance, as previously mentioned, we pretested the survey with individuals internal and external to GAO to enhance the clarity of our questions, which minimizes the likelihood of errors arising from differences in how questions might be interpreted and helps to reduce the variability in responses that should be qualitatively the same. To help reduce nonresponse, another source of non-sampling error, we asked ICI and SPARK officials to send reminder emails to their members on multiple occasions to further encourage them to complete the surveys. In reviewing the survey data, we performed automated checks to identify inappropriate answers. We further reviewed the data for ambiguous responses and followed up with respondents to clarify their responses when necessary. To assess the quality of the data captured in both surveys, we included questions in the surveys that asked respondents to identify the data sources they consulted and any data limitations. On the basis of our application of recognized survey design practices and follow-up procedures and subject to the limitations outlined below, we determined that the survey data were of sufficient quality for our purposes.

Key data limitations for the IRA transfer agent and 401(k) plan service provider surveys include our lack of direct access to the target population, the potential for respondents to submit multiple responses, and the lack of generalizable responses.

- First, it is possible that individuals outside of our target population completed the surveys because survey respondents in our target population could have forwarded the survey link to others. However, to help address this possibility, we built checks into the surveys to confirm who received them. For example, both surveys included questions that asked respondents to confirm their roles (i.e., IRA transfer agent, 401(k) plan record keeper).

- Second, because we conducted the surveys anonymously, we could not verify that respondents did not submit more than one survey response. However, to mitigate this concern, ICI and SPARK officials specifically asked their members to submit only one response.
- Third, the transfer agents and plan service providers that completed the surveys are voluntary members of ICI and SPARK, respectively. Therefore, they may differ from companies that are not members of these organizations in terms of their knowledge of or concern about the issues addressed in the surveys, which has implications on their survey responses. As a result, the data and views reported in the surveys are not generalizable.

APPENDIX II: TABLE COMPARING SOURCES OF DATA ON UNCLAIMED RETIREMENT SAVINGS TRANSFERRED TO STATES IN 2016

Table 5. Sources of Data on Unclaimed Retirement Savings Transferred to States in 2016

Data source	Coverage	Number of transfers of retirement savings[a] in 2016	Dollar value of transfers of retirement savings in 2016 (rounded)
GAO survey of 50 states and D.C.	22 states responded, with populations that make up 57% of the U.S. population. 17 provided data on retirement savings transferred.	53,725 properties	$35 million[b]

Data source	Coverage	Number of transfers of retirement savings[a] in 2016	Dollar value of transfers of retirement savings in 2016 (rounded)
GAO survey of 401(k) plan service providers	7 companies responded; these companies provide services for more than[c] 13% of total 401(k) assets nationwide. 5 provided data on transfers to states. 2 reported they do not make such transfers.	16,221 individuals	$2 million
GAO survey of IRA transfer agents, mutual fund companies, and related providers	21 transfer agents, covering 4% of total IRA assets nationwide.	1,057 individuals	$13 million
Data shared by additional Individual Retirement Account (IRA) providers[d]	4 IRA providers that manage 20% of total IRA assets nationwide.	1,606 accounts	$17 million[e]

Source: GAO analysis of survey and industry data, including 2016 population data from the U.S. Census and 2015 data on market size from Cerulli. | GAO-19-88.

[a] These transfer data reflect retirement savings related properties transferred, individuals who had some or all of their savings transferred, and accounts transferred. The exact measure used varied depending on the entity that shared the data. The retirement savings of one individual could be transferred to the states in more than one transfer because different assets are sent separately. For example, the savings in a single IRA could be split up by investment funds and transferred to the state as multiple, separate properties which belong to one owner. State data may understate the actual total number of properties transferred in 2016 because the data exclude properties sent in aggregate—some states permit holders to send small properties as a group, without identifying the underlying individual account owners. The data across all of our surveys cannot be added together because there could be double counting between the accounts transferred by IRA providers, for example, and the properties received by states.

[b] The dollar value of transfers is the minimum value because savings transferred in shares of a mutual fund may not have an associated value recorded at the time of transfer. For example, the dollar value of mutual fund shares transferred to several states responding to our survey is not reflected in this number.

[c] Of seven survey respondents, just six provided data on their assets under management, meaning that this percentage of the total market under management by survey respondents underreports the actual percentage.

[d] These providers shared IRA transfer data outside of our survey of IRA providers.

[e] The dollar value of transfers is imprecise because two companies provided estimates and one provided 2015 data.

Appendix III: Actions States Take to Maintain the Value of Unclaimed Property and to Locate and Protect Owners

Table 6. Actions States Take to Maintain the Value of Unclaimed Property and to Locate and Protect Owners, Based on 22 State Responses to a GAO Survey

	State Survey Response	
	Always or sometimes	Never
State actions to maintain value of unclaimed property		
Apply state-paid interest on the value of unclaimed property (not including interest earned by the asset)	7	14
Delay liquidation of property	16	6
Immediate liquidation of property	10	12
State actions to locate owners of unclaimed property		
Staff identify and attempt to contact owners	17	2
Direct mailing to individuals with unclaimed property	19	3
Check the Social Security Administration's Death Master File and search for beneficiaries	6	13
Hire a third party to search the Death Master File and search for beneficiaries	5	17
Post unclaimed property information on www.MissingMoney.com	19	3
Post unclaimed property information on your state's own searchable website	21	1
Use Lexis Nexis to search for property owners	20	2
Publicize the unclaimed property office via television	19	2
Publicize the unclaimed property office at public events (e.g., state fairs)	20	2
Advertise the unclaimed property office in the newspaper	17	3
Advertise specific properties in the newspaper	10	11
State actions to protect owners of unclaimed property		
Limit finder-fees	17	5
Require that investigators, asset locators and/or heir-finders are licensed in your state	11	11
Limit heir-finder or related services before property is transferred to the state	7	15
Limit heir-finder or related services after property is transferred to the state	19	3

Source: GAO survey data from 22 states. | GAO-19-88. Note: State responses of "Don't Know" are not included above. Some states did not respond to each item, so answers do not always total 22.

APPENDIX IV: COMMENTS FROM THE INTERNAL REVENUE SERVICE

DEPUTY COMMISSIONER

DEPARTMENT OF THE TREASURY
INTERNAL REVENUE SERVICE
WASHINGTON, D.C. 20224

December 14, 2018

Charles A. Jeszeck
Director, Education, Workforce, and Income Security Issues
United States Government Accountability Office
441 G Street, NW
Washington, DC 20548

Dear Mr. Jeszeck:

Thank you for the opportunity to review the draft report of the Government Accountability Office entitled "***Retirement Accounts: Federal Action Needed to Clarify Tax Treatment of Unclaimed 401(k) Plan Savings Transferred to States***" (GAO-19-88, Job Code 101190). As noted in your report, states receive millions in unclaimed retirement savings each year from a variety of sources, including employer-sponsored plans and IRAs, and in a variety of forms, such as cash and securities. The IRS shares enforcement responsibility for the Employee Retirement Income Security Act of 1974 with the Department of Labor, and we look forward to future collaboration with the Department of Labor as we address these retirement issues.

The IRS and the Department of the Treasury previously provided input to the Department of Labor on their Field Assistance Bulletins (FABs) 2004-02 and 2014-01 regarding "Fiduciary Duties and Missing Participants in Terminated Defined Contribution Plans." Those FABs included discussion regarding payments from terminated defined contribution plans to state unclaimed property funds. More recently, the IRS issued Rev. Rul. 2018-17 and Rev. Rul. 2018-90, which address tax withholding and reporting obligations in the case of traditional IRAs that are paid to state unclaimed property funds. Also, Treasury's 2018-2019 Priority Guidance Plan contains a "Retirement Benefits" project entitled "Guidance on Missing Participants."

The draft report makes two recommendations to the IRS. With respect to the first recommendation, the IRS will work with the Department of the Treasury to consider clarifying if transfers of unclaimed retirement savings from employer-based plans (such as 401(k) plans) to states are distributions, what, if any, tax reporting and withholding requirements apply, and when they apply. With respect to the second recommendation, the IRS will work with the Department of the Treasury to consider adding retirement savings transferred to states from terminating defined contribution plans to the list of permitted reasons for rolling over savings after the 60-day rollover period in a form consistent with the rules adopted on the taxation of transfers of unclaimed retirement savings.

Sincerely,

Kirsten B. Wielobob,
Deputy Commissioner for
Services and Enforcement

APPENDIX V: COMMENTS FROM THE DEPARTMENT OF LABOR

U.S. Department of Labor

Assistant Secretary for
Employee Benefits Security Administration
Washington, D.C. 20210

DEC 0 3 2018

Charles A. Jeszeck
Director, Education, Workforce and Income Security
Government Accountability Office
Washington D.C. 20548

Dear Mr. Jeszeck:

Thank you for the opportunity to review the Government Accountability Office's draft report entitled "Federal Action Needed to Clarify Tax Treatment of Unclaimed 401(k) Plan Savings Transferred to States." The draft report contained one recommendation for the Department of Labor. Specifically, you recommend that the Secretary of Labor specify the circumstances, if any, under which uncashed distribution checks from active retirement plans can be transferred to state unclaimed property funds.

Under the Employee Retirement Income Security Act (ERISA), plan fiduciaries have a duty to pay workers their promised retirement benefits when due. Plan fiduciaries have a related duty to maintain accurate records, including plan participant contact information, and must search for missing plan participants. The goal of the Employee Benefits Security Administration's (EBSA) enforcement activities and guidance initiatives in this area is to help plans locate and pay retirement benefits to missing participants and beneficiaries. In our view, eliminating, or at least very substantially reducing, the number of uncashed distribution checks is the best solution.

EBSA has received letters from state treasurers and controllers concerning their unclaimed property funds and my staff has personally met with representatives of several states. We have also met with representatives of plans, employers, financial services groups, and consumer groups. Additionally, legislative proposals have been introduced in Congress. As you might expect, different stakeholders have different perspectives on the issues involved.

There may be ways that state unclaimed property funds can help us do more in this area. We plan to continue to evaluate whether there are circumstances in which transfer of uncashed distribution checks from an ongoing plan to a state unclaimed property fund advances the goal of reuniting missing participants with their retirement savings. The fact that not all state unclaimed property laws are the same presents challenges for identifying a uniform, nationwide approach. Guidance in this area also may require notice and comment rulemaking, and will need to be coordinated with the Department of the Treasury/Internal Revenue Service on inter-related tax compliance issues.

Thank you again for sharing your draft report and recommendation. Please be assured that we are focused on solutions that serve the best interests of America's workers.

Sincerely,

Preston Rutledge
Assistant Secretary

In: Retirement
Editor: Thomas M. Osborne
ISBN: 978-1-53615-703-1

Chapter 6

RETIREMENT BENEFITS FOR FEDERAL LAW ENFORCEMENT PERSONNEL*

Katelin P. Isaacs

SUMMARY

Federal employees who perform specific duties, as defined in statute, are classified as law enforcement officers (LEOs) for the purpose of federal retirement benefits. LEOs and a few legislatively designated groups, including federal firefighters and air traffic controllers, are eligible for enhanced retirement benefits under the Civil Service Retirement System (CSRS), for individuals hired before 1984, or the Federal Employees' Retirement System (FERS), for individuals hired in 1984 or later.

The availability of enhanced retirement benefits for LEOs and similar groups is linked to an expectation of limited federal service. This limited service is due, in turn, to the rigorous physical demands of law enforcement duties and the mandatory retirement age to which these individuals are subject. LEO enhanced retirement benefits are designed to provide adequate retirement income for federal employees with careers

---

* This is an edited, reformatted and augmented version of Congressional Research Service, Publication No. R42631, dated September 5, 2017.

that end at an earlier age with fewer years of service than regular civilian federal employees.

In general, law enforcement personnel are subject to mandatory retirement at age 57, or as soon as 20 years of service have been completed after age 57. The maximum age of entry, which is intended to ensure full retirement benefits upon reaching mandatory retirement age, is typically age 37. Under both CSRS and FERS, law enforcement personnel are eligible for their enhanced benefits at the age of 50 provided they have completed the minimum requirement of 20 years of service. Under FERS, law enforcement personnel with 25 years of service are eligible for retirement regardless of age.

Law enforcement personnel in CSRS and their employing agencies each contribute 7.5% of payroll. CSRS law enforcement personnel accrue benefits at the rate of 2.5% per year for their first 20 years of service and 2% for each year after the 20th year of service. Law enforcement personnel in FERS accrue benefits at the rate of 1.7% per year for the first 20 years of service and 1% per year for each year thereafter. FERS contribution rates vary by date of hire. Law enforcement personnel in FERS first hired before 2013 contribute 1.3% of pay (plus Social Security contributions), and their agencies contribute 30.1% of pay. Under P.L. 112-96, FERS law enforcement personnel first hired in 2013 contribute 3.6% of pay (plus Social Security contributions), and their agencies contribute 28.4% of pay. Finally, under P.L. 113-67, FERS law enforcement personnel first hired in 2014 or later contribute 4.9% of pay (plus Social Security contributions), but their agencies still contribute 28.4% of pay. FERS accrual rates remain unchanged for law enforcement personnel first hired in 2013 or later (including individuals first hired in 2014 or later).

Many employees in law enforcement occupations are not recognized as LEOs by their agencies and OPM for the purposes of federal retirement coverage and, consequently, are not eligible to receive enhanced retirement benefits. Several employee groups and unions representing individuals in these occupations have sought enhanced retirement benefits through additional legislation. Recent Congresses have responded by introducing legislation that would provide enhanced retirement benefits to additional personnel. Though granting more groups such benefits may alleviate problems of attrition and perceived inequity across law enforcement occupations, it would also increase personnel costs for employing agencies as well as overall federal expenditures on civilian federal retirement benefits.

INTRODUCTION

Federal law enforcement officers, as defined in statute, and a few related occupations—such as federal firefighters and air traffic controllers—are eligible for enhanced retirement benefits. Congress decided that these occupations should be composed of young men and women who possess the strength and endurance necessary to perform the required duties. Enhanced retirement benefits help to maintain this type of workforce by permitting employees in these positions to retire earlier and accrue pension benefits faster during earlier years of service than regular civilian federal employees. Many individuals and employee groups who work in law enforcement-related positions, but who have not qualified as law enforcement officers for retirement purposes, have sought enhanced benefits through legislation in recent Congresses. Incorporating additional occupations may address problems of attrition and perceived inequity across law enforcement-related positions. However, expanding access to enhanced retirement benefits also generates concerns over additional expenditures on federal retirement benefits.

FEDERAL LAW ENFORCEMENT OFFICERS AND RELATED PERSONNEL

Currently, the definition of a federal law enforcement officer (LEO) for retirement purposes is limited to an employee who performs certain duties defined in statute under either the Civil Service Retirement System (CSRS), which covers federal employees hired before 1984, or the Federal Employees' Retirement System (FERS), which covers federal employees hired in 1984 or later. Individuals employed in positions that meet the statutory definition of a LEO, as well as certain personnel who have obtained LEO-equivalent benefits through direct legislation, are eligible to retire earlier with fewer years of service and receive a benefit accrual rate during the first 20 years of service that is higher than the benefit accrual rate for regular federal civilian employees. LEOs and employees who have enhanced retirement benefits also contribute more to their own benefits than regular civilian federal employees and are subject to a mandatory retirement age.

Statutory Definition of a Law Enforcement Officer

Under CSRS, a LEO is an employee whose *primary* duties are "the investigation, apprehension, or detention of individuals suspected or convicted of offenses against the criminal laws of the United States, including an employee engaged in this activity who is transferred to a supervisory or administrative position."[1]

The definition of a LEO under FERS is nearly identical to the CSRS definition, though more specific. In addition to an employee whose *primary* duties are "the investigation, apprehension, or detention of individuals suspected or convicted of offenses against the United States," the FERS definition includes an employee whose *primary* duties are "the protection of officials of the United States against threats to personal safety."[2] The FERS statutory definition of a LEO also provides an explicit standard for rigorous duty. For those employees whose *primary* duties are as described above, these duties must be "sufficiently rigorous that employment should be limited to young and physically vigorous individuals."[3]

---

[1] 5 U.S.C. §8331(20). "Primary duties" are defined by the U.S. Code of Federal Regulations (5 C.F.R. §831.802) as "those duties of a position which—(a) Are paramount in influence or weight; that is, constitute the basic reasons for the existence of the position; (b) Occupy a substantial portion of the individual's working time over a typical work cycle; and (c) Are assigned on a regular and recurring basis. Duties that are of an emergency, incidental, or temporary nature cannot be considered "primary" even if they meet the substantial portion of time criterion."

[2] 5 U.S.C. §8401(17).

[3] 5 U.S.C. §§8401(14) and 8401(17), respectively. A "rigorous position" is defined in federal regulations (5 C.F.R. §3307(e)) as "a position the duties of which are so rigorous that employment opportunities should, as soon as reasonably possible, be limited (through establishment of a maximum entry age and physical qualifications) to young and physically vigorous individuals."

Additional Regulations Defining LEOs

The implementing regulations for the Office of Personnel Management (OPM), which administers CSRS and FERS benefits, establish that the definition of a law enforcement officer "does not include an employee whose primary duties involve maintaining law and order, protecting life and property, guarding against or inspecting for violations of law, or investigating persons other than persons who are suspected or convicted of offenses against the criminal laws of the United States."[4]

Furthermore, qualification for enhanced retirement benefits does not depend on the law enforcement mission of an agency, nor does it depend on the classification of a position within an occupational series of the Federal Classification and Job Grading System. Effectively, this has excluded police officers, guards, and inspectors from the definition of "law enforcement officer" for federal retirement purposes.

Administrative Process for Determining LEO Status

Typically, for a group of employees to be eligible for enhanced retirement benefits under CSRS or FERS, the employing agency must determine that the duties of the position meet the statutory definition of a LEO and submit their evaluation to OPM. OPM rarely overturns the decision of the head of an agency but retains the right to do so.[5] Alternatively, some groups whose agencies and OPM have determined that they do not meet the statutory definition of a LEO have gained access to enhanced retirement benefits through direct legislation that either added them to the statutory definition of a LEO or provided benefits similar to those received by LEOs. If an employee feels that he or she has been unjustly excluded from the LEO definition and the concomitant retirement

---

[4] 5 C.F.R. §831.920.

[5] U.S. Government Accountability Office, *Federal Law Enforcement Retirement: Information on Enhanced Retirement Benefits for Law Enforcement Personnel*, GAO-09-727, July 2009. (Hereafter cited as GAO-09-727.)

benefits, that individual may appeal the final decision of the relevant agency to the Merit Systems Protection Board.[6]

Table 1 provides a list of groups of employees eligible for enhanced retirement benefits as a LEO or similar position. The left column includes examples of groups of employees that meet the statutory definition of a LEO under CSRS or FERS. The right column lists employee groups that have either been added to the LEO definition or granted enhanced retirement benefits through direct legislation. As described above, LEO determinations are made on the basis of position duties or by direct legislation. Therefore, the list in Table 1 is presented for illustrative purposes and is not intended to be exhaustive.

Table 1. Major Occupational Groups Eligible for Enhanced Benefits

Meet LEO Definitional Criteria via OPM Administrative Process	Added to LEO Definition or Provided LEO-Equivalent Benefits via Direct Legislation
Border Patrol Agents	Air Traffic Controllers
Drug Enforcement Administration Special Agents	Bureau of Prisons Correction Institute Staff
FBI Special Agents	Customs and Border Protection Officers
Federal Air Marshals	Firefighters
Immigration Enforcement Agents and Detention/Deportation Officers	Nuclear Materials Couriers
IRS Special Agents	U.S. Park Police[a]
U.S. Marshals	U.S. Secret Service Officers Uniformed Division[a]
U.S. Park Rangers	U.S. Capitol Police
U.S. Secret Service Special Agents	U.S. Supreme Court Police

Source: Compiled by the Congressional Research Service using information from the U.S. Office of Personnel Management and U.S. Government Accountability Office.

Notes: This list of LEO employee groups is presented for illustrative purposes and is not intended to be exhaustive. LEO determinations are made on the basis of position duties and/or by direct legislation.

[a]Applies in the case of FERS coverage only. These groups were covered by the District of Columbia Police Officers' and Firefighters' Retirement System prior to 1984 rather than CSRS.

[6] 5 C.F.R. §§831.308 and 841.308.

Table 2. Major Occupational Groups Added to the Definition of a LEO or Provided with LEO-Equivalent Benefits via Direct Legislation

Air Traffic Controllers	P.L. 92-297	1972
Bureau of Prisons Correction Institute Staff	P.L. 84-854	1956
Customs and Border Protection Officers	P.L. 110-161	2008
Firefighters	P.L. 92-382	1972
Nuclear Materials Couriers	P.L. 105-261	1998
U.S. Park Police	P.L. 100-238	1988
U.S. Secret Service Agents Uniformed Division	P.L. 100-238	1988
U.S. Capitol Police	P.L. 101-428	1990
U.S. Supreme Court Police	P.L. 106-553	2000

Source: Compiled by the Congressional Research Service using information from the U.S. Statutes at Large.

Table 2 provides further details on major occupational groups that have either been added to the LEO definition or granted enhanced retirement benefits through direct legislation. The center column lists the public law that provides enhanced retirement benefits for each group. The far right column shows the year in which each law was enacted.

In the remainder of this chapter, the above-mentioned groups are referred to collectively as law enforcement personnel. Differences in retirement benefits pertaining to any specific occupational group are noted.

Legislative Rationale for Enhanced Retirement Benefits

The duties of law enforcement personnel place unique physical and psychological demands on individuals employed in those positions. Because physical and mental health decline with age, Congress deemed it necessary to maintain a youthful workforce to ensure the quality of law enforcement services. Law enforcement personnel are subject to a mandatory retirement age to maintain this goal, which leads to an expectation of limited federal service for these employees. Consequently,

Congress has established enhanced retirement benefits for individuals in these occupations.

The provision of enhanced retirement benefits for law enforcement personnel was initially implemented with two primary intentions. The first was to create a retirement system under which it is financially reasonable for officers to retire at an earlier age with fewer years of service than regular civilian federal employees. Second, the enhanced retirement benefits, which encourage entry at a young age, continuous service, and early retirement, are intended to help maintain a young and vigorous federal law enforcement workforce. Enhanced retirement benefits, however, are not intended as compensation for the stress and hazard of the duties that federal law enforcement personnel perform.[7]

In 1947, Congress first legislated enhanced retirement benefits and an early retirement age, but only for the Federal Bureau of Investigation (FBI) agents.[8] At the time, the agency was losing agents to more lucrative employment in nonfederal positions.[9] A more generous retirement program was considered necessary to retain youthful individuals for career service. Shortly thereafter, many federal employee groups with comparable duties to FBI agents began to petition for enhanced benefits.

In 1948, the House Committee on Post Office and Civil Service submitted a report to Congress expressing that it would not oppose granting benefits to groups of employees similar to the FBI agents that Congress had previously approved for enhanced benefits[10]. The committee report stated that "it is only fair to grant such retirement benefits that are provided for under the bill to law-enforcement agents in all parts of the Government at an earlier age, because it is physically impossible to carry

[7] U.S. General Accounting Office, Statement of H.L. Krieger, Director, Federal Personnel and Compensation Division, on a General Accounting Office report entitled 'Special Retirement Policy for Federal Law Enforcement and Firefighter Personnel Needs Reevaluation,' FPCD-76-97, February 24, 1977, September 27, 1977. P.L. 93-350 deleted hazard as a criterion for entitlement.

[8] P.L. 80-168.

[9] U.S. General Accounting Office, *Special Retirement Policy for Federal Law Enforcement and Firefighter Personnel Needs Reevaluation*, FPCD-76-97, February 1977.

[10] U.S. House of Representatives, Committee on Post Office and Civil Service, *Amending the Civil Service Retirement Act to Provide Annuities for Certain Federal Employees*, H.Rept. 2034 (Washington: Government Printing Office, May 1948).

on the necessary strenuous activities after reaching 50 years of age."[11] Rather than recognize individual groups, Congress developed a blanket definition to authorize benefits for these occupational groups. The legislation that followed defined a "law enforcement officer" and expanded the provision of enhanced retirement benefits to individuals employed in the relevant occupations.[12]

Following the 1948 decision by Congress, legislation has done little to alter the definition of a LEO for retirement purposes. FERS was enacted in 1986 (P.L. 99-335) and sought to mimic the policies put in place by its predecessor, CSRS. Consequently, the definition of a law enforcement officer under FERS is similar to the definition under CSRS and maintains enhanced retirement benefits for those personnel.

Retirement Coverage for Federal Law Enforcement Personnel

For retirement purposes, most federal employees are covered under either the Civil Service Retirement System, for those hired before 1984, or the Federal Employees' Retirement System, for those hired in 1984 or later. Congress passed the Civil Service Retirement Act of 1920 (P.L 66-215) to create a pension plan for civilian federal employees. The Social Security system followed in 1935 to create a retirement plan for private-sector workers. Federal employees were excluded from Social Security until Congress passed the Social Security Amendments of 1983 (P.L. 98-21) and the Federal Employees' Retirement System Act of 1986 (P.L. 99-335), which together incorporated all civilian federal employees, hired in 1984 or after, into Social Security as part of a new federal retirement system. Additionally, FERS covers employees who were hired before 1984 and were covered by CSRS but elected to switch to FERS during the "open seasons" that Congress authorized in 1987 and 1998.

[11] Ibid., p. 2.
[12] P.L. 80-879.

Civil Service Retirement System

The CSRS annuity is the primary retirement benefit available to eligible individuals under CSRS. Employees covered by CSRS generally do not pay Social Security taxes, nor do they claim Social Security benefits. The CSRS annuity is a monthly pension based on years of service, the average of the three highest consecutive years of pay, and the accrual rate for each year of service. Employees covered under CSRS may participate in the Thrift Savings Plan (TSP), but they receive no matching contributions from employing agencies. The TSP is a defined contribution retirement plan much like plans authorized under Section 401(k) of the Internal Revenue Code for private-sector employers. Contributions to the TSP are at the discretion of the employee up to an annual limit.[13]

Federal Employees' Retirement System

Retirement benefits under FERS have three components: the FERS basic annuity, Social Security, and TSP. Employees covered by FERS pay Social Security taxes and receive Social Security benefits. The annuity, as under CSRS, is a monthly pension based on years of service, the average of the three highest consecutive years of pay, and the accrual rate for each year of service. However, the annuity portion is smaller compared with CSRS, as it is supplemented with Social Security and TSP. Like CSRS, employees may participate in TSP, but FERS employees are also eligible for matching contributions from their employer up to 5% of pay.[14]

---

[13] For more details on the Thrift Savings Plan, see CRS Report RL30387, *Federal Employees' Retirement System: The Role of the Thrift Savings Plan*.

[14] Ibid.

ELIGIBILITY AND BENEFIT AMOUNTS UNDER CSRS AND FERS

Age and Length of Service Requirements

Under both CSRS and FERS, the date an employee is eligible to retire and receive an annuity depends on his or her age and years of service. As described above, to provide quality law enforcement services, and in consideration of the physical and psychological demands imposed on law enforcement personnel, Congress has deemed it necessary to maintain a young and vigorous workforce. For that reason Congress has made provisions for a mandatory retirement age and, subsequently, a maximum age of entry for law enforcement personnel. Law enforcement personnel may be eligible for enhanced benefits after achieving the minimum retirement age and years of service.

Mandatory Retirement

Congress has set in statute a mandatory retirement age for law enforcement personnel. Under both CSRS and FERS, law enforcement personnel are required by law to retire at the age of 57 or as soon as 20 years of service have been completed after the age of 57.[15] The maximum retirement age for an air traffic controller (ATC) with 20 years of service is 56.[16] An employee may be exempt from the mandatory retirement age until the age of 60, or 61 for an air traffic controller, if the head of an employing agency determines that "the public interest so requires."[17] Additionally, the President, by executive order, may exempt a law enforcement officer from mandatory separation if the President determines it is in the public interest to do so.[18]

---

[15] 5 U.S.C. §8335(b) for CSRS. 5 U.S.C. §8425(b) for FERS.
[16] 5 U.S.C. §8335(a) for CSRS. 5 U.S.C. §8425(a) for FERS.
[17] 5 U.S.C. §8335(b) for CSRS. 5 U.S.C. §8425(b) for FERS.
[18] 5 U.S.C. §8335(f) for CSRS. 5 U.S.C. §8425(e) for FERS.

Maximum Age of Entry

Though federal law generally prohibits federal agencies from establishing a maximum age for individuals appointed to positions as federal employees, there is an exception in the case of law enforcement personnel.[19] To ensure that law enforcement personnel are eligible for retirement benefits at the mandatory retirement age, certain agencies have also been allowed to implement a maximum age of entry.[20]

The head of a federal agency may establish a maximum age of entry—typically 37—for an individual who is appointed to a position as a LEO. This is the highest age at which an individual can be hired into a law enforcement position and complete 20 years of service by the time he or she reaches the mandatory retirement age of 57.

Some exceptions to the maximum age of entry at age 37 have been made. The U.S. Customs and Border Protection, for instance, increased the maximum age of entry by three years to the age of 40 for veterans entering Border Patrol agency positions.[21]

Minimum Retirement Age

Under both CSRS and FERS, the minimum retirement age is 50 for law enforcement personnel with 20 years of service. Under FERS, employees are eligible for retirement at any age after completing 25 years of service.

---

[19] 5 U.S.C. §3307 designates that air traffic controllers, U.S. Park Police, law enforcement officers, firefighters, nuclear materials couriers, and customs and border protection officers may be subject to a maximum age of entry.

[20] Ibid.

[21] GAO-09-727. The Government Accountability Office states, "Some agencies have extended their maximum hiring age for LEOs to around 40 to facilitate the hiring of certain highly-skilled armed services veterans who have completed a military career" (p. 10). The Secretary of Homeland Security, like other agency heads, may provide for an exemption from the mandatory retirement age of 57 for Border Patrol agents until the age of 60 under certain conditions as authorized under 5 U.S.C. §8425(c). See 5 C.F.R. §842.1006. Mandatory separation at the age of 60 would allow Border Patrol agents who enter service at (or before) the age of 40 to accrue the 20 years of service required for LEO retirement.

Required Contributions

CSRS and FERS both require law enforcement personnel and their agencies to contribute a larger percentage of pay to their retirement system compared to regular civilian employees. Specifically, law enforcement personnel contribute an additional 0.5% of pay compared to regular federal employees hired at the same time.

Contributions under CSRS

Regular federal employees covered by CSRS contribute 7.0% of pay to CSRS. The employing agencies contribute another 7.0%. Law enforcement personnel contribute 7.5% of pay, as do their agencies.

Contributions under FERS

Regular federal employees first hired before 2013 contribute 0.8% of pay to FERS. Employing agencies currently contribute 13.7% of payroll on behalf of regular FERS employees hired before 2013. Under P.L. 112-96, regular federal employees first hired in 2013 contribute 3.1% of pay. P.L. 113-67 further increased the FERS contribution for regular federal employees first hired in 2014 or later to be 4.4% of pay. Employing agencies of regular FERS employees hired in 2013 or later (including individuals hired in 2014 or later) currently contribute 11.9% of pay.

By comparison, law enforcement personnel first hired before 2013 contribute 1.3% of pay, while their agencies currently contribute 30.1% of pay. Under P.L. 112-96, law enforcement personnel first hired in 2013 contribute 3.6% of pay to FERS. P.L. 113-67 increased the FERS contribution rate for law enforcement personnel first hired in 2014 or later to 4.4% of pay. Agencies employing law enforcement personnel hired in 2013 or later (including individuals hired in 2014 or later) currently contribute 28.4% of pay.[22]

---

[22] Office of Personnel Management, "Federal Employees' Retirement System: Normal Cost Percentages," 80 *Federal Register* 15036-15037, March 20, 2015. FERS agency contribution rates may be adjusted in future fiscal years based on changes in OPM's annual actuarial calculations of the dynamic normal cost of FERS benefits as well as any changes in required employee contribution rates. For a discussion of the dynamic normal cost of

Pension Plan Benefits

Annuities under both CSRS and FERS are computed according to (1) the number of years of service completed under the retirement plan; (2) the retiree's average annual salary for the three consecutive years of highest pay; and (3) the accrual rate at which benefits accumulate for each year of service.

High-Three Average Salary

Under both CSRS and FERS, the salary used in the annuity calculation is the average of the highest three consecutive years of base pay. This is commonly called "high-three" average salary. In some cases, special pay provisions provide higher rates of pay for law enforcement personnel.[23] To the extent that these pay schemes increase the basic pay of employees, there will be accompanying increases in retirement benefits.

Accrual Rates

The accrual rate is the pension benefit earned for each year of service, expressed as a percentage of the salary base. Under both CSRS and FERS, law enforcement personnel accrue benefits at a higher rate than do regular federal employees in their first 20 years of service.

Under CSRS, the accrual rates increase with years of service. A regular CSRS employee earns 1.5% of high-three average pay for each of the first five years of service, 1.75% for years 6-10, and 2% for each year beyond the 10th year. For their first 20 years of service, CSRS law enforcement personnel accrue benefits at the rate of 2.5% per year and 2% for each year after the 20th year of service.

Under FERS, a regular federal employee accrues benefits in one of two scenarios. The employee either accrues benefits at the rate of 1% per year of service or, if the employee has at least 20 years of service and works

---

FERS benefits, including the calculation of agency contributions, see CRS Report RL30023, *Federal Employees' Retirement System: Budget and Trust Fund Issues*.

[23] U.S. Office of Personnel Management, *Federal Law Enforcement Pay and Benefits: Report to Congress*, July 2004.

until the age of 62, accrues benefits at the rate of 1.1% per year of service. Law enforcement personnel accrue FERS benefits at the rate of 1.7% per year for the first 20 years of service and 1% per year for each year thereafter.

Pension Formulas

General Formula for Federal Employees

Generally, the annuity for a federal employee is

Annual Pension = Years of Service × High-Three Salary × Accrual Rate

Formula for Law Enforcement Personnel under CSRS

Under CSRS, using the appropriate accrual rates, the annuity for law enforcement personnel would be

CSRS Annual Pension = [Years of Service (not exceeding 20 years) × High-Three Salary × 0.025] + [Years of Service (exceeding 20) × High-Three Salary × 0.02]

Air traffic controllers (ATCs) have a special provision under CSRS, which guarantees them a minimum benefit. An ATC is entitled to receive the greater of the annuity calculated under the CSRS formula or 50% of his or her high-three average salary.[24]

Formula for Law Enforcement Personnel under FERS

Similarly under FERS, the annuity for law enforcement personnel would be

---

[24] 5 U.S.C. §8339(e).

FERS Annual Pension = [Years of Service (not exceeding 20 years) x High-Three Salary x 0.017] + [Years of Service (exceeding 20) x High-Three Salary x 0.01]

For example, law enforcement personnel retiring with 25 years of service would receive a pension equal to

FERS Annual Pension = [20 x High-Three Salary x 0.017] + [5 x High-Three Salary x 0.01]

Federal Law Enforcement Personnel with Both CSRS and FERS Coverage

Individuals who chose to transfer from coverage under CSRS to FERS with five or more years of creditable civilian service as of the effective date of the transfer, excluding service covered by both CSRS and Social Security deductions, will have a CSRS component to their annuity.[25] The CSRS component will be calculated based on the standard CSRS annuity formula for law enforcement personnel. For the FERS component, service years under CSRS do not count toward the 20-year limit on the 1.7% accrual rate.

The FERS Supplement

The FERS basic annuity was designed as a complement to Social Security retirement benefits. FERS employees, including law enforcement personnel, who retire before they are eligible for Social Security may receive a temporary supplement that is paid from the time of retirement until the Social Security eligibility age of 62. The amount of the supplement is equal to an estimate of the amount of Social Security benefits accrued from federal service. The supplement ends at the age of 62 regardless of whether the individual claims Social Security benefits at that time. Similar to Social Security benefits received before the full

[25] 5 C.F.R. §846.304.

retirement age,[26] the supplement is subject to an earnings test and reduced if the retiree has earnings above a specified limit.[27]

Cost-of-Living Adjustments

To offset inflation and preserve the purchasing power of retirees' income, CSRS and FERS annuities include a cost-of-living adjustment (COLA). All CSRS retirees and survivors, law enforcement personnel included, receive COLAs. The COLA is based on the rate of inflation as measured by the Consumer Price Index for Urban Wage Earners and Clerical Workers (CPI-W). The CSRS COLA is equal to the annual change in the CPI-W, which is the same COLA calculation used for Social Security benefits.

Under FERS, the COLA is also contingent on changes in the CPI-W. If the annual change in the CPI-W is less than 2.0%, then the FERS COLA will match this inflation change. If the annual change in the CPI-W is between 2.0% and 3.0%, then the FERS COLA is capped at 2.0%. For annual change in the CPI-W greater than 3.0%, the FERS COLA is equal to the annual change in the CPI-W less 1 percentage point. Under FERS, nondisabled retirees under the age of 62 do not receive COLAs. However, law enforcement personnel under the age of 62, retiring in accordance with the age and eligibility requirements, receive the COLAs.[28] Because FERS employees are eligible for Social Security, they also receive a separate Social Security COLA applied to their Social Security benefits.[29]

---

[26] The Social Security full retirement age is the age at which unreduced Social Security retirement benefits are first payable. The Social Security full retirement age ranges from 65 to 67, depending on the individual's year of birth. For more details, see CRS Report R42035, *Social Security Primer*.

[27] 5 U.S.C. §8421.

[28] For more details on COLAs for CSRS and FERS annuities, see CRS Report 94-834, *Cost-of-Living Adjustments for Federal Civil Service Annuities*.

[29] For more details on COLAs for Social Security benefits, see CRS Report 94-803, *Social Security: Cost-of-Living Adjustments*.

Replacement Rates

The replacement rate is often used to measure the income adequacy of retirement benefits. The measure is a ratio of annual retirement benefit to annual preretirement earnings. The annual retirement benefit typically includes the retiree's pension and his or her Social Security benefit.

Under CSRS, law enforcement personnel do not receive Social Security benefits, and so the replacement rate can be calculated using only the annuity benefit. Because of the more generous annuity, law enforcement personnel will have a higher replacement rate than regular federal employees. CSRS law enforcement personnel who retire with 20 years of service at the age of 50 will have a replacement rate of 50%, and those with 25 years of service will have a replacement rate of 60%.[30] A regular CSRS employee with 20 years of service would have a replacement rate of 36.25%.[31]

The FERS annuity was designed as a complement to Social Security and TSP. Considering all three components of FERS introduces significant variation in the replacement rate. Estimates of the replacement rate for an employee earning enhanced benefits range from 54% to 91%, depending on work history and TSP contributions of the worker.[32] Focusing only on the annuity portion, law enforcement personnel with 20 years of service would replace 34% of preretirement earnings with their annuity, and with 25 years of service would replace 39%. A regular federal employee with 20 years of service would earn an annuity equal to 20% of his or her preretirement earnings.

---

[30] For example, *(20 × 0.025 × High-Three Salary)/High-Three Salary = 0.50 or 50%; [(20 × 0.025 × High-Three Salary) + (5 × 0.02 × High-Three Salary)]/High-Three Salary = 0.60 or 60%.*

[31] For example, *(5 × 0.015 × High-Three Salary + 5 × 0.0175 × High-Three Salary + 10 × 0.02 × High-Three Salary)/High-Three Salary = 0.3625 or 36.25%.* Current law limits the maximum CSRS annuity for regular CSRS employees and law enforcement personnel to 80% of high-three salary (5 U.S.C. §8339(f)).

[32] U.S. Government Accountability Office, *Capitol Police: Retirement Benefits, Pay, Duties, and Attrition Compared to Other Federal Police Forces*, GAO-12-58, January 2012.

Table 3. Summary of Retirement Benefits for Federal Law Enforcement Personnel

	CSRS		FERS	
	Law Enforcement Personnel	**Regular Employees**	**Law Enforcement Personnel**	**Regular Employees**
Minimum Retirement Age	50a	60b	50c	60d
Mandatory Retirement Age	57e	N/A	57[e]	N/A
Maximum Entry Age	37[f]	N/A	37[f]	N/A
Accrual Rates by Years of Service	2.5% for years 1-20 2% for years 21+	1.5% for years 1-5 1.75% for years 6-10 2% for years 11+	1.7% for years 1-20 1% for years 21+	1%[g]
Agency Contribution	7.5%	7%	30.1% for those hired before 2013 28.4% for those hired in 2013 or later[h]	13.7% for those hired before 2013 11.9% for those hired in 2013 or later[h]
Employee Contribution	7.5%	7%	1.3% for those hired before 2013 3.6% for those hired in 2013 4.9% for those hired in 2014 or later	0.8% for those hired before 2013 3.1% for those hired in 2013 4.4% for those hired in 2014 or later
Replacement Rate With 20 Years of Service	50%	36.25%	34%[i]	20%[i]
TSP Agency Matching	No	No	Yes	Yes

Source: Congressional Research Service.

Table 3. (Continued)

[a] Applies to those with 20 years of service.

[b] Applies to those with 20 years of service. Those with 30 years of service may retire at the age of 55 and those with only 5 years of service may retire at the age of 62.

[c] Applies to those with 20 years of service. Otherwise employees are eligible for retirement at any age upon completing 25 years of service (Continued)

[d] Applies to those with 20 years of service. Those with 30 years of service may retire at a minimum retirement age that increases with birth year. For those born in 1970 or later the FERS minimum retirement age is 57 with 30 years of service. Those with only 5 years of service may retire at the age of 62.

[e] Applies to those with 20 years of service, or as soon as they have completed 20 years of service if not completed by the age of 57 (or 56 for an air traffic controller).

[f] In some agencies the maximum entry age has been increased up to three years for veterans.

[g] For employees with at least 20 years of service and who continue working until the age of 62, the accrual rate is 1.1%.

[h] *Office of Personnel Management, "Federal Employees' Retirement System: Normal Cost Percentages,"* 80 *Federal Register* 15036-15037, March 20, 2015. The FERS agency contribution rate for air traffic controllers first hired before 2013 is 31.8%. For air traffic controllers first hired in 2013 or later, the FERS agency contribution rate is 30.1%.

[i] Includes only the annuity and applies to those with 20 years of service.

Table 3 provides a summary of various aspects of civilian federal retirement benefits under both CSRS and FERS. It also compares the CSRS and FERS program rules for regular civilian federal employees and federal law enforcement personnel.

EXTENDING ENHANCED BENEFITS TO OTHER OCCUPATIONAL GROUPS

Many employees in law enforcement occupations are not recognized as LEOs by their agency and OPM, and consequently they are not eligible to receive enhanced retirement benefits. Several employee groups and unions representing individuals in these occupations have sought enhanced benefits through additional legislation. Generally, this legislation either proposes to include these groups as LEOs for retirement purposes or grant them LEO-equivalent benefits. For instance, in the 113th Congress, legislation has been introduced that would expand the definition of LEO—and, therefore, provide enhanced retirement benefits—to include (1) employees who investigate or apprehend individuals suspected or convicted of offenses against the criminal laws of the United States; (2) employees who carry firearms; and (3) Internal Revenue Service (IRS) employees whose duties are primarily the collection of delinquent taxes and the securing of delinquent returns (e.g., H.R. 1362, the Law Enforcement Officers Retirement Equity Act of 2013; H.R. 1525, the Save America Comprehensive Immigration Act of 2013).[33]

Two primary reasons are offered in support of extending enhanced benefit entitlement for law enforcement positions that are currently excluded[34]

- High attrition rates are among those currently not receiving enhanced benefits.
- Employees perform duties that are similar to law enforcement personnel currently receiving enhanced benefits, which may create the appearance of inequity.

Extending enhanced retirement benefits to other occupational groups would result in higher costs to employing agencies and the federal government. The majority of personnel pursuing enhanced benefits in the future would be covered under FERS and would have most of the costs of their enhanced benefits covered by higher agency contributions. Currently, agencies are required to contribute an additional 14.4% of basic pay for law enforcement personnel in comparison with regular FERS employees. Agency contributions are based on OPM's annual actuarial calculations of

---

[33] In the 110th, 111th, and 112th Congresses, legislation was also introduced to extend enhanced retirement benefits to Pentagon Force Protection Agency officers, Assistant U.S. Attorneys, Customs and Border Patrol Agriculture Inspectors, and Internal Revenue Service Revenue Officers. For instance, in the 112th Congress, see S. 985, S. 1543, and H.R. 327; in the 111th Congress, see H.R. 264; and in the 110th Congress, see H.R. 2878, S. 1729, H.R. 1073, and H.R. 750.

[34] GAO-09-727.

the dynamic normal cost of FERS benefits as well as the required employee contributions under current law. These agency contributions may be subject to change in the future.[35]

[35] Changes to FERS agency contribution rates for FY2012 by employee category were announced in OPM's Benefits Administration Letter Number 11-304, *Changes to FERS Contribution Rates for Fiscal Year 2012*, June 2011, available at http://www.opm.gov/retire/pubs/bals/2011/11-304.pdf. These agency contribution rates remain unchanged for FY2013 (see OPM's Benefits Administration Letter 12-104, *Federal Employees Retirement System-Revised Annuity Employees (RAE)*, October 2012, available at http://www.opm.gov/retire/pubs/bals/2012/12-104.pdf). For a discussion of the dynamic normal cost of FERS benefits, including the calculation of agency contributions, see CRS Report RL30023, *Federal Employees' Retirement System: Budget and Trust Fund Issues*.

In: Retirement
Editor: Thomas M. Osborne

ISBN: 978-1-53615-703-1

Chapter 7

RAILROAD RETIREMENT BOARD: RETIREMENT, SURVIVOR, DISABILITY, UNEMPLOYMENT, AND SICKNESS BENEFITS*

Zhe Li

SUMMARY

The Railroad Retirement Board (RRB), an independent federal agency, administers retirement, survivor, disability, unemployment, and sickness insurance for railroad workers and their families. During FY2017, the RRB paid nearly $12.5 billion in retirement, disability, and survivor benefits to approximately 548,000 beneficiaries and paid $105.4 million in unemployment and sickness benefits to approximately 28,000 claimants. Of the total $12.5 billion benefit payments in the same fiscal year, 60.0% was paid to retired workers, 8.0% to disabled workers, 14.4% to spouses, and 16.8% to survivors.

The Railroad Retirement Act (RRA) authorizes retirement, disability, and survivor benefits for railroad workers and their families. RRA is financed primarily by payroll taxes, financial interchanges from Social

* This is an edited, reformatted and augmented version of Congressional Research Service, Publication No. RS22350, dated March 1, 2019.

Security, and transfers from the National Railroad Retirement Investment Trust (NRRIT). Railroad retirement payroll taxes have two tiers: the Tier I tax is essentially the same as the Social Security payroll tax and the Tier II tax is set each year based on the railroad retirement system's asset balances, benefit payments, and administrative costs. In FY2017, the gross RRA funding was about $12.7 billion.

Railroad retirement annuities are also divided into two tiers. Tier I annuities are designed to be nearly equivalent to Social Security benefits and are based on both railroad retirement and Social Security-covered employment. However, Tier I annuities are more generous than Social Security benefits in certain situations. For example, at the age of 60, railroad workers with at least 30 years of covered railroad work may receive unreduced retirement annuities. Tier II annuities are similar to private pensions and based solely on covered railroad service. Tier II annuities are paid in addition to Tier I annuities.

Railroad disability annuities may be payable to totally disabled railroad workers who are permanently disabled from all work and occupational disabled workers who are found to be permanently disabled from their regular railroad occupations. Eligible spouses and survivors of railroad workers may receive a certain portion of Tier I and Tier II benefits, but divorced spouses and surviving divorced spouses are eligible for only a certain portion of Tier I benefits.

The Railroad Unemployment Insurance Act (RUIA) authorizes unemployment and sickness benefits for railroad workers. RUIA is financed solely by railroad employers, whose contributions are based on the taxable earnings of their employees. Eligibility for railroad unemployment and sickness benefits is based on recent railroad service and earnings. The maximum daily unemployment and sickness benefit payable in the benefit year that began July 1, 2018, is $77, and the maximum benefit for a biweekly claim is $770. Normal benefits are paid for up to 26 weeks in a benefit year. The railroad unemployment and sickness system remains affected by sequestration, as unemployment benefits will continue to be reduced through at least September 30, 2019.

INTRODUCTION

The Railroad Retirement Board (RRB),[1] an independent federal agency, administers retirement, survivor, disability, unemployment, and

[1] The Railroad Retirement Board (RRB) consists of three members appointed by the President with the advice and consent of the Senate to staggered five-year terms. One member is

sickness insurance for railroad workers and their families under the Railroad Retirement Act (RRA) and the Railroad Unemployment Insurance Act (RUIA).[2] These acts cover workers who are employed by railroads engaged in interstate commerce and related subsidiaries, railroad associations, and railroad labor organizations. Lifelong railroad workers receive railroad retirement benefits instead of Social Security benefits; railroad workers with nonrailroad experience receive benefits either from railroad retirement or Social Security, depending on the length of their railroad service.

The number of railroad workers has been declining since the 1950s, although the rate of decline has been irregular and recent years have seen increases in railroad employment after reaching an all-time low of 215,000 workers in January 2010. Recently, railroad employment peaked in April 2015 to 253,000 workers, the highest level since November 1999, and then declined through FY2017, falling to 221,000 workers.[3] The total number of beneficiaries under the RRA and RUIA decreased from 623,000 in FY2008 to 574,000 in FY2017, and total benefit payments increased from $10.1 billion to $12.6 billion during the same time.[4] During FY2017, the RRB paid nearly $12.5 billion in retirement, disability, and survivor benefits to approximately 548,000 beneficiaries.[5] Almost $105.4 million in unemployment and sickness benefits were paid to approximately 28,000 claimants.[6]

---

appointed on the recommendation of the railroad industry, one on the recommendation of railroad labor, and the chair is appointed to represent the public.

[2] The RRB also administers aspects of the Medicare program and has administrative responsibilities under the Social Security Act and the Internal Revenue Code.

[3] Railroad Retirement Board, *2018 Annual Report*, p. 33, at https://www.rrb.gov/sites/default/files/2018-08/ 2018_Annual_Report.pdf.

[4] Ibid., p. 49. The total number of beneficiaries counted each beneficiary only once, even though they may have received more than one type of benefit. In FY2009, there were 626,000 beneficiaries, mainly due to the increase in unemployment benefit payments.

[5] Retirement, disability, and survivor benefits include age, disability, and supplemental annuities paid to employees, as well as annuities paid to spouses, divorced spouses, and survivors. Railroad Retirement Board, *2018 Annual Report*, p. 8, at https://www.rrb.gov/sites/default/files/2018-08/2018_Annual_Report.pdf.

[6] In FY2017, gross unemployment and sickness benefits totaled about $130 million. Net benefits to unemployment and sickness claims totaled almost $105.4 million after adjustment for recoveries of benefit payments, including injury settlements, some of which were made in

This chapter explains the programs under RRA and RUIA, including how each program is financed, the eligibility rules, and the types of benefits available to railroad workers and family members. It also discusses how railroad retirement relates to the Social Security system.

RAILROAD RETIREMENT, SURVIVOR, AND DISABILITY BENEFITS

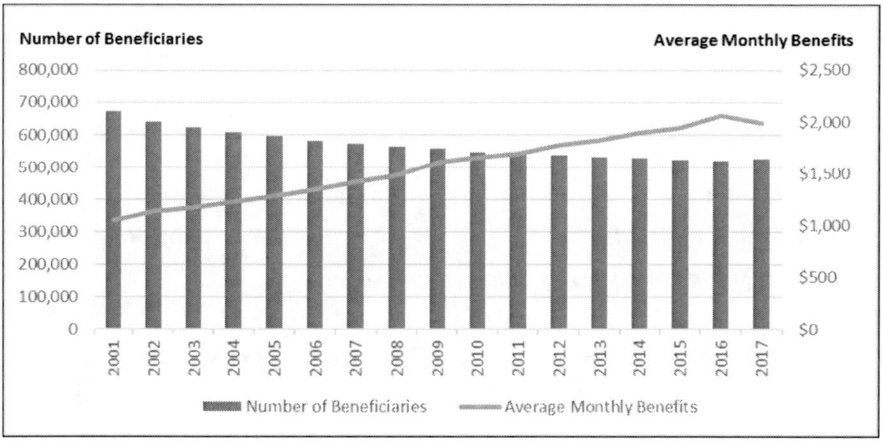

Source: Railroad Retirement Board, Bureau of the Actuary, Benefits and Beneficiaries, January 2001 to December 2017, Table 1.

Notes: The number of beneficiaries is beneficiaries in current-payment status at the end of each year. Average monthly benefits are estimated based on the number of beneficiaries and total amount of benefit payments in each year.

Figure 1. Number of RRA Beneficiaries and Average Monthly Benefits, 2001-2017.

The RRA authorizes retirement, survivor, and disability benefits for railroad workers and their families.[7] In December 2017, there were a total of 526,100 RRA beneficiaries, decreasing from 672,400 in 2001. This decline might partly result from the decline in railroad employment in the

prior years. Railroad Retirement Board, *2018 Annual Report*, p. 8, at https://www.rrb.gov/sites/default/files/2018-08/2018_Annual_Report.pdf.

[7] 45 U.S.C. §§231 et seq.

past five decades.[8] The average monthly benefit for each beneficiary was about $1,986 in 2017, which increased from $1,043 in 2001, reflecting the growth in average wages and prices (see Figure 1).

Financing

The railroad retirement, disability, and survivor program is mainly financed by payroll taxes, financial interchanges from Social Security, and transfers from the National Railroad Retirement Investment Trust (NRRIT) (see Figure 2), all of which accounted for 93.9% of the $12.7 billion gross funding of the RRA program during FY2017. The remaining 6.1% of the program was financed by federal income taxes levied on railroad retirement benefits,[9] interest on investment and other revenue, and general appropriations to pay the costs of phasing out vested dual benefits.

Payroll taxes, which provided 47.0% of gross RRA funding in FY2017, are the largest funding source for railroad retirement, survivor, and disability benefits.[10] Railroad retirement payroll taxes are divided into two tiers—Tier I and Tier II taxes. The Tier I tax is the same as the Social Security payroll tax: railroad employers and employees each pay 6.2% on earnings up to $132,900 in 2019.[11] The Tier II tax is set each year based on the railroad retirement system's asset balances, benefit payments, and administrative costs.[12] In 2019, the Tier II tax is 13.1% for subject to U.S.

[8] The railroads employed 617,000 workers in 1970, declined to 220,000 in 1997, and remained below 253,000 afterward. See https://www.railserve.com/employment.html.

[9] Regular railroad retirement annuities consisting of Tier I, Tier II, and vested dual benefit components have been

[10] Gross RRA funding does not include funding sources offset by reductions in National Railroad Retirement Investment Trust (NRRIT) assets, salaries, and expenses for the RRB Office of the Inspector General, and reductions in contingency liability and unexpended appropriations.

[11] P.L. 111-312. During 2011 and 2012, Congress provided a temporary reduction of two percentage points in the Social Security payroll tax rate paid by employees, from 6.2% to 4.2%.

[12] Under the Railroad Retirement and Survivors' Improvement Act of 2001 (P.L. 107-90), Tier II taxes on both employers and employees are automatically adjusted according to the average account benefits ratio. The average account benefits ratio (ABR) is the average of the 10 most recent annual ABRs. The ABR is the ratio of the combined fair market value of Railroad Retirement Account (Tier II tax revenues) and NRRIT assets as of the close of the

federal income tax since 1984. Supplemental annuities have been subject to federal income tax since 1966. The portion of the Tier I component of railroad retirement annuity that is equivalent to Social Security benefits is treated the same as a Social Security benefit for federal income tax purpose. The non-Social Security equivalent benefit of the Tier I benefit, Tier II benefits, vested dual benefits, and supplemental annuity payments are treated like contributory pensions for federal income tax purposes. Only the amount of the contributory pension that exceeds the amount of contributions made by the wage earner is taxable. Railroad retirement annuities are not taxable by states in accordance with Section 14 of the Railroad Retirement Act (45 U.S.C. § 231m). For more information, see "Tax Withholding and Railroad Retirement Payments," at https://www.rrb.gov/Benefits/IncomeTax/TXB-25. employers and 4.9% for employees on earnings up to $98,700. Tier II taxes are used to finance Tier II benefits, the portion of Tier I benefits in excess of Social Security retirement benefits (such as unreduced early retirement benefits for railroad employees with at least 30 years of railroad service), and supplemental annuities.[13]

Tier I payroll taxes are deposited in the Social Security Equivalent Benefit Account (SSEBA), which pays the Social Security level of benefits and administrative expenses allocable to those benefits. The SSEBA also receives or pays the financial interchange transfers between the railroad retirement and Social Security systems. The financial interchange with Social Security provided 32.6% of gross RRA funding in FY2017. The purpose of the financial interchange is to place the Social Security trust funds in the same position they would have been in, if railroad

fiscal year to the total RRB benefits and administrative expenses paid from the Railroad Retirement Account and the NRRIT in that fiscal year. A higher average ABR will result in a lower Tier II tax rate and consequently lower future tax income, whereas a lower average ABR result in higher Tier II tax rates and income. For more information, see CRS Report RS22782, *Railroad Retirement Board: Trust Fund Investment Practices*.

[13] For information about supplemental annuities, see "Other Retired Worker Benefits: Supplemental Annuities and Vested Dual Benefits."

employment had been covered under Social Security since that program's inception.[14]

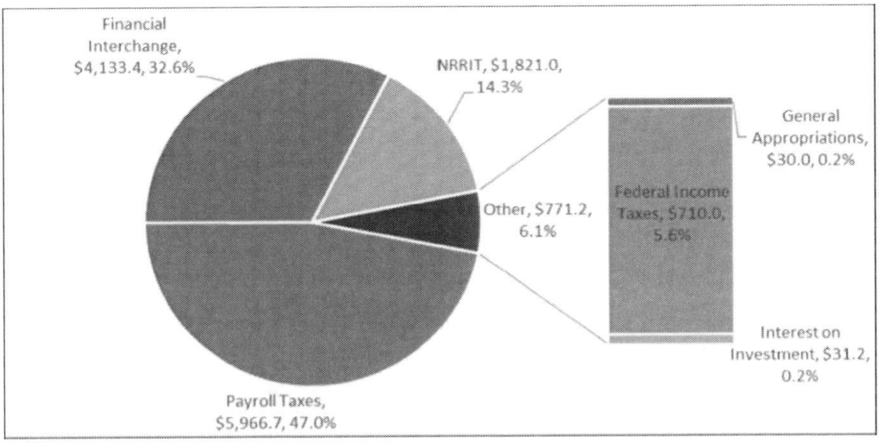

Source: Railroad Retirement Board, *2018 Annual Report*, page 8, at https://www.rrb.gov/sites/default/files/2018- 08/2018_Annual_Report.pdf.

Notes: Gross funding was $12.7 billion in FY2017. Numbers may not add due to rounding.

Figure 2. Financial Sources for Railroad Retirement, Disability and Survivor Program, FY2017. (Dollar amounts are in millions).

Tier II tax revenues that are not needed to pay current benefits or associated administrative costs are held in the National Railroad Retirement Investment Trust (NRRIT), which is invested in both government securities and private equities.[15] NRRIT transfers provide another revenue source for railroad benefits, and they were 14.3% of gross RRA funding in FY2017. Prior to the Railroad Retirement and Survivors'

---

[14] The railroad retirement system and the Social Security system have been coordinated financially since 1951 (P.L. 82 234). The financial interchange involves computing the amount of Social Security taxes that would have been collected on railroad employment, and computing the amount of additional benefits that Social Security would have paid to railroad retirement beneficiaries during the same fiscal year. When benefit reimbursements exceed payroll taxes, the difference, with an allowance for interest and administrative expenses, is transferred from the Social Security trust funds to the Social Security Equivalent Benefits Account. If taxes exceed benefit reimbursements (this has not happened since 1951), a transfer would be made in favor of the Social Security trust funds.

[15] For additional information on the NRRIT, see CRS Report RS22782, *Railroad Retirement Board: Trust Fund Investment Practices*.

Improvement Act of 2001 (P.L. 107-90), surplus railroad retirement assets could only be invested in U.S. government securities—just as the Social Security trust funds must be invested in securities issued or guaranteed by the U.S. government. The 2001 act established the NRRIT to manage and invest the assets in the Railroad Retirement Account in the same way that the assets of private-sector and most state and local government pension plans are invested. The remainder of the railroad retirement system's assets, such as assets in SSEBA, continues to be invested solely in U.S. government-issued or -granted securities.

The combined fair market value of Tier II taxes and NRRIT assets is designed to maintain four to six years' worth of RRB benefits and administrative expenses. To maintain this balance, the Railroad Retirement Tier II tax rates automatically adjust as needed. This tax adjustment does not require congressional action, according to Section 204 of the 2001 act.

Eligibility and Types of Benefits

To be insured for railroad benefits, a worker must generally have at least 10 years of covered railroad work or 5 years performed after 1995 and "insured status" under Social Security rules (generally 40 earnings credits)[16] based on combined railroad retirement and Social Security-covered earnings. An insured railroad worker's family may be entitled to receive railroad retirement benefits. If a worker does not qualify for railroad retirement benefits, his or her railroad work counts toward Social Security benefits. Of the total $12.5 billion benefit payments during FY2017, 60.0% (or $7.5 billion) were paid in retirement annuities to retired workers, 8.0% (or $1.0 billion) in disability annuities, 14.4% (or

[16] A worker may earn up to four earnings credits per calendar year. In 2019, a worker earns one credit for each $1,360 of covered earnings, up to a maximum of four credits for covered earnings of $5,440 or more. Earnings credits are also called *quarters of coverage*. This amount increases each year to account for wage growth. For additional information, see CRS Report R43542, *How Social Security Benefits Are Computed: In Brief*.

$1.8 billion) in spouse annuities, and 16.8% (or $2.1 billion) in survivor annuities.[17]

Tier I Retirement Annuities

Tier I annuities are designed to be nearly equivalent to Social Security Old Age, Survivors, and Disability Insurance benefits. Tier I annuities are calculated using the Social Security benefit formula and are based on both railroad retirement and Social Security-covered employment.[18] However, Tier I annuities are more generous than Social Security benefits in certain situation. For example, at the age of 60, railroad workers with at least 30 years of covered railroad work may receive unreduced retirement annuities.[19] At the full retirement age (FRA), which is gradually increasing from 65 to 67 for Social Security and railroad retirement beneficiaries, insured workers with fewer than 30 years of service may receive full retirement annuities.[20] Alternatively, workers with fewer than 30 years of service may, starting at the age of 62, receive annuities that have been reduced actuarially for the additional years the worker is expected to spend in retirement. Tier I benefit reductions for early retirement are similar to those in the Social Security system. As the FRA rises, so will the reduction for early retirement.[21] If a railroad employee delays retirement past FRA, Tier I annuities are increased by a certain percentage for each month up until the age of 70, which is identical to the benefit increase provided by Delayed Retirement Credits under the Social Security system.[22]

---

[17] Less than 1% of the total railroad retirement, disability, and survivor benefits were paid for supplemental annuities and lump-sum death benefits.

[18] For additional information on the Social Security benefit formula, see CRS Report R43542, *How Social Security Benefits Are Computed: In Brief.*

[19] Early retirement reductions are applied in the Tier I annuity of 30-year employees who first became eligible for the annuity on July 1, 1984, or later and retired at the age of 60 or 61 before 2002.

[20] Full retirement age (FRA) is rising from 65 for those born before 1938 to 67 for those born after 1959. For additional information on the FRA, see CRS Report R41962, The Social Security Retirement Age: In Brief.

[21] The reduction at the age of 62, Social Security's earliest eligibility age, is rising from 20% to 30% as the FRA rises from age 65 to age 67.

[22] For additional information on the Social Security benefit formula, see CRS Report R43542, *How Social Security Benefits Are Computed: In Brief.*

In general, Social Security benefits are subtracted from Tier I annuities, because work covered by Social Security is counted toward Tier I annuities. Beneficiaries insured by both systems receive a single check from the RRB. Railroad retirement annuities may also be reduced for certain pensions earned through federal, state, and local government work that is not covered by Social Security.[23] For early retirees who continue to work for a nonrailroad employer while receiving the retirement benefit during the year prior to FRA, Tier I benefits are reduced by $1 for every $2 earned above an exempt amount ($17,040 in 2018).[24] After Tier I benefits are first paid, they increase annually with a cost-of-living adjustment (COLA) in the same manner as Social Security benefits.[25]

Retirement annuities are not payable to workers who continue to work in a covered railroad job or who return to railroad work after retirement.

Tier II Retirement Annuities

Tier II retirement annuities are paid in addition to Tier I annuities and any private pension and retirement saving plans offered by railroad employers. They are similar to private pensions and based solely on covered railroad service. Tier II annuities for current retirees are equal to seven-tenths of 1% of the employee's average monthly earnings in the 60 months of highest earnings, times the total number of years of railroad service.[26] Tier II annuities are increased annually by 32.5% of the Social Security COLA.

---

[23] For additional information, see CRS In Focus IF10203, *Social Security: The Windfall Elimination Provision (WEP) and the Government Pension Offset (GPO)*.

[24] If the employee or spouse has a Tier I reduction for Social Security benefits, the Tier I annuity is not reduced for excess earnings. During the calendar year that a retiree will reach the FRA, the formula for calculating the early retirement reduction changes: benefits are reduced $1 for every $3 earned above an exempt amount ($45,360 in 2018) until the beneficiary reaches FRA. Earnings while a Tier I annuitant may be used to recompute a beneficiary's annuity, which may result in the beneficiary receiving a higher annuity after FRA due to these earnings. For additional information on the increase in Social Security benefits at FRA to account for benefits lost due to earnings, see CRS Report R41242, *Social Security Retirement Earnings Test: How Earnings Affect Benefits*.

[25] For additional information on the Social Security COLA, see CRS Report 94-803, *Social Security: Cost-of-Living Adjustments*.

[26] The formula for the gross Tier II amount is 0.007 × (total earnings in the 60 months of highest earnings ÷ 60) × Years of service. If the highest earnings in the 60 months are greater than

Tier II annuities are not (in contrast to Tier I annuities) reduced if a worker receives Social Security benefits or a government pension that was not covered by Social Security. For railroad retirees and spouses who work for their last pre-retirement nonrailroad employer while receiving retirement benefits,[27] Tier II annuities are reduced by $1 for every $2 earned, capped at 50% of the Tier II annuity. There is no cap to the earnings-related reduction in railroad Tier I or Social Security benefits. In addition, the earnings-related reduction applies to all Tier II beneficiaries regardless of age, whereas for railroad Tier I and Social Security benefits, the earnings-related reduction applies only until the beneficiary reaches FRA.

Other Retired Worker Benefits: Supplemental Annuities and Vested Dual Benefits

Tier II payroll taxes also finance a supplemental annuity program. Supplemental annuities are payable to employees first hired before October 1981, aged 60 with at least 30 years of covered railroad service or aged 65 and older with at least 25 years of covered railroad service, and a current connection with the railroad industry.[28]

In addition, general revenues finance a vested dual benefit for those who were insured for both railroad retirement and Social Security in 1974 when the two-tier railroad retirement benefit structure was established.[29] Neither supplemental annuities nor vested dual benefits are adjusted for changes in the cost of living during retirement. Supplemental annuities are subject to the same earnings reductions as Tier II benefits; vested dual benefits are subject to the same earnings reductions as Tier I benefits.

---

the Tier II taxable maximum base, then the formula use the Tier II taxable maximum base instead.

[27] Work that begins on the same day as the annuity beginning date is not last pre-retirement nonrailroad employment.

[28] Workers have a current connection with the railroad industry if they worked in a covered railroad job for at least 12 months of the 30 months before death or receipt of a railroad annuity. The current connection is not broken during employment at certain U.S. government agencies or in other special circumstances.

[29] The payment of vested dual benefits depends on the time and amount of such appropriations. If the appropriation in a fiscal year is for less than the estimated total vested dual benefit payments, individual payments will be reduced.

Disability Annuities

Railroad workers may be eligible for disability annuities if they become disabled regardless of whether the disability is caused by railroad work. The RRB determines whether a worker is disabled based on the medical evidence provided during the application process. Railroad workers found to be totally and permanently disabled from *all work* may be eligible for Tier I benefits at any age if the worker has at least 10 years of railroad service.[30] Totally disabled workers may also receive Tier II benefits at the age of 62 if they have 10 or more years of service. Occupational disability annuities are also payable to workers found to be permanently disabled from their regular railroad occupations, if the worker is at least 60 years old with 10 years of service (or any age with 20 years of service), and with a current connection to the railroad industry. A five-month waiting period after the onset of disability is required before any disability annuity can be payable.

Disability annuities are not payable if a worker is currently employed in a covered railroad job. Disability benefits are suspended if a beneficiary earns more than a certain amount after deducting certain disability-related work expenses.[31] The Tier I portion of disability benefits may be reduced for the receipt of workers compensation or government disability benefits.

Spouse Annuities

In any month that a worker collects a railroad retirement or disability annuity, his or her spouse may also be eligible for a spousal annuity equal to or greater than the benefit he or she would have received if the worker's railroad work had been covered by Social Security. A spouse is eligible for a spousal annuity when he or she reaches the same minimum age required

---

[30] Employees with five years to nine years of covered railroad service, if at least five years were performed after 1995, may qualify for Tier I benefits before retirement age only if they also meet certain Social Security earnings requirements. For information on Social Security disability insurance, see CRS In Focus IF10506, *Social Security Disability Insurance (SSDI)*.

[31] The earnings threshold is $950 in 2019 and is indexed to average national wage growth. Disability work restrictions cease when a disabled employee attains full retirement age, when disability annuities convert to retirement annuities. This transition is effective on earlier than FRA if the annuitant had 30 years of railroad service.

for the worker (i.e., either at the age of 60 or 62, depending on years of the worker's service). At any age, a spouse may be eligible for a spousal annuity if he or she cares for the worker's unmarried child under the age of 18 (or a child of any age that was disabled before the age of 22). An individual must have been married to the railroad worker for at least one year before he or she applies for the spousal annuities, with certain exceptions. A qualifying spouse receives 50% of the worker's Tier I benefit before any reductions (or, if higher, a Social Security benefit based on his or her own earnings). Spouses may also receive 45% of the worker's Tier II benefit before any reductions.

Divorced spouses of retired or disabled railroad workers may also be eligible for spousal annuities. A divorced spouse may receive 50% of the worker's Tier I benefit before reductions, but no Tier II benefits. To qualify, the former spouse must have been married to the worker for at least 10 years and must not currently be married (remarriages if any must have terminated); both the worker and former spouse must be at least 62 years old.[32]

For spouses, as for railroad workers, Social Security benefits are subtracted from Tier I annuities. The Tier I portion of a spouse annuity may also be reduced for receipt of any pension from government employment not covered by Social Security based on the spouse's own earnings.[33] Spouses are subject to reductions based on the primary worker's earnings as well as on their own earnings. For example, for early retirement, spouses are subject to different benefit reductions from

---

[32] A divorced spouse can receive an annuity even if the employee has not retired, provided they have been divorced for a period of not less than two years, the employee and former spouse are at least age 62, and the employee is fully insured under the Social Security Act using combined railroad and Social Security earnings. Although a spouse is eligible for an annuity at any age if caring for the employee's unmarried child, who is under age 18 or disabled at any age who became disabled before age 22, a divorced spouse is not eligible for an annuity on such basis unless the employee is deceased.

[33] For spouses subject to the public pension reduction, the Tier I benefit is reduced by two-thirds of the amount of the public pension. For more information, see CRS Report RL32453, *Social Security: The Government Pension Offset (GPO)*.

workers.[34] Finally, spouse annuities are reduced by the amount of any railroad benefits earned based on their own work.

Survivor Annuities

After the worker's death, surviving spouses, former spouses, children, and other dependents may be eligible to receive survivor annuities, which are paid in addition to any private life insurance offered by railroad employers. To be insured for survivor annuities, the worker must have had a current connection with the railroad industry at the time of death. Railroad survivor annuities are generally higher than comparable Social Security benefits because railroad workers' families may be entitled to Tier II annuities as well as Tier I annuities (as noted above, Tier I annuities are equivalent to Social Security benefits). In cases where no monthly survivor annuities are paid, a lump-sum payment may be made to certain survivors.[35]

The widows and widowers of railroad workers may be eligible to receive survivor annuities. At FRA, a surviving spouse may be eligible for 100% of the worker's Tier I annuity (or his or her own Social Security or railroad retirement Tier I benefit, if higher). The widow(er) may also receive up to 100% of the worker's Tier II annuity. As early as the age of 60 (or age 50, if disabled), widows and widowers may receive reduced survivor annuities.[36] A qualifying widow(er) must have been married to the deceased railroad worker for at least nine months, with certain exceptions.[37] At any age, a widow(er) caring for a deceased worker's child under the age of 18 may receive a survivor annuity equal to 75% of the

[34] For spouses, the reduction at the age of 62 is gradually rising from 25% to 35% as the FRA increases from age 65 to 67, whereas for workers, the reduction is rising from 20% to 30%.

[35] A lump-sum death payment is made in cases in which the worker had at least 10 years of railroad service; if less than 10 years, at least five years of service after 1995 and a current connection to the railroad industry; and there is no person eligible for monthly survivors benefits either because there are no eligible survivors or the widow(er) has not reached the minimum age for benefits. The lump-sum death payment is limited to $255 if the employee did not have 120 months of service in the railroad industry before 1975.

[36] For widow(er)s, the reduction at the age of 60 (Social Security's earliest eligibility age for widowed spouses) is rising from 17.10% to 20.36% as the FRA increases from 65 to 67. For a disabled widow(er), the maximum reduction is 28.5%, even if the annuity begins at age 50.

[37] Exceptions are provided in some cases such as accidental death or death in the line of duty.

worker's Tier I annuity, as well as up to 100% of the worker's Tier II annuity. Widow(er)s who are the natural or adoptive parent of the deceased worker's child do not have to meet the length of marriage requirement.

Survivor annuities may also be payable to a surviving divorced spouse or remarried widow(er). To qualify for benefits, a surviving divorced spouse has to be married to the employee for at least 10 years and is unmarried or remarried after age 60 (age 50 for disabled surviving divorced spouse).[38] A surviving divorced spouse who is unmarried can qualify for benefits at any age if caring for the employee's child who is under age 16 or disabled.[39] Benefits are limited to the amounts Social Security would pay (Tier I only) and therefore are less than the amount of the survivor annuity otherwise payable.

Railroad workers' children may also receive survivor annuities. To qualify, a child must be unmarried and under the age of 18 (or 19 if still in high school). Disabled adult children may qualify if their disability began before the age of 22. Eligible children receive 75% of the worker's Tier I annuity and 15% of the worker's Tier II annuity.[40] In addition, if a worker's parent was dependent on the worker for at least half of the parent's support, he or she may receive 82.5% of the worker's Tier I annuity and 35% of the worker's Tier II annuity after reaching age 60.

Survivor annuities are not payable to a current railroad employee, and survivor annuities are reduced by any railroad retirement benefit the survivor has earned through his or her own railroad work.

---

[38] For a surviving divorced spouse or remarried widow(er), the maximum age reduction is 28.5%, which is the same as the maximum reduction for a disabled remarried widow(er) or disabled surviving divorced spouse even if the annuity begins at age 50.

[39] The 10-year marriage requirement does not apply to surviving divorced spouse with child in care.

[40] Social Security provides children's benefits when a railroad worker is totally disabled, retired, or deceased. The Railroad Retirement Act only provides children's benefits if the employee is deceased. However, under a special minimum guaranty provision, railroad families will not receive less in monthly benefits than they would have if railroad earnings were covered by Social Security. Therefore, if a retired railroad worker has children who would otherwise be eligible for a benefit under Social Security, the worker's retirement annuity would be increased to reflect what Social Security would pay for the family.

Table 1. Railroad Retirement, Survivor, and Disability Annuities, June 2018

Type of Annuity	Number of Benefits[a]	Percentage of Total Benefits	Average Monthly Benefit ($)
Age-Based	189,262	29.5%	$2,806.4
Disability -Under Full Retirement	25,795	4.0%	$2,744.3
Disability -At or Above FRA Age (FRA)	47,012	7.3%	$2,466.6
Supplemental	120,409	18.8%	$41.5
Spouse	141,993	22.1%	$1,047.0
Divorced Spouse	5,126	0.8%	$652.8
Aged Widow(er)	85,297	13.3%	$1,709.1
Disabled Widow(er)	3,440	0.5%	$1,360.1
Widowed Mother and Father	592	0.1%	$1,875.7
Remarried Widow(er)	2,936	0.5%	$1,108.5
Divorced Widow(er)	9,690	1.5%	$1,113.3
Children	8,339	1.3%	$1,109.2
Partition Payments[b]	1,841	0.3%	$316.9
Total Benefits	641,732[c]	100.0%	$1,636.8[d]

Source: Railroad Retirement Board, Bureau of the Actuary, Quarterly Benefit Statistics, April-June 2018, Table 1, https://rrb.gov/sites/default/files/2018-09/stat_qbs0618.pdf.

Notes: Numbers may not add due to rounding.

a. Total number of benefits paid includes multiple benefits paid to individual beneficiaries. Benefits were paid to 512,045 beneficiaries.

b. The court-ordered partitioned portion of the Tier II, vested dual and supplemental benefit payments can be made to spouses and divorced spouses when the railroad worker is deceased or not otherwise entitled to an annuity.

c. The total number of benefits does not include the number of dependent parents' annuities, which was 21 in current payment status.

d. Estimated based on total number and amount of benefits.

Survivors receive the same reductions as retired workers for Social Security benefit receipt; they also have reductions from government pension receipts that are not covered by Social Security.[41] A family maximum applies to survivor benefits, usually applicable when three or more survivors receive benefits on a worker's record (not counting divorced spouses).[42]

In summary, Table 1 provides data on railroad retirement, survivor, and disability annuities as of June 2018.

RAILROAD UNEMPLOYMENT AND SICKNESS BENEFITS

Railroad workers may qualify for daily unemployment and sickness benefits under the Railroad Unemployment Insurance Act (RUIA).[43] These monetary benefits are paid in addition to any paid leave or private insurance an employee may have. For sickness benefits, a worker must be unable to work because of illness or injury. Sickness benefits are distinct from disability benefits because they are intended to cover a finite, temporary period of time. Workers may not earn any money while receiving unemployment or sickness benefits.

Figure 3 displays the monthly number of beneficiaries with unemployment and sickness benefits from January 2002 to July 2018, respectively. Although the number of sickness beneficiaries stayed relatively stable over time, the number of unemployment insurance beneficiaries increased significantly during and after the most recent economic recession from 2007 to 2009.

---

[41] For survivors subject to the public pension reduction, the Tier I benefit is reduced by two-thirds of the amount of the public pension. For more information, see CRS Report RL32453, *Social Security: The Government Pension Offset (GPO).*

[42] Social Security Administration, "Formula for Family Maximum Benefit," see https://www.ssa.gov/OACT/COLA/ familymax.html.

[43] 45 U.S.C. §§351-369.

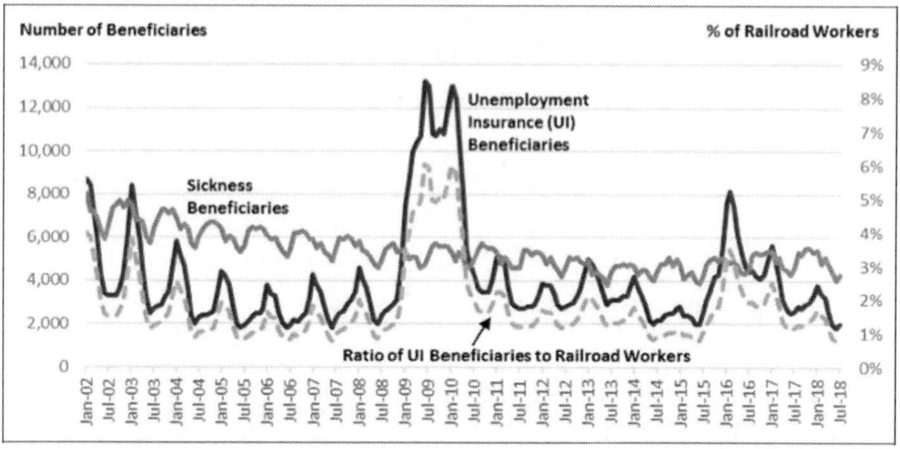

Source: Railroad Retirement Board, Bureau of the Actuary, Benefits and Beneficiaries, January 2002 to July 2018, Table 2.

Figure 3. Number of RUIA Beneficiaries, 2002-2018.

Financing

Railroad unemployment and sickness benefits are financed solely by railroad employers' payroll taxes, based on the taxable earnings of their employees. Employers' tax rates depend on the past rates of unemployment and employees' sickness claims. For calendar year 2018, the employer tax rate ranges from 2.2% to 12.0% on the first $1,560 of each employee's monthly earnings.

The payroll tax proceeds not needed immediately for unemployment and sickness insurance benefits or operating expenses are deposited in the Railroad Unemployment Insurance Account maintained by the Treasury. This account, together with similar unemployment insurance accounts for each state, forms a Federal Unemployment Insurance Trust Fund whose deposits are invested in U.S. government securities, and the Railroad Unemployment Insurance Account receives interest based on these deposits. During FY2017, payroll tax contributions from railroad employers totaled $126.4 million and interest income was about $4 million.

The RUIA provides for employers to pay a surcharge if the Railroad Unemployment Insurance Account falls below an indexed threshold amount.[44] The surcharge is added to the employer's tax rate. However, the total tax rate plus the surcharge cannot exceed the maximum rate of 12.0%, unless the surcharge is 3.5%, in which case the maximum tax rate is increased to 12.5%. From 2004 through 2010, the surcharge was 1.5%. The surcharge in 2011 was 2.5% and 1.5% in 2012 with no surcharges in 2013 or 2014. The surcharge in 2018 was 1.5%, the same as the level in the past three years.

Eligibility and Benefits

Eligibility for railroad unemployment and sickness benefits is based on recent railroad service and earnings. The annual benefit year begins on July 1. Eligibility is based on work in the prior year, or the base year. To qualify in the benefit year beginning July 1, 2018, railroad workers must have base year earnings of $3,862.50 in calendar year 2017, counting no more than $1,545 per month.[45] New railroad workers must also have at least five months of covered railroad work in the base year. To receive unemployment benefits, a worker must be ready, willing, and able to work.

The maximum daily unemployment and sickness benefit payable in the benefit year that began July 1, 2018, is $77, and the maximum benefit for a biweekly claim is $770. However, due to sequestration pursuant to the Budget Control Act of 2011 (P.L. 112-25, as amended), the maximum daily benefit of $77 is reduced by 6.2% to $72.23 and the maximum biweekly benefit is reduced by 6.2% to $722.26 through September 30, 2019.[46] Railroad workers receive these benefits only to the extent that they

---

[44] 45 U.S.C. §358(a)(14).

[45] Railroad Retirement Board, "Railroad Unemployment and Sickness Benefits," at https://www.rrb.gov/index.php/ Benefits/UB9.

[46] Railroad unemployment benefits are paid biweekly for up to 10 days of unemployment. Certain railroad sickness benefits are also subject to regular Tier I railroad retirement taxes, resulting in a further reduction of 7.65% (Social Security and Medicare payroll taxes). Applying the 6.2% reduction to these sickness benefits will result in a maximum 2-week

are higher than other benefits they receive under the RRA, the Social Security Act, or certain other public programs, including workers compensation.

Unemployment and sickness beneficiaries may receive normal benefits for up to 26 weeks in a benefit year or until the benefits they receive equal their creditable earnings in the base year if sooner.[47] Employees with at least 10 years of covered railroad service may qualify for extended benefits for 13 weeks after they have exhausted normal benefits. Table 2 displays the number and average weekly amount of RUIA benefits paid in June 2018.

Workers who apply for unemployment benefits are automatically enrolled in a free job placement service operated by railroad employers and the RRB.[48]

Table 2. Railroad Unemployment and Sickness Benefits, June 2018

Type of Benefits	Number of Normal Benefits	Number of Extended Benefits	Average Weekly Benefit
Unemployment	2,863	573	$334.25
Sickness	6,388	1515	$335.50

Source: Railroad Retirement Board, Bureau of the Actuary, Quarterly Benefit Statistics, April-June 2018, Table 3, https://rrb.gov/sites/default/files/2018-09/stat_qbs0618.pdf.

total of $667.01.The rate of reduction due to sequestration is set annually and may continue past September 30, 2019.

47 There is essentially a one-week waiting period for unemployment and sickness benefits. There is a two-week waiting period for unemployment benefits if a worker participates in a legal strike.

48 For more information, see RRB, "Free Placement Service," at https://www.rrb.gov/Free_Placement_Service.

In: Retirement
Editor: Thomas M. Osborne
ISBN: 978-1-53615-703-1

Chapter 8

RAILROAD RETIREMENT BOARD: TRUST FUND INVESTMENT PRACTICES*

Zhe Li

SUMMARY

The Railroad Retirement Board (RRB), an independent federal agency, administers retirement, survivor, disability, unemployment, and sickness insurance for railroad workers and their families. Railroad retirement payroll taxes include two tiers—Tier I and Tier II taxes. The Tier I tax finances the Tier I railroad retirement benefit that is equivalent to Social Security benefits and the Tier II tax finances the Tier II benefit, Tier I benefits in excess of Social Security benefits, and supplemental annuities.

Since 2002, Tier II tax revenues in excess of obligatory RRB benefits and associated administrative costs have been invested in private stocks, bonds, and other investments. Prior to the Railroad Retirement and Survivors' Improvement Act of 2001 (RRSIA; P.L. 107-90), surplus railroad retirement assets could only be invested in U.S. government securities—just as the Social Security trust funds must be invested. The

---

* This is an edited, reformatted and augmented version of Congressional Research Service, Publication No. RS22782, dated January 10, 2019.

RRSIA established the National Railroad Retirement Investment Trust (NRRIT; hereinafter, the Trust) to manage and invest part of the RRB's assets in much the same way that the assets of private-sector and most state and local government pension plans are invested. The remainder of RRB's assets continues to be invested solely in U.S. government securities.

Congress structured the Trust in an effort to ensure investment independence and limit political interference. It also aimed to increase railroad retirement system funding, add enhanced benefits, potentially reduce taxes, and protect system financing in case of market downturns. The Trust's assets are invested in a diversified portfolio, both to minimize investment risk and avoid disproportionate influence over an industry or firm. The Trust is a tax-exempt entity independent of the federal government, and it is not subject to the same oversight as federal agencies. However, the RRSIA requires an annual management report to Congress.

From its inception in February 2002 to September 30, 2017, $21.3 billion has been transferred to the Trust from the RRB and $21.1 billion has been transferred from the Trust to pay railroad retirement benefits. At the end of FY2017, the net asset value of the Trust was $26.5 billion.

The Trust's investments have generally followed the markets' recent performance. From FY2003 to FY2017, the Trust's annual returns averaged 8.3%, slightly higher than expectations of the bill's drafters, who assumed nominal annual returns of 8.0%. As the Trust's investment portfolio diversified over time, its administrative expenses steadily increased, to 36 basis points in FY2011, but fell to 31 basis points in FY2017, and remain low when compared with other mutual funds.

The combined fair market value of Tier II taxes and Trust assets is designed to maintain four to six years' worth of RRB benefits and administrative expenses. To maintain this balance, the Railroad Retirement Tier II tax rates automatically adjust as needed. This tax adjustment does not require congressional action. The Railroad Retirement Tier II tax rates increased in 2013 and most recently in 2015.

BACKGROUND

The Railroad Retirement Act authorizes retirement, survivor, and disability benefits for railroad workers and their families.[1] The Railroad

---

[1] 45 U.S.C. §231 et seq. For additional information on the RRB, see CRS Report RS22350, *Railroad Retirement Board: Retirement, Survivor, Disability, Unemployment, and Sickness Benefits*.

Retirement Board (RRB), an independent federal agency, administers these benefits. Workers covered by the RRB include those employed by railroads engaged in interstate commerce and related subsidiaries, railroad associations, and railroad labor organizations. These benefits are earned by railroad workers and their families in lieu of Social Security.

Railroad retirement benefits are divided into two tiers. Tier I benefits are generally computed using the Social Security benefit formula, on the basis of earnings covered by either the Railroad Retirement or Social Security programs. In some cases, RRB Tier I benefits can be higher than comparable Social Security benefits. For example, RRB beneficiaries may receive unreduced Tier

I retirement benefits as early as aged 60 if they have at least 30 years of railroad service; Social Security beneficiaries may receive unreduced retirement benefits only when they reach their full retirement ages, currently rising from aged 65 to 67. RRB Tier II benefits are similar to private pension benefits and are based only on railroad work.[2]

The Tier I railroad retirement benefit that is equivalent to Social Security benefits is mainly finance by Tier I payroll taxes (typically the same rate as the 12.4% Social Security payroll tax) and Social Security's financial interchange transfers.[3] Tier II benefits, Tier I benefits in excess of Social Security benefits, and supplemental annuities[4] are mainly financed by Tier II payroll taxes (currently 13.1% on employers and 4.9% on

---

[2] Railroad employers also finance a supplemental annuity program for certain railroad employees hired before October 1981. General revenues finance a vested dual benefit for certain railroad employees who were eligible for benefits before 1975.

[3] The financial interchange is intended to place the Social Security Trust Funds in the same position in which they would have been had railroad employment been covered by the Social Security since Social Security's inception. This involves computing the amount of Social Security taxes that would have been collected on railroad employment, and computing the amount of additional benefits which Social Security would have paid to railroad retirement beneficiaries during the same fiscal year. When benefit reimbursements exceed payroll taxes, the difference, with an allowance for interest and administrative expenses, is transferred from the Social Security Trust Funds to the Social Security Equivalent Benefits Account. If taxes exceed benefit reimbursements (this has not happened since 1951), a transfer would be made in favor of the Social Security Trust Funds.

[4] Supplemental annuities are payable to employees first hired before October 1981, aged 60 with at least 30 years of covered railroad service or aged 65 and older with at least 25 years of covered railroad service, and a current connection with the railroad industry.

employees) and transfers from the National Railroad Retirement Investment Trust (NRRIT; hereinafter, the Trust).

HISTORY OF THE TRUST

Beginning in 2002, Tier II tax revenues in excess of obligatory benefits and associated administrative costs have been transferred from the Railroad Retirement Accounts to the Trust, which is invested in private stocks, bonds, and other investments. Prior to the Railroad Retirement and Survivors' Improvement Act of 2001 (RRSIA; P.L. 107-90), surplus railroad retirement assets could be invested only in U.S. government securities—just as the Social Security trust funds must be invested.[5] The RRSIA established the Trust to manage and invest assets in the Railroad Retirement Account in much the same way that the assets of private-sector retirement plans are invested. The RRB also receives transfers from the Trust, as needed, to pay railroad retirement and survivor benefits. Assets in the Social Security Equivalent Benefits Account, which are used for RRB Tier I benefits that are equivalent to Social Security benefits, continue to be invested solely in U.S. government bonds, as required by law.

Since February 2002 when railroad retirement funds were first invested through the Trust, a total of $21.3 billion has been transferred to the Trust from the RRB,[6] and $21.1 billion in earnings have been transferred from the Trust to the RRB to pay railroad benefits and administrative expenses.[7] From its inception to the end of FY2017, the Trust has earned a total of

---

[5] The Social Security trust funds may not be invested in private markets. For additional information on current practices, see CRS In Focus IF10564, *Social Security Trust Fund Investment Practices*.

[6] National Railroad Retirement Investment Trust (NRRIT), *Annual Management Report for Fiscal Year 2017*, p. 10. The Trust has received no transfers from the RRB since the end of FY2004.

[7] Ibid., p. 11.

$26.3 billion. At the end of FY2017, the market value of the Trust's managed assets was $26.5 billion.[8]

STRUCTURE OF THE TRUST

Independence

Congress structured the Trust to be independent and free of political interference. As such, the Trust is a tax-exempt entity independent of the RRB and is not part of the federal government. It has no responsibilities for administering RRB benefits. The Trust's trustees are required to act solely in the interest of the RRB and the railroad retirement system participants. The fiduciary rules governing the trustees are similar to those required by the law that governs the private pension system, the Employee Retirement Income Security Act (ERISA).[9]

The board of the Trust is made up of seven trustees who have expertise in managing financial investments and pension plans. Three of the trustees are selected by railroad labor unions, three by railroad management, and one by the other six trustees. Each trustee serve a three-year term. A professional staff handles the Trust's day-to-day operations.

Independent investment managers invest the Trust's assets according to the investment guidelines established by the trustees. Each investment manager

- may control no more than 10% of the Trust's assets;
- must vote all proxies he or she holds in the Trust's portfolio in the sole interest of railroad retirement participants and beneficiaries;

[8] Ibid. As of the end of FY2017, the value of total RRB assets was $27.8 billion, with $26.5 billion held by the Trust and $1.3 billion held in reserve accounts at the Department of the Treasury.

[9] For additional information on ERISA, see CRS Report 95-926, *Regulating Private Pensions: A Brief Summary of ERISA*.

- must certify each year that all proxies have been voted in the sole interest of railroad retirement participants and beneficiaries; and
- must record votes and provide them to the Trust upon request.[10]

Goals

Congress designed the Trust to increase RRB funding. Investing railroad retirement funds in private markets was expected to yield higher average annual returns than investing solely in government securities. The higher returns were intended to pay for the enhanced benefits that were established in the RRSIA and to potentially reduce future tax rates for railroad employers and employees.[11]

Impact on Railroad Retirement Tier II Tax Rates

Under the RRSIA, Tier II taxes on both employers and employees are automatically adjusted according to the average account benefits ratio. The average account benefits ratio (ABR) is the average of the 10 most recent annual ABRs. The ABR is the ratio of the combined fair market value of Railroad Retirement Account and Trust assets as of the close of the fiscal year to the total RRB benefits and administrative expenses paid from the Railroad Retirement Account and the Trust in that fiscal year. A higher average ABR will result in a lower Tier II tax rate and consequently lower future tax income, whereas a lower average ABR result in higher Tier II tax rates and income.

Depending on the average ABR, Tier II taxes for employers can range between 8.2% and 22.1% and the Tier II tax rate for employees is capped at 4.9%. Since the Trust's inception, Tier II tax rates have been lowered

[10] NRRIT, *Annual Management Report for Fiscal Year 2017.*

[11] U.S. Congress, House Committee on Transportation and Infrastructure, *Railroad Retirement and Survivors Improvement Act of 2001*, report to accompany H.R. 1140, 107th Cong., 1st sess., May 24, 2001, H.Rept. 107-82, part 1 (Washington: GPO, 2001), pp. 14-15. Hereinafter cited as H.Rept. 107-82, part 1.

twice and increased twice (see Figure 1). In 2005, the Tier II tax rate on employers was automatically lowered from 13.1% to 12.6% and the tax rate on employees was lowered from 4.9% to 4.4%. Tier II tax rates were lowered again in 2007 to 12.1% on employers and 3.9% on employees. In 2013, tax rates were raised to 12.6% and 4.4% on employers and employees, respectively, and in 2015, the rates were raised to their current levels of 13.1% on employers and 4.9% on employees. The maximum amount of earnings subject to Tier II taxes is $98,700 in 2019.

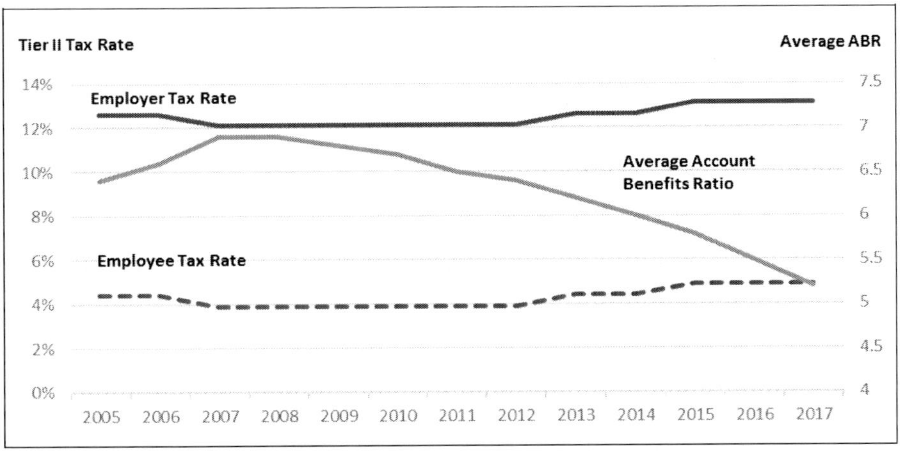

Source: National Railroad Retirement Investment Trust, *Annual Management Report for Fiscal Year 2006-2017.*

Notes: The Average ABR was measured at the end of each fiscal year (September 30 of each calendar year), and the Tier II tax rate was applied to railroad employers and employees in each calendar year.

Figure 1. Average Account Benefits Ratio (ABR) and Tier II Tax Rates, 2005-2017.

Investment Guidelines

The Trust's assets are invested in a diversified portfolio, both to minimize investment risk and avoid disproportionate influence over a particular industry or firm. The investment guidelines adopted by the trustees include target asset allocations developed by the Trust's investment staff in consultation with an independent investment advisory firm. Outside investment managers hired by the Trust invest the assets according to these guidelines. The resulting investment performance is monitored by the trustees and the Trust's Chief Investment Officer.

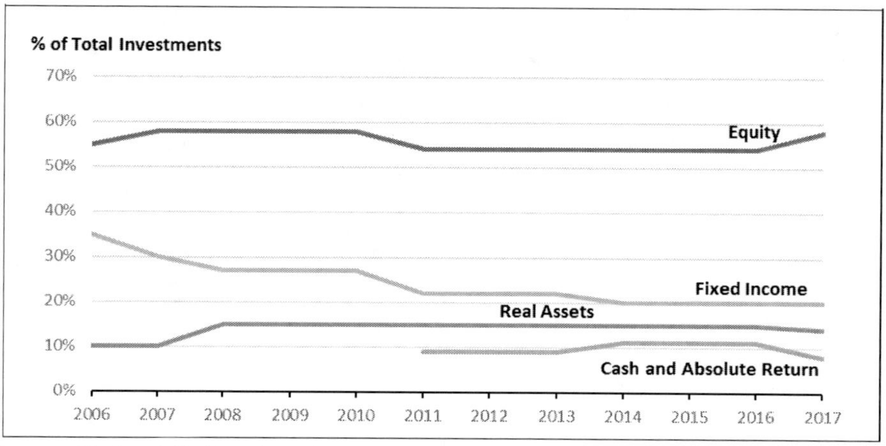

Source: National Railroad Retirement Investment Trust, *Annual Management Report for Fiscal Year 2006-2017.*

Note: Real assets include investments in real estate and commodities.

Figure 2. NRRIT Target Asset Allocations, 2006-2017.

The Trust's target asset allocations change over time to reflect current market expectation (see Figure 2).[12] For example, over the past decade, the Trust has continued its effort in moving away from fixed income investment, with a decline from 35% of total investments in FY2006 to 20% in FY2017. The target proportion of total investments in equity—domestic, international, and private equity—has been relatively stable between FY2006 and FY2017, ranging from 54% to 58%. The percentage of total investments in private equity increased from 5% in FY2006 to 10% in FY2008, and remained at this level thereafter. At the same time, fixed income was reduced and investments into real assets, cash, and absolute

[12] At the Trust's inception, the initial asset allocation policy established target weights between 2002 and 2006 were 47% in domestic equity, 21% in international equity, and 32% in fixed income. National Railroad Retirement Investment Trust, *Annual Management Report for Fiscal Year 2007*, at https://www.goiam.org/wp-content/uploads/2015/08/uploaded Files_TCUnion_Railroad_Retirement_Updates_2007_Annual_Report.pdf.

return assets were increased. The investment in real assets, including real estate and commodities, increased from 10% of total investments in FY2006 to 15% in FY2008 and then the proportion remained relatively stable. Cash and absolute return investments were adopted in FY2011, and they have accounted for around 10% of total investments since then. The current investment guidelines are shown in detail in Table 1.

Table 1. Current Trust Target Asset Allocations and Ranges (effective beginning October 1, 2017)

Asset Class	Target Allocation	Target Allocation Range
Equity	58%	
Domestic	24%	19%-29%
International	24%	19%-29%
Private	10%	5%-15%
Fixed Income	20%	
Domestic	14%	10%-18%
International	4%	2%-6%
Private Debt	2%	0%-4%
Real Assets	14%	
Commodities	4%	2%-6%
Real Estate	10%	5%-15%
Other	8%	
Absolute Return	7%	3%-11%
Cash	1%	0%-3%

Source: National Railroad Retirement Investment Trust, *Annual Management Report for Fiscal Year 2017,* 2017, p. 15, https://www.rrb.gov/sites/default/files/2018-03/NRRIT_rpt_FY2017.pdf. See pages 15-17 for detailed definitions of assets.

Oversight

The Trust is an independent nongovernmental entity, and it is not subject to the same oversight as federal agencies. The RRSIA outlines specific reporting requirements, including an annual management report to Congress. The report must include a statement of financial position, a statement of cash flows, a statement on internal accounting and administrative control systems, and any other information necessary to inform Congress about the operations and financial condition of the Trust. The financial statements must be audited by independent public accountants. A copy of the annual report and audit must be submitted to the President, the RRB, and the Director of the Office of Management and Budget (OMB). The RRB has the authority to bring a civil action to enforce provisions of the act.

Over the past decade, the RRB Office of Inspector General (OIG) has expressed concerns about the effectiveness of the oversight of the Trust. In 2008, the OIG argued that the annual financial audit required "is not adequate to support the RRB's enforcement responsibility because such audits are not intended to provide information about all areas of risk that could indicate the need for enforcement action."[13] The OIG noted that there are fewer safeguards protecting the Trust than there are for the retirement investments of federal government and private-sector workers. For example, there is no requirement for performance audits of the Trust, which would assess program effectiveness, economy and efficiency, internal control, and compliance with the law.

In 2011, the OIG reiterated its concerns with the oversight of the Trust and stated,

> The lack of NRRIT investment fund management accountability, transparency, and stringent financial oversight can be precursors to fraud, waste and abuse. Within the Federal agency spectrum there is no comparable example where Federal program assets are completely outside the jurisdiction of a Federal agency's appointed Inspector General. However, the NRRIT fund which supports the Railroad Retirement program remains outside the purview of those appointed to protect the interests of the program's beneficiaries and the tax-paying public.[14]

---

[13] Railroad Retirement Board, Office of Inspector General, *Statement of Concern: National Railroad Retirement Investment Trust Lack of Provision for Performance Audits*, March 31, 2008, https://www.rrb.gov/sites/default/files/ 2017-05/nrritStatement.pdf.

[14] Railroad Retirement Board, Office of the Inspector General, *Office of the Inspector General's Proposal to Improve Business Efficiency at the Railroad Retirement Board*, September 21, 2011, p. 5, https://rrb.gov/sites/default/files/2017- 05/SR_092111.pdf.

In a recent report in FY2018, the OIG asserted that lack of access to the Trust's auditor continued to be a concern,

> This lack of cooperation and communication prevents OIG auditors from obtaining sufficient appropriate audit evidence regarding the RRB's financial statements....During fiscal year 2014, [OIG] recommended that an independent committee be established to identify a functional solution that would enable communication between OIG and NRRIT's auditors. Although RRB management did not concur with this recommendation, [OIG] will continue to cite this issue and the need for corrective action.[15]

Accounting in the Federal Budget

As required in the RRSIA, Trust purchases and sales initially were treated as exchanges of assets of equal value, thus did not produce direct budgetary cost or income.[16] The law did not prescribe the treatment of unrealized capital gains and losses on the Trust's investments. The Congressional Budget Office (CBO) and OMB agreed that any capital loss or gain resulting from changes in market prices would be recognized in the year in which the price change occurs, and interest payments and dividends would be recorded as offsetting receipts.[17] As a result, income and capital gains reduce outlays and the deficit, and losses increase them. This reflects the change in real economic resources available to the government as the value of the Trust changes. As for future performance, both CBO and

---

[15] RRB Office of Inspector General, *Independent Auditor's Report* in *Performance and Accountability Report of FY2018*, p. 9, at https://www.rrb.gov/sites/default/files/2018-11/Report%20on%20the%20Railroad%20Retirement%20Board%27s%20Financial%20Statements%20%20Fiscal%20Year%202018%20%287.2%20MB%29_0.pdf.

[16] For budgetary purposes, purchases or sales by the Trust are treated as a means of financing, which are not considered as outlays or receipts, so they are nonbudgetary. This differs from long-standing budgetary rules, which usually treat an investment in nonfederal securities as the purchase of an asset, recording both an obligation and an outlay equal to the purchase price during the year of the purchase.

[17] For more information on accounting for government investment in private markets, see Congressional Budget Office, *Evaluating and Accounting for Federal Investment in Corporate Stocks and Other Private Securities*, January 2003, http://www.cbo.gov/sites/default/files/cbofiles/ftpdocs/40xx/doc4023/01-08-03-stocks.pdf.

OMB use risk-adjusted rate of return assumptions—that is, they assume that the Trust's investments will earn the comparable Treasury bond rate.

PERFORMANCE OF THE TRUST

To date, the Trust's average annual performance slightly exceeds expectations expressed by the RRSIA's drafters, which had assumed that Trust investments would earn an average annual rate of return of 8.0%.[18] From FY2003 to FY2017, the Trust's annual rates of return, net of fees, have averaged 8.3%. For the first half of the Trust's existence, its returns largely exceeded expectations. Prior to FY2008, the average rate of return on Trust investments was 14.7% and the average rate of return exceeded the expected rate of 8.0% through FY2010. The Trust then had negative rates of return in FY2008 (-19.1%) and FY2009 (-0.7%) but rebounded with an 11.2% rate of return in FY2010 followed by a slightly negative rate of return of -0.1% in FY2011. The FY2012 rate of return of 16.4% brought the average annual rate of return of the Trust above the expected level of 8.0% for the first time in two years (since FY2010). The rate of return was 13.4% in FY2017.[19]

Comparison to Benchmarks

The Trust's annual rates of return have generally compared favorably to its benchmarks. A benchmark is a standard used for comparison when measuring investment performance, and the NRRIT strategic policy benchmark is based on a series of benchmarks corresponding to each of the

[18] H.Rept. 107-82, part 1, p. 14.

[19] NRRIT, *Annual Management Report for Fiscal Year 2017*, p. 14, https://www.rrb.gov/sites/default/files/2018-03/ NRRIT_rpt_FY2017.pdf.

major asset classes in the Trust.[20] For example, the current benchmark for the Trust's investments in domestic equities is the Russell 3000 Index.[21]

As shown in Figure 3, in the majority of years between FY2003 and FY2017, Trust performances exceeded its strategic policy benchmarks. In FY2006 and FY2007, the Trust's performances was roughly equal to its benchmarks, whereas in FY2008, FY2009, FY2011, and FY2016, the Trust's investments had lower returns than its strategic policy benchmarks. In FY2017, the Trust's rate of return of 13.4% (net of fees) exceeded the benchmark of 12.3%.[22]

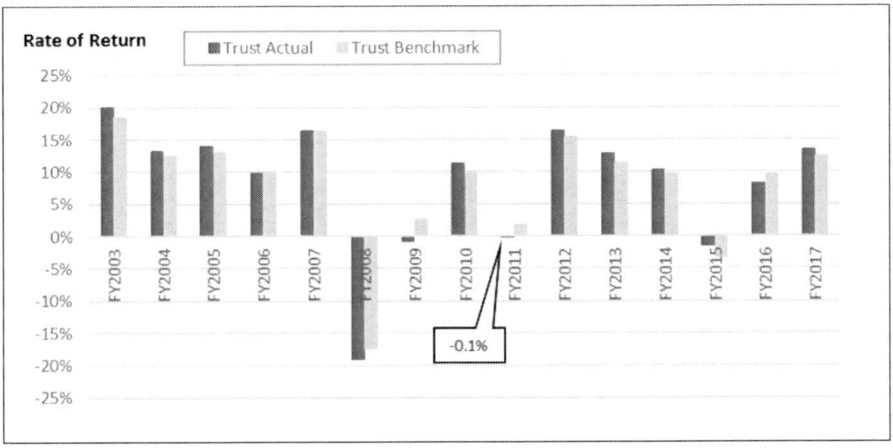

Source: National Railroad Retirement Investment Trust, *Annual Management Report for Fiscal Year 2017*, p. 14; and previous editions.

Note: Rates of return were net of fees.

Figure 3. Actual Trust Rates of Return Compared with Strategic Policy Benchmarks (FY2003 to FY2017).

---

[20] Benchmarks for each of the Trust's asset classes are provided in NRRIT, *Annual Management Report for Fiscal Year 2017*, Appendix B.

[21] Additional information on the Russell 3000 Index is available on the website of Russell Investments at http://www.ftse.com/Analytics/FactSheets/temp/44c7ed53-1026-4910-9fda-55fb203f8744.pdf.

[22] NRRIT, *Annual Management Report for FY2017*, p. 14; and previous editions.

Administrative Expenses

Table 2. Trust Expense Ratios (FY2003-FY2017)

Fiscal Year	Basis Points
2003	2
2004	4
2005	9
2006	15
2007	24
2008	25
2009	26
2010	33
2011	36
2012	30
2013	29
2014	29
2015	27
2016	28
2017	31

Source: National Railroad Retirement Investment Trust, *Annual Management Report for Fiscal Year 2017*, p. 18; and previous editions.

Notes: One basis point is equal to 1/100th of 1% of the average net assets of a fund. For example an expense ratio of 29 basis points indicates that expenses were 0.29% of average net assets.

The Trust's administrative expenses steadily increased through FY2011 as its investment portfolio diversified. However, as shown in Table 2, beginning in FY2012, the Trust's administrative expense ratio decreased, mirroring a national trend of decreasing expense ratios for mutual and money market funds. The Trust's administrative expenses remain low compared with industry standards.

In FY2017, the Trust's expense ratio was 31 basis points (expenses were 0.31% of average net assets).[23] In comparison, in 2017, average expense ratios were 59 basis points for equity funds, 48 basis points for bond funds, 70 basis points for hybrid funds, and 25 basis points for money market funds.[24]

---

[23] NRRIT, *Annual Management Report for Fiscal Year 2017*, p. 18.

[24] Investment Company Institute, *Trends in the Fees and Expenses of Mutual Funds, 2017,* April 2018, http://www.ici.org/pdf/per24-03.pdf.

In: Retirement
Editor: Thomas M. Osborne
ISBN: 978-1-53615-703-1

Chapter 9

MILITARY RETIREMENT: BACKGROUND AND RECENT DEVELOPMENTS (UPDATED)*

Kristy N. Kamarck

SUMMARY

The military retirement system is a government-funded, noncontributory, defined benefit system that has historically been viewed as a significant incentive in retaining a career military force. The system currently includes monthly compensation for qualified active and reserve retirees, disability benefits for those deemed medically unfit to serve, and a survivor annuity program for the eligible survivors of deceased retirees. The amount of compensation is dependent on time served, basic pay at retirement, and annual Cost-of-Living-Adjustments (COLAs). Military retirees are also entitled to nonmonetary benefits including exchange and commissary privileges, medical care through TRICARE, and access to Morale, Welfare and Recreation (MWR) facilities and programs.

Currently, there are three general categories of military retiree, active component, reserve component, and disability retiree. Active component personnel are eligible for retirement (i.e., vested) after completing 20

* This is an edited, reformatted and augmented version of Congressional Research Service, Publication No. RL34751, dated September 13, 2018.

years of service (YOS). Reserve personnel are eligible after 20 years of creditable service based on a points system, but do not typically begin to draw retirement pay until age 60. Finally, those with a disability retirement do not need to have served 20 years to be eligible for retired pay; however, they must have been found unqualified for further service due to a permanent, stable disability.

In FY2017, approximately $57 billion was paid to 2.3 million military retirees and survivors. Given the size of the program, some have viewed military retirement as a place where substantial budgetary savings could be made. Others have argued that past modifications intended to save money have had a deleterious effect on military recruiting and retention. Military retirees, families, and veterans' service organizations closely monitor potential changes to the retirement system. When considering alternatives to the current system, Congress may choose to consider the balance among the benefits of the military retirement system as a retention incentive, budget constraints, and the needs and concerns of their constituents.

OVERVIEW

The military retirement system is a government-funded benefit system that has been viewed historically as a significant incentive in retaining a career military force. The system includes a defined benefit (i.e., pension) element for all retirees and a defined contribution element for certain eligible retirees. The defined benefit includes a monthly annuity for qualified active and reserve retirees paid out of the Military Retirement Fund. The defined contribution benefit includes government-matching payments into an individual retirement Thrift Savings Plan (TSP) account. The amount of the retirement annuity depends on time served and basic pay at retirement. It is adjusted annually by a Cost-of-Living Adjustment (COLA) to ensure that the annuity is protected from the adverse consequences of inflation. Military retirees are also entitled to nonmonetary benefits, which include exchange and commissary privileges, medical care through TRICARE, and access to Morale, Welfare and Recreation facilities and programs.

The non-disability military retirement system has evolved since the late 1800s to meet four main goals.

- To keep the military forces of the United States young and vigorous and ensure promotion opportunities for younger members.
- To enable the armed forces to remain competitive with private-sector employers and the federal Civil Service.
- To provide a reserve pool of experienced military manpower that can be called upon in time of war or national emergency to augment active forces.
- To provide economic security for former members of the armed forces during their old age.

Among active duty personnel, eligibility for a monthly pension is generally based on a service requirement of at least 20 years of (active) service. For reserve component personnel, the system is based on *points,* and reservists do not generally begin to receive retired pay until the age of 60. Both the active duty and reserve component retirement systems *vest* at 20 years of qualifying service.[1] However, some members who are retired with a physical disability may receive a pension regardless of the amount of time they have spent on active duty. Disability retirement offers a choice between two retirement compensation options: one based on years of service (longevity) and one on the severity of the disability.

In FY2017, approximately $53.5 billion was paid to approximately 2 million military retirees, and an additional $3.9 billion was paid to 319,431 survivors.[2] As shown in Table 1, the number of military retirees and the cost of their retirement benefits have increased over the past decade.

---

[1] Vesting in the military retirement system is commonly referred to as "cliff vesting." Until the 20-year point, there is generally no vesting. At 20 years, the servicemember becomes fully vested. However, individuals can receive retirement benefits with fewer than 20 years of service under the disability retirement system and under Temporary Early Retirement Authority (Section 4403, P.L. 102-484, October 23, 1992).

[2] Department of Defense, *FY2017 DOD Statistical Report on the Military Retirement System,* Office of the Actuary, July 2018, p. 23.

Table 1. DOD Retired Military Personnel, Survivors, and Program Costs, FY2006-FY2017

Fiscal Year	Retired Pay Recipients and Total Program Cost	Regular Retirees from an Active Duty Military Career	Disability Retirees	Reserve Retirees	Survivor Benefit Recipients
2017	2,315,806	1,469,751	118,029	408,595	319,431
	$57.4 billion	$45.51 billion	$1.59 billion	$6.40 billion	$3.95 billion
2016	2,312,880	1,472,140	116,141	401,580	323,019
	$57.01 billion	$45.22 billion	$1.56 billion	$6.23 billion	$3.98 billion
2015	2,308,073	1,474,116	112,260	395,808	325,889
	$56.49 billion	$44.93 billion	$1.52 billion	$6.08 billion	$3.96 billion
2014	2,297,889	1,473,315/	107,751	389,750	327,073
	$55.13 billion	$43.92 billion	$1.46 billion	$5.85 billion	$3.91billion
2013	2,284,233	1,470,803	103,160	383,490	326,780
	$54.00 billion	$43.72 billion	$1.43 billion	$5.62 billion	$3.85 billion
2012	2,272,295	1,472,087	95,910	376,052	328,246
	$52.61 billion	$42.05 billion	$1.38 billion	$5.36 billion	$3.81 billion
2011	2,260,112	1,471,219	94,886	366,823	327,184
	$50.65 billion	$40.53 billion	$1.36 billion	$5.06 billion	$3.70 billion
2010	2,211,580	1,467,936	92,704	356,602	299,478
	$50.12 billion	$40.19 billion	$1.38 billion	$4.89 billion	$3.65 billion
2009	2,196,397	1,468,377	91,460	344,393	297,558
	$49.16 billion	$39.54 billion	$1.38 billion	$4.65 billion	3.60 billion
2008	2,170,803	1,466,705	85,502	328,664	296,580
	$45.66 billion	$36.90 billion	$1.29 billion	$4.20 billion	$3.27 billion
2007	2,146,961	1,461,724	85,306	312,647	293,193
	$43.57 billion	$35.51 billion	$1.29 billion	$3.86 billion	$2.92 billion

Sources: Department of Defense, Fiscal Year 2017 DOD Statistical Report on the Military Retirement System, Office of the Actuary, July 2018. Statistical documents available by fiscal year for FY2005-FY2017, available at http://actuary.defense.gov/.

Notes: Total Program Cost is total DOD obligations for that Fiscal Year. Survivors include the spouse, children, and others with insurable interests that are entitled to survivor benefits from the DOD Military Retirement Fund.

Congress grapples with constituent concerns as well as budgetary constraints in considering military retirement issues. In the past, some have viewed military retirement as a place where substantial savings could be made, arguing that the military retirement compensation is overly generous relative to pension systems in the civilian sector. In particular, they note that active duty military personnel become eligible for retirement at a relatively young age. In FY2017, the average active duty non-disability[3] enlisted retiree is 42 years old and has 21 years of service at retirement; the average officer is 46 years old and has about 23 years of service at retirement.[4] Others argue that the military retirement system is fair given the unique demands of military service, pointing out the high operational tempo and repetitive tours of duty in overseas combat areas that servicemembers have endured over the past 15 years. In addition, some have argued that past modifications to the system intended to save money have had a deleterious effect on military recruiting and retention, particularly in times of strong economic performance.

While congressionally mandated changes to the military retirement system have been infrequent, any potential changes are closely monitored by current servicemembers, retirees, survivors and the veterans' service organizations that support them.

RETIREMENT SYSTEM ELIGIBILITY AND PAY CALCULATIONS

There are currently three separate but related retirement systems within the DOD: one for active duty members, one for reservists, and one for those who become medically disabled and are unable to complete a 20-year military career due to their disability. Each of these systems has distinct eligibility requirements and formulas for calculating the retirement annuity.

Retirement pay calculations are based on the date when the servicemember first entered active duty and their *pay base* at the time of retirement.[5] The defined benefit portion of the active and reserve

---

[3] These figures are for all of DOD non-disability retirees, excluding reserve retirees.

[4] Department of Defense, *Fiscal Year 2017 DOD Statistical Report on the Military Retirement System*, Office of the Actuary, July 2018, pp. 83 and 97.

[5] The "pay base" is either the amount of basic pay being received at the time of retirement (for those in the Final Basic Pay System) or the average of the highest 36 months of basic pay received (for those in the High-3 System). See 10 U.S.C. §§1406 and 1407. Basic pay is the principal element of Regular Military Compensation (RMC). The other elements include the

component retirement systems *cliff-vests* after 20 years of service. This means servicemembers who leave the service prior to completing 20 years of eligible service typically will not receive any non-disability retirement benefit.[6] This contrasts with eligibility for disabled veterans, who are vested on their disability retirement date regardless of years of service.

Active Component Retirement[7]

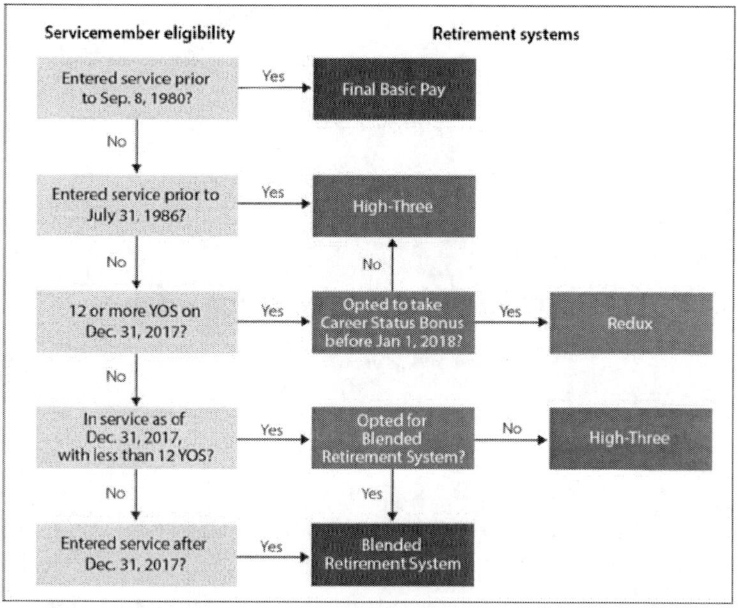

Source: CRS, derived from Title 10, United States Code.
Note: YOS = Years of Service.

Figure 1. Active Duty, Non-Disability (Longevity) Retirement Eligibility Flowchart.

Basic Allowance for Housing (BAH) and the Basic Allowance for Subsistence (BAS), which are nontaxable allowances. Basic pay is between 65% and 75% of RMC. RMC excludes all special pay and bonuses, reimbursements, educational assistance, and any value associated with nonmonetary benefits such as health care, commissaries, and post exchanges. For additional discussion of military pay and RMC, see CRS Report RL33446, *Military Pay: Key Questions and Answers*, by Lawrence Kapp and Barbara Salazar Torreon.

[6] Some individuals may qualify for longevity retirement prior to attaining 20 years of service under Temporary Early Retirement Authority (TERA).

[7] This is also frequently referred to as regular non-disability retirement.

For active duty military personnel, there are four methods of calculating retired pay based on longevity: the Final Basic Pay System, "High Three," Redux, and the Blended Retirement System (BRS) (see Table 4 for a comparison of the benefits under each method). The applicable retirement calculation is based on the date when the servicemember first entered active duty, their pay base at the time of retirement, their years of service, and whether they chose the Redux system or the BRS (if eligible). Figure 1 shows how eligibility for retirement calculations is determined.

Final Basic Pay (prior to September 8, 1980)

For persons who entered military service before September 8, 1980, the pay base is the final monthly basic pay received by the servicemember at the time of retirement multiplied by 2.5% for each year of service.[8] The minimum amount of retired pay to which a member is entitled under this formula is therefore 50% of the retired pay computation base (20 years of service times 2.5%). For example, a servicemember who retires at 25 years receives 62.5% of the computation base (25 years of service times 2.5%).[9]

The Final Basic Pay cohort that entered the military before September 8, 1980, had 30 years of service in 2010. It was expected that all members of this group would be retired by 2016.[10]

High Three

Those who entered service *on or after* September 8, 1980, and *before* January 1, 2018, are eligible to elect the High Three system. For this

---

[8] Partial years of service are credited as well, with each month equivalent to one-twelfth of a year. Military Retirement Reform Act of 1986, Section 1405(b), P.L. 99-348, July 1, 1986.

[9] Historically, the maximum, reached at the 30-year mark, was 75% of the computation base (30 years of service times 2.5%). However, the John Warner National Defense Authorization Act for Fiscal Year 2007 (P.L. 99-348 §§601 and 642) extended the previous pay table to 40 years, allowed additional longevity raises, and provided additional retirement credit for service beyond 30 years at the rate of 2.5% per year. In the FY2015 Carl Levin and Howard P. "Buck" McKeon National Defense Authorization Act. (P.L. 113-291 §622), Congress reinstated a cap on retired pay of general and flag officers at the Executive Level II salary ($183,300 for 2015). This change applies only to years served after December 31, 2014.

[10] Department of Defense, *Valuation of the Military Retirement System, September 30, 2006*, DOD Office of the Actuary, November, 2007, p. 12.

system the computation base is the average of the highest 3 years (36 months) of basic pay rather than the final basic pay. Otherwise, calculations are the same as under the Final Basic Pay method.

Redux

The *Redux* military retirement system was initiated with the Military Retirement Reform Act of 1986 (P.L. 99-348). The Redux formula reduced the amount of retired pay for which military servicemembers who entered the armed forces on or after August 1, 1986, were eligible. This system was broadly unpopular and by 1997 Congress began to take note of potential recruiting and retention problems associated with the change.[11] In 1998, the Clinton Administration announced that it supported Redux repeal.[12] The National Defense Authorization Act for Fiscal Year 2000 (P.L. 106-65 §§641 and 642) repealed *compulsory* Redux. It allowed post-August 1, 1986, entrants to retire under the High Three system *or* opt for Redux plus an immediate $30,000 cash payment. The FY2016 NDAA, enacted on November 25, 2015, terminated the Redux option.

Those who entered the service during the time when Redux was an option were required to select one of the following two options for calculating their retired pay within 180 days of reaching 15 years of service.

Option 1: Pre-Redux

Eligible servicemembers can opt to have their retired pay computed in accordance with the preRedux formula, described above as High Three.

Option 2: Redux

Eligible servicemembers can opt to have their retired pay computed in accordance with the Redux formula and receive an immediate $30,000

---

[11] Department of Defense, Military Compensation Background Papers: Compensation Elements and Related Manpower Cost Items, Their Purposes and Legislative Backgrounds, April 2005, p. 707.

[12] U.S. Congress, Senate Special Committee on Aging, Developments in Aging: 1999 and 2000, Volume 1, 107th Cong., 2nd sess., S.Rept. 107-158 (Washington, DC: GPO, 2001).

cash bonus called a Career Status Bonus.[13] Those who select the Career Status Bonus (CSB) must remain on active duty until they complete 20 years of service or forfeit a portion of the bonus.

The Redux Formula

Redux is different from the High Three formula in two major ways.

- Retirees under age 62: First, for retirees under the age of 62, the retired pay multiplier will be reduced by 1% for each year of creditable service less than 30 years. Under this formula, a 20-year retiree will receive 40% of his or her retired pay computation base upon retirement (20 years of service multiplied by 2.5% minus 10%), and a 25-year retiree will receive 57.5% of the computation base (25 years of service multiplied by 2.5% minus 5%). A 30-year retiree will receive 75% of the retired pay computation base (30 years of service multiplied by 2.5% minus 0%, the same as the High Three retiree). The Redux formula, therefore, is "skewed" in favor of the longer serving military member, theoretically providing an incentive to remain on active duty longer before retiring.
- Retirees 62 and older: Second, when a retiree reaches the age of 62, his or her retired pay will be recomputed based on the old formula (2.5% of the retired pay computation base for each year of service). Thus, beginning at 62, the 20-year retiree receiving 40% of his or her pay base under the Redux formula will begin receiving 50% of his or her pay base; the 25-year retiree's annuity will jump from 57.5% of the pay base to 62.5%; and the 30-year retiree's annuity, already at 75% of the pay base under both the old and new formulas will not change.[14]

Blended Retirement System (BRS)

In the FY2016 NDAA, based on recommendations from the Military Compensation and Retirement Modernization Commission (MCRMC), Congress adopted a new retirement system, shifting from a purely defined benefit system to a blended defined benefit plus defined contribution system. Servicemembers with 12 or fewer years of service as of December 31, 2017, were afforded an opportunity to choose the BRS. The BRS is mandatory for individuals who entered the service on or after January 1, 2018. For these servicemembers, the computation base for the defined

---

[13] 37 U.S.C. §354. The bonus can actually be paid in several annual installments if the recipient so wishes, for tax purposes.

[14] Note that this change is an increase in monthly retired pay, not a lump sum at the age of 62.

benefit will be the average of the highest three years (36 months) of basic pay, as in the High Three System; however, the multiplier is reduced to 2.0 from 2.5. This means that the pay base is the high three average at the time of retirement multiplied by 2.0% for each year of service. Therefore a servicemember retiring at 20 years would receive 40% of his or her pay base under the new formula and a 30-year retiree would receive 60% of his or her pay base.

The Lump Sum Payment

The Blended Retirement System also allows servicemembers to receive a portion of their retired pay in a lump sum. An individual entitled to retired pay may, no later than 90 days before the date of retirement, elect to receive

> A lump sum payment of the discounted present value at the time of the election of an amount of the covered retired pay[15] that the eligible person is otherwise entitled to receive for the period beginning on the date of retirement and the date the eligible person attains the eligible person's retirement age.[16]

For those who elect to receive a lump sum payment, after reaching the eligibility age for social security (usually 67), they will again receive 100% of their regular monthly annuity, which will be adjusted for annual cost of living increases.[17] The law also allows retirees to take their lump sum payment as a single payment or up to four annual installments. The lump sum is discounted to the present value based on the annual rate published by DOD in June of each year and which goes into effect on January 1 of

[15] Covered retired pay is defined as retired pay under title 10, title 14, the National Oceanic and Atmospheric Administration Commissioned Officer Corps Act of 2002 (33 U.S.C. §301 et seq.), and the Public Health Service Act (42 U.S.C. §201 et seq.)

[16]. P.L. 114-92 §633. "Retirement age" has the meaning given to the term in Section 2016(1) of the Social Security Act.

[17]. See https://www.ssa.gov/planners/retire/retirechart.html.

the following year.[18] Lump sum payments are considered earned income and are taxed accordingly.

Calculating the Lump Sum Payment

An eligible retiree can elect one of two options for calculating the lump sum.

- A lump sum of 50% of the discounted present value of retired pay between the date of retirement and the date of social security eligibility and a monthly annuity of 50% of the monthly retired pay they are otherwise entitled to. So for example, if a retiree was entitled to $4,000 per month in retired pay, the retiree would continue to receive a monthly annuity of $2,000 and would receive a lump sum equal to the discounted present value of the remaining annuity between the time of retirement and the normal social security retirement age.
- A lump sum of 25% of the discounted present value of retired pay between the date of retirement and the date of social security eligibility and a monthly annuity of 75% of the monthly retired pay they are otherwise entitled to. So for example, if a retiree was entitled to $4,000 per month in retired pay, the retiree would continue to receive a monthly annuity of $3,000 and would receive a lump sum payment equal to the discounted present value of the remaining annuity between the time of retirement and the normal social security retirement age.

Members under the BRS with a disability retirement do not have the option of receiving a portion of retired pay as a discounted lump sum. Reserve component members may elect the discounted lump sum option from the date the member first becomes eligible for retired pay (typically 60 years old) until the normal social security retirement age (typically 67). Based on an external study, the DOD Board of Actuaries assumes that

[18] The discounted present value will be determined in accordance with the rate that is an inflation adjusted, 7-year average of the Department of the Treasury High-Quality Market (HQM) Corporate Bond Spot Rate Yield Curve at a 23-year maturity plus an adjustment factor of 4.28 percentage points. The inflation-adjustment applied is the Department of the Treasury "Breakeven Inflation Spot Rate Yield Curve." Department of Defense, *Implementation of the Blended Retirement System*, Memorandum, January 27, 2017, https://militarypay.defense.gov/Portals/3/Documents/BlendedRetirementDocuments/FINAL_BRSImplementationGuidance.pdf. Department of Defense, *Blended Retirement System Lump-sum Government Discount Rate for 2018*, Memorandum, May 26, 2017, http://militarypay.defense.gov/ Portals/3/Documents/BlendedRetirementDocuments/BRS%20Lump%20Sum%20Government%20Discount%20Rate%20Memo%20(2018).pdf?ver=2017-06-13-121230- 790.

approximately 5.2% of officers and 22.8% of enlisted members under the BRS will elect the lump sum option.[19]

BRS Defined Contributions

Congress's decision to include a defined contribution element in the BRS was driven by the finding that under the legacy retirement systems, 83% of enlisted and 51% of officers did not complete the 20 years of service and thus received no retirement compensation for their service.[20] This was at odds with retirement benefits in the private sector where firms increasingly offer a variety of defined contribution packages and are required by law to vest employees within a much shorter time period.[21]

Under the BRS, individuals entering service after January 1, 2018, are automatically enrolled in the Thrift Savings Plan (TSP) at an individual contribution level of 3% from his or her monthly basic pay or inactive duty pay beginning the first pay period after the member's 60th day of service. At that time, the services will also begin automatic monthly contributions of 1% of basic pay to the servicemember's TSP account. In addition, DOD will match servicemembers' contributions up to 4% of the servicemember's basic pay starting at two years and one day after the member first enters service and ending at 26 years of service.[22] The servicemember is required to make individual total contributions of 5% in order to receive government matching of 4% (see Table 2 for government matching percentages). The servicemember is fully vested after two complete years of service and able to take ownership of the 1% contributions as well as any subsequent matching contributions. Any earnings on government contributions are immediately vested when they

---

[19] DOD Office of the Actuary, Valuation of the Military Retirement System, September 30, 2016, June 2018 p. 107.

[20] Military Compensation and Retirement Modernization Commission Final Report, January 2015. p. 23.

[21] The Employee Retirement Income Security Act (ERISA) requires firms to vest employees in company-provided defined benefit retirement plans either gradually over a period of seven years or by five years for cliff-vesting. In addition, a defined contribution plan must cliff vest within three years or up to six years for gradual vesting.

[22] This 4% is in addition to the 1% automatic government contribution, therefore the total government contribution would not exceed 5% of the member's basic pay.

accrue. Servicemembers are immediately fully vested in any personal TSP contributions.

The services will also automatically enroll new servicemembers in the TSP program for individual contributions at a default amount of their basic pay unless the servicemember opts out. If the servicemember declines to make individual contributions, he or she will automatically be reenrolled every year at the default amount of 3% individual contribution. This requires the individual to make an active decision every year to not contribute to the TSP.

Table 2. Government Automatic and Matching Contributions

Individual Contribution Rate of Basic Pay or Inactive Duty Pay	Government Automatic Contribution Rate of Basic Pay or Inactive Duty Pay	Government Matching Contribution Rate of Basic Pay or Inactive Duty Pay	Total Rate of TSP Monthly Contribution of Basic Pay or Inactive Duty Pay
0%	1%	0%	1%
1%	1%	1%	3%
2%	1%	2%	5%
3%	1%	3%	7%
4%	1%	3.5%	8.5%
5%	1%	4%	10%

Source: Department of Defense, Guidance for Implementation of the Blended Retirement System for the Uniformed Services, Memorandum from the Deputy Secretary of Defense, January 27, 2017.

Continuation Pay

In order to provide a mid-career retention incentive under the BRS, Congress authorized continuation pay for members who are between 8 to 12 years of service, in return for a three-year service obligation.[23] The pay may be distributed in a lump sum, or in a series of not more than four payments.[24] The law allows an active duty (regular component) member or reserve component member who is performing Active Guard or Reserve

[23] Congress first required a four-year obligation for continuation pay in the 12th year of service in the FY2016 NDAA (Section 634). This was amended in the FY2017 NDAA to provide more flexibility in the timing of this pay as "not less than 8 and not more than 12 years of service" and changed the service obligation to a minimum of 3 additional years of service following acceptance of continuation pay.

[24] 37 U.S.C. §356(d).

duty[25] to receive a minimum amount of continuation pay equal to 2.5 times their monthly basic pay. For reserve component members not on active duty, the minimum continuation pay is equal to at least 0.5 times the monthly basic pay of an active component member of similar rank and longevity. The law also authorizes an additional amount of continuation pay, at the discretion of the Secretary concerned (see Table 3). For active component members that would be the amount of monthly basic pay multiplied by no more than 13.[26] This flexibility awarded to military department Secretaries on the amount of additional continuation pay is intended to aid force-shaping by allowing the Secretaries to offer higher continuation payments to those in occupational specialties that are undermanned.

Table 3. Potential Continuation Pay Multipliers (by Component and Duty Status)

Component and Status	Minimum Continuation Pay	Additional Discretionary Continuation Pay
Active Component	2.5 times monthly base pay	Up to 13 times monthly base pay
Reserve Component on Active Duty as defined in 10 U.S.C. §101(d)(6)	2.5 times monthly base pay	Up to 6 times monthly base pay
Reserve Component *not* on Active Duty as defined in 10 U.S.C. §101(d)(6)	0.5 times monthly base pay	Up to 6 times monthly base pay

Source: 37 U.S.C. §356.

Note: Monthly base pay for reservists is calculated as the monthly base pay of an active component member of similar rank and longevity.

---

[25] As defined in 10 U.S.C. §101(d)(6).

[26] Section 634 of P.L. 114-92 states, "(b) AMOUNT.—The amount of continuation pay payable to a full TSP member under subsection (a) shall be the amount that is equal to—(1) in the case of a member of a regular component—'(A) the monthly basic pay of the member at 12 years of service multiplied by 2.5; plus "B) at the discretion of the Secretary concerned, the monthly basic pay of the member at 12 years of service multiplied by such number of months (not to exceed 13 months) as the Secretary concerned shall specify in the agreement of the member under subsection (a). (2) in the case of a member of a reserve component—(A) the amount of monthly basic pay to which the member would be entitled at 12 years of service if the member were a member of a regular component multiplied by 0.5; plus (B) at the discretion of the Secretary concerned, the amount of monthly basic pay described in subparagraph (A) multiplied by such number of months (not to exceed 6 months) as the Secretary concerned shall specify in the agreement of the member under subsection (a)."

Table 4. Retirement System Comparisons

	Final Basic Pay	**High Three**	**Redux**	**Blended Retirement System**
Applies to	Servicemembers entering before September 8, 1980	Servicemembers entering from Sept. 8, 1980, through July 31, 1986, and persons entering after July 31, 1986, but opting not to accept the 15-year CSB	Servicemembers entering after July 31, 1986, and accepting 15-year Career Status Bonus with additional 5-year service obligation	Servicemembers entering on or after January 1, 2018, and those with 12 or fewer YOS on December 31, 2017, who choose to opt in.
Basis of Computation	Final rate of monthly basic pay	Average monthly basic pay for the highest 36 months of basic pay	Average monthly basic pay for the highest 36 months of basic pay	Average monthly basic pay for the highest 36 months of basic pay
Defined Benefit Multiplier	2.5% per YOS	2.5% per YOS	2.5% per YOS, less 1% for each year of service less than 30 (restored at age 62)	2.0% per YOS
Defined Contribution	Individual contributions to TSP, no matching	Individual contributions to TSP, no matching	Individual contributions to TSP, no matching	1.0% minimum contribution into TSP from Service with up to 4.0% matching contributions
Lump Sum Option	Monthly annuity only	Monthly annuity only	Monthly annuity only	Option for partial lump sum payment at retirement with full monthly annuity restored at eligibility age for full social security payments
Additional Continuation Benefit	None	None	$30,000 CSB payable at the 15-year anniversary with 5-year obligation to remain on active duty	Minimum incentive pay between 8 to12 YOS w/3-year service obligation

Sources: Adapted by CRS from Military Compensation Background Papers, Department of Defense, Seventh Edition, November 2011, and FY2016 NDAA.

Notes: YOS = Years of Service; CSB = Career Status Bonus.

Under the blended system, reserve component members within the window of eligibility would receive the minimum continuation pay as discussed above (2.5 or 0.5 times the monthly basic pay of an active component member), plus an additional amount at the discretion of the Service Secretary that would be the amount of monthly basic pay multiplied by no more than six.

Reserve Component Retirement[27]

There are many similarities between the active and reserve retirement systems. First, reserve component (RC) members must also complete 20 *qualifying years* of service to become eligible for a defined retirement benefit.[28] Second, the reserve retirement system also accrues at the rate of 2.5% per *equivalent year* of qualifying service (explained below) at retirement eligibility for those who entered service prior to January 1, 2018, and 2.0% for those who enter on or after January 1, 2018. The primary difference between the reserve and the active system is the points system used to calculate qualifying years and equivalent years of service, as well as the age at which the retirement annuity begins. Also, Redux is not an option for reservists.

For retirement purposes, a *qualifying year* of service is a year in which a member of the RC earns at least 50 retirement *points*. Points are awarded for a variety of reserve activities

- one point for each day of active service, which includes annual training;[29]
- fifteen points a year for membership in the Ready Reserve;
- one point for each inactive duty training (IDT) period;[30]

---

[27] Also referred to as non-regular retirement. For additional information on reserve pay and benefits, see CRS Report RL30802, *Reserve Component Personnel Issues: Questions and Answers,* by Lawrence Kapp and Barbara Salazar Torreon.

[28] *Reserve Component* generally describes the six reserve components of the Department of Defense: the Army National Guard, the Army Reserve, the Navy Reserve, the Marine Corps Reserve, the Air National Guard and the Air Force Reserve.

[29] Annual training is a two-week period of active service that usually results in 14 or 15 retirement points.

- one point for each period of funeral honors duty; and
- one point for every three satisfactorily completed credit hours of certain military correspondence courses.

With multiple opportunities to earn points, a participating member of the selected reserve normally can accrue the requisite 50 points per year and thus earn a qualifying year for retirement. The maximum number of points per year, exclusive of active duty, has varied over time but is currently capped at 130 points.[31] When active duty points are added to this total, the reservist cannot earn more than 365 points a year. The number of points is critical in determining both the number of years of qualifying service and the number of equivalent years of service for retired pay calculation purposes.

A reservist may retire after completing 20 years of qualifying service; there is no minimum age. However, the reservist will usually not become eligible for retired pay until age 60, at which time he or she also becomes eligible for military medical care.[32] Upon retirement, the individual is normally transferred to the Retired Reserve and is entitled to a number of military benefits to include commissary and exchange privileges; access to Morale, Welfare and Recreation programs and facilities; and limited space available travel on military aircraft. Reservists in the Retired Reserve, but not yet retired pay eligible, are referred to as *Gray Area* retirees. Time spent in the Retired Reserve counts for longevity purposes and ultimately results in higher retired pay. For example, a lieutenant colonel who transitions to the Retired Reserve at age 45 will have their retired pay at age 60 calculated on the basic pay of a lieutenant colonel with an additional 15 years of longevity.

---

[30] A day of inactive duty for training typically includes two Unit Training Assemblies (UTAs). The normal drill weekend consists of four UTAs and therefore results in four retirement points. A year of weekend drills earns 48 UTAs/retirement points.

[31] P.L. 110-181 §648.

[32] Section 647 of the FY2008 National Defense Authorization Act (P.L. 110-181) reduced the age for receipt of retired pay by three months for each aggregate of 90 days of specified duty performed after January 28, 2008 (the date of enactment of the FY2008 NDAA). This authority was not made retroactive to September 11, 2001. The retired pay eligibility age cannot be reduced below 50 and eligibility for medical benefits remains at age 60.

The date the reservist became a member of the armed forces determines whether their retired pay is calculated based on the Final Basic Pay, High Three, or Blended Retirement System. Those entering before September 8, 1980, will retire under the Final Basic Pay system while those entering after September 8, 1980 but before January 1, 2018, will retire under the High Three system. Those who first perform Reserve Component service (with no prior regular or reserve service) on or after January 1, 2018, will retire under the Blended Retirement System. Those reservists with prior service who have accumulated less than 12 *equivalent years of service* (< 4,320 points) may elect the BRS.

Calculation of Reserve Retired Pay

The actual calculation parallels the active duty system but requires adjustment to reflect the part-time nature of reserve duty. For example, consider a reserve component lieutenant colonel with 5,000 points who joined the military in January 1980 and transferred to the Retired Reserve in 2000 after completing 20 qualifying years of service. In 2015, after reaching 60 years of age, and becoming eligible to receive retired pay, the process for calculating her retired pay would be

- Step 1: Divide the total points by 360 to convert the points to *equivalent years of service* (5,000 / 360 = 13.89).
- Step 2: Multiply the equivalent years of service by the 2.5% multiplier (13.89 times 0.025 = 0.3472). Using the Final Basic Pay option, the 2015 pay base for a lieutenant colonel with 35 years of service (20 years of qualifying service plus 15 years in the Retired Reserve) is $8,762.40 per month.[33]
- Step 3: Multiply the pay base by the retired pay multiplier ($8,762.40 times 0.3472) to produce a monthly retirement annuity of $3,042 per month.

[33] 2015 Military Pay Chart at http://www.dfas.mil.

Disability Retirement[34]

Servicemembers who, due to a disqualifying medical condition, are no longer able to perform their military duties, may qualify for disability retirement, commonly referred to as a *Chapter 61 retirement.* Eligibility is based on having a permanent and stable disability rated at 30% or more under the standard schedule of rating disabilities in use by the Department of Veterans Affairs at the time of determination.[35] Some disability retirees are retired before becoming eligible for longevity retirement, while others have completed 20 or more years of service.

Formulas for Calculating Disability Retired Pay

A servicemember retired for disability may select one of two available options for calculating their monthly retired pay.[36]

- Longevity Formula. Retired pay is computed by multiplying the years of service times 2.5% or 2.0% (for those joining on or after January 1, 2018) and then times the pay base (either final pay or high three, as appropriate).
- Disability Formula. Retired pay is computed by multiplying the DOD disability percentage by the pay base.

The maximum retired pay calculation under the disability formula cannot exceed 75% of basic pay.[37] Disability retirees are not authorized to receive a lump sum payment under the Blended Retirement System.

Retired pay computed under the disability formula is subject to federal income tax, unless one or more of the following conditions applies: (1) the

[34] For additional information on DOD's disability process, see CRS Report RL33991, *Disability Evaluation of Military Servicemembers*, by Christine Scott and Don J. Jansen.

[35] 10 U.S.C. §1201 (b) (3) (B). Prior to the FY2008 NDAA (P.L. 110-181 §1641), disability retirement required at least eight years of service or a disability that resulted from active duty or was incurred in the line of duty during war or national emergency. Under current statute, members must be on active duty for more than 30 days and the disability was either 1) not noted at the time of the member's entrance on active duty (unless clear and unmistakable evidence demonstrates that the disability existed before the member's entrance on active duty and was not aggravated by active military service); 2) the proximate result of performing active duty; 3) incurred in line of duty in time of war or national emergency; or 4) incurred in line of duty after September 14, 1978.

[36] 10 U.S.C. §1401.

[37] 10 U.S.C. §1401.

member's disability is the result of a combat-related injury, or (2) the individual was eligible to receive disability retirement payments prior to September 25, 1975, or (3) the individual was in the Armed Services prior to September 25, 1975, and later became eligible for disability retired pay.[38] Retired pay under the longevity formula (for those entering after September 24, 1975) is taxable only to the extent that it exceeds what the individual would receive for a combat related injury under the disability formula.

Extraordinary Heroism Pay

Retired enlisted members of military services with less than 30 years of service may be eligible for a 10% increase in retired pay when credited with extraordinary heroism in the line of duty as determined by the Secretary of his or her service.[39] This increase is subject to a maximum of 75% of the member's retired or retainer pay base. In 2002, Congress extended this benefit to enlisted members of the reserve component who are eligible for reserve retired pay.[40]

Military Retired Pay, Social Security, and Federal Income Tax

Military retirees receive full Social Security benefits in addition to their military retired pay. Current military personnel do not contribute a portion of their salary as part of the military retirement pay accrual.

---

[38] 26 U.S.C. §104. The term "combat-related injury" means personal injury or sickness which is incurred (1) as a direct result of armed conflict, (2) while engaged in extrahazardous service, or (3) under conditions simulating war; or which is caused by an instrumentality of war.

[39] See 10 U.S.C. §3991(a)(2) (Army), §6330(c)(3) (Navy and Marine Corps), and §8991(a)(2) (Air Force); and Department of Defense, *Financial Management Regulation*, DOD 7000.14-R Volume 7B, Chapter 1, March 2018.

[40] P.L. 107-314.

However, they have paid taxes into the Social Security trust fund since January 1, 1957 and are entitled to full Social Security benefits based on their military service. Military retired pay and Social Security are not offset against each other.

Military retired pay is not subject to withholding for Social Security tax. However, all non-disability retired pay is subject to withholding of federal income tax. A portion of the Social Security benefit may also be subject to federal income tax for individuals who have other income.

RETIRED PAY AND THE COST-OF-LIVING ADJUSTMENT (COLA)

Table 5. Cost-of-Living Adjustments 2007-2017

COLA Date	Pre-Aug. 1986 COLA	Post-Aug. 1986 COLA	COLA Date	Pre-Aug. 1986 COLA	Post-Aug. 1986 COLA
Dec. 1, 2007	2.3%	2.3% w/o CSB 1.3% w/ CSB	Dec 1, 2013	1.5%	1.5% w/o CSB 0.5% w/ CSB
Dec 1, 2008	5.8%	5.8% w/o CSB 4.8% w/ CSB	Dec 1, 2014	1.7%	1.7% w/o CSB 0.7% w/ CSB
Dec 1, 2009	0.0%	0.0% w/o CSB 0.0% w/ CSB	Dec 1, 2015	0.0%	0.0% w/o CSB 0.0% w/ CSB
Dec 1, 2010	0.0%	0.0% w/o CSB 0.0% w/ CSB	Dec 1, 2016	0.3%	0.3% w/o CSB 0.0% w/ CSB
Dec 1, 2011	3.6%	3.6% w/o CSB 2.6% w/ CSB	Dec 1, 2017	2.0%	2.0% w/o CSB 1.0% w/ CSB
Dec 1, 2012	1.7%	1.7% w/o CSB 0.7% w/ CSB			

Source: Office of the Under Secretary of Defense (Comptroller), DOD 7000.14-R Financial Management Regulation, Vol. 7B, Chapter 8, July 2018.

Notes: CSB = Career Status Bonus. The COLA increase for most retired pay is effective December 1, 2017, will apply to payments through calendar year 2018.

Military retired pay is adjusted for inflation by statute (10 U.S.C. §1401a). The Military Retirement Reform Act of 1986, in conjunction with changes contained in the FY2000 National Defense Authorization Act (P.L. 106-65), provides for COLAs as indicated below. Congress has not modified the COLA formula since 1995.[41] However, policymakers regularly discuss COLA modifications, typically with the aim of reducing costs and, hence, the payments to retirees. COLAs for 2007 to 2017 are shown in Table 5.

COLAs for Pre-August 1, 1986, Entrants

For military personnel who first entered military service before August 1, 1986, each December a COLA equal to the percentage increase in the Consumer Price Index between the third quarters of successive years will be applied to military retired pay for the annuities paid beginning each January 1.[42] This number is rounded to the nearest one-tenth of 1%.[43] The COLA is applied to the monthly benefit amount and the final payment is rounded down to the nearest $1.00.[44]

COLAs for Personnel Who Entered Service On or After August 1, 1986

For those personnel who first entered military service on or after August 1, 1986, their COLAs will be calculated in accordance with either of two methods, as noted below.

Non-Redux Recipients

Those personnel who opted to have their retired pay computed in accordance with the pre-Redux (High Three) formula will have their COLAs computed as described above for pre-August 1, 1986, entrants.

---

[41] The actual index used to adjust COLA is the CPI-W; the index for urban wage earners and clerical workers. It represents the buying habits of approximately 32% of the non-institutional population of the United States, *Military Compensation Background Papers*, Seventh Edition, November 2011, p. 637.

[42] The CPI is calculated and published by the Bureau of Labor Statistics.

[43] 10 U.S.C. 1401a.

[44] 10 U.S.C. 1412.

Redux/$30,000 Cash Bonus Recipients

Those personnel who opt to have their retired pay computed in accordance with the Redux formula, have their COLAs computed using a different formula. Annual COLAs are held one percentage point below the actual inflation rate. So for example, the December 2017 COLA increase was 2.0% and Redux retirees saw a COLA increase of 1.0%. When a retiree reaches the age of 62, there is a one-time recomputation of his or her annuity to make up for the lost purchasing power caused by holding of annual COLA adjustments to the inflation rate minus one percentage point.[45] This recomputation of COLA, in combination with the recomputation of the retired pay multiplier (discussed earlier), is a one-time increase in the member's monthly retired pay to parity with that of a similarly retired member who did not take the Redux option. After the recomputation at age 62, however, future COLA increases continue to be computed annually on the basis of the inflation rate minus one percentage point.

CONCERNS ABOUT THE FUTURE OF MILITARY RETIREMENT

Some advocacy groups and servicemembers have expressed concerns about the implementation of the Blended Retirement System, in particular in relation to the reduced multiplier for the defined benefit (monthly annuity) and the lump sum payment option. These include the potential impacts of the BRS on recruitment and retention, as well as on the financial well-being of military personnel.

For example, there is some uncertainty as to whether the reduced multiplier for the defined benefit remains a strong enough retention incentive for mid-career personnel. A recent study for the Marine Corps that modeled potential retention outcomes found relatively small effects on force profiles, with officer retention being somewhat more sensitive than

[45] 10 U.S.C. §1410.

enlisted retention.[46] The study also noted that retention may vary by occupational specialty—supporting the notion that flexibility may be needed for the services to vary the continuation pay, to offer other retention bonuses, or to lengthen minimum service requirements for high-demand fields.

In terms of financial well-being, the study found that, in general, those who retire after a 20-year career and contribute to the TSP throughout their career, will have lower take-home pay from retirement to age 60 than those in the legacy retirement system, but will be better off after the age of 60 when eligible to start drawing from the TSP without penalty.[47] The total lifetime benefit was estimated to be slightly higher under the legacy retirement system than under the BRS.[48] Since the average military retiree upon retirement is in his or her 40s, many choose to pursue a second civilian career and may also accrue retirement savings and benefits from his or her new employer. Estimates of retirement savings are sensitive to the amount a member contributes to the TSP and the return on investment for TSP accounts. One of the ways that Congress addressed these concerns was to require financial literacy training for servicemembers in the FY2016 NDAA with the authorization for the new retirement system.[49]

MILITARY RETIREMENT BUDGETING AND COSTS

Military retirement costs, which include all payments to current retirees and survivors, have been rising modestly each year, due to a predictable, slow rise in the number of retirees and survivors coupled with cost of living increases. All DOD budgets through FY1984 reflected the costs of retired pay actually being paid out to personnel who had already retired. That is, Congress appropriated the amount of money required to

[46] Grefer, James et al., The Military Compensation and Retirement Modernization Commission's Blended Retirement Plan: Implications for Marine Corps Force Management Objectives, CNA, October 2016.

[47] Ibid., p. v.

[48] Ibid., p. 70.

[49] P.L. 114-92 §661.

pay current retirees each year as part of each annual defense appropriations bill.

Since FY1985, the *accrual accounting* concept has been used to budget for the costs of military retired pay. The unfunded liability resulting from the change in accounting practices is discussed in the next section. Under the accrual accounting system, the DOD budget for each fiscal year includes a contribution to a Military Retirement Fund (MRF)[50] sufficient to finance future retirement payouts to *current* uniformed personnel when they retire, not the amount of retired pay actually paid to current retirees. These annual *accrual* contributions accumulate in the MRF, along with interest earned on them.[51] Therefore, changes to military end-strength, increases or decreases in basic pay tables, or changes to retirement pay formulas, in any given year will result in same-year DOD budget obligations for military retired pay. Once military personnel retire, payments to them are made from the accumulated amounts in the MRF, not from the annual DOD budget.

The amount that DOD must contribute to the MRF each year to cover future retirement costs is determined by an independent, presidentially appointed, Department of Defense Retirement Board of Actuaries, which decides how much is needed to cover future retirement costs as a percentage of military basic pay. Estimated future retirement costs are modeled based on the past rates at which active duty military personnel stayed in the service until retirement and on assumptions regarding the overall U.S. economy, including interest rates, inflation rates, and military pay levels. The model helps determine the level percentage of basic pay for each active servicemember that must be contributed from the DOD budget every year to cover future retirement costs—approximately 30 cents on

[50] The Military Retirement Fund is located in the Income Security Function of the federal budget. Individual retirees receive their retired pay from the Defense Finance and Accounting Service (DFAS). Technically, however, because this money paid to individuals comes not from the DOD budget, but from the fund, it is paid out of the Income Security function of the federal budget. Actual payments to current retirees thus show up in the federal budget as outlays from the federal budget as a whole, not from DOD.

[51] The money in the fund is invested in nonnegotiable government securities.

every dollar of basic pay for full-time members.[52] This is called the normal cost percentage (NCP) and is shown in Table 6.

Table 6. DOD's Normal Cost Percentages (NCPs) for FY2017

Benefit Formula	Full-time (active component)	Part-time (reserve component)
Final Pay	35.4%	24.8%
High-3	32.3%	23.5%
CSB/Redux	31.7%	NA
BRS	23.7%	18.3%

Source: DOD Office of the Actuary, Valuation of the Military Retirement System, September 30, 2016, June 2018 p. 19.

Note: Because the multiplier for those retiring under the Blended Retirement System is reduced from 2.5 to 2.0, the NCP for those retiring under the new system is lower than the NCPs under legacy systems. Estimates of the magnitude of cost savings vary under the new system; however, all estimates suggest increased annual savings for DOD as the BRS is implemented.

The Military Retirement Fund also receives intergovernmental transfers from the General Fund of the Treasury to fund the initial unfunded liability of the military retirement system. This is the total future cost of military retired pay that will result from military service performed prior to the implementation of accrual accounting in FY1985.

Sources of Military Retirement Fund (MRF) Income

The MRF receives income from three sources 1) normal cost payments (NCPs) from the Services and U.S. Treasury; (2) U.S. Treasury payments to amortize the unfunded liability and for the normal cost of concurrent receipt benefits; and (3) investment (interest) income.[53]

---

[52] According to the DOD actuary, "mathematically, a NCP is calculated by devising the present value of future benefits for the entire cohort by the present value of future basic pay, evaluated at the assumed interest rate." *Valuation of the Military Retirement System, September 30, 2016*, June 2018 p. 19.

[53]. The FY2004 NDAA (P.L. 108-136 §641) which authorized concurrent receipt of military retired pay and veterans disability benefits also required the U.S. Department of the Treasury to pay into the Fund at the beginning of each year the normal cost arising from increased concurrent receipt benefits. See CRS Report R40589, *Concurrent Receipt: Background and Issues for Congress,* by Kristy N. Kamarck.For more information on concurrent receipt, see CRS Report R40589, *Concurrent Receipt: Background and Issues for Congress,* by Kristy N. Kamarck.

Unfunded Liability

Current debates over both federal civilian and military retirement have included some discussion of *unfunded liability*, which consists of future retired pay costs incurred before the creation of the Military Retirement Fund in FY1985. The initial unfunded liability as of September 30, 1984 was $528.7 billion.[54] The unfunded liability at the end of FY2016 was $742.6 billion.[55] These obligations are being liquidated by the payment to the fund each year of an amount from the General Fund of the Treasury and are currently expected to be fully amortized by FY2025.[56]

Congressional action to change basic pay, retired pay, or associated benefits (e.g., concurrent retirement disability pay[57], or survivor benefit program) may affect the unfunded liability. For example, the implementation of the Blended Retirement System *reduced* the unfunded liability by $800 million, while the FY2017 NDAA provision authorizing an extension of the Special Survivor Indemnity Allowance (SSIA) for certain survivors of military members *raised* the unfunded liability by $200 million.[58] The FY2017 NDAA extended the SSIA as a permanent benefit which annual COLA increases. The DOD Actuary estimates that this change will raise NCPs by approximately 0.1 percentage point and lead to an actuarial loss of approximately $8 billion to the Military Retirement Fund.[59]

---

[54] Department of Defense Office of the Actuary, FY2016 Valuation of the Military Retirement System, September 30, 2016, June 2018, p. 21.

[55] Ibid., p. 5.

[56] Ibid., p. 21.

[57] See CRS Report R40589, Concurrent Receipt: Background and Issues for Congress, by Kristy N. Kamarck.

[58] Department of Defense Office of the Actuary, FY2016 Valuation of the Military Retirement System, September 30, 2016, June 2018, p. 26.

[59] Ibid., p. 9.

APPENDIX: RETIREMENT REFORM RECOMMENDATIONS IN PRIOR REVIEWS

Every four years, the President is required by law to direct a comprehensive review of the military compensation system and to forward the review, along with his recommendations, to Congress.[60] This review is known as the Quadrennial Review of Military Compensation (QRMC). The Military Compensation and Retirement Modernization Commission (MCRMC) served as the 12th QRMC.[61] The sections below summarize the recommendations of these commissions.

10th QRMC Recommendations

In the 10th Quadrennial Review of Military Compensation (QRMC), one of the directed areas of assessment was "the implications of changing expectations of present and potential members of the uniformed services relating to retirement."[62] To accomplish this, the QRMC suggested a major revision of both the active and reserve retirement systems. Selected options were:

- A defined benefit plan similar to the current High Three system that would vest personnel at 10 years of service, with benefits to begin either at age 60 (for personnel who have served less than 20 years of service) or age 57 (for those that served more than 20 years of service). Retirees could opt to receive the retirement annuity immediately upon retirement but the annuity would be reduced by 5% for each year under age 57.

---

[60] 37 U.S.C. §1008(b).

[61] Presidential memorandum, Subject: Twelfth Quadrennial Review of Military Compensation, January 9, 2015.

[62] Presidential memorandum, Subject: Tenth Quadrennial Review of Military Compensation, August 2, 2005.

- Combined with the above defined benefit plan would be a defined contribution plan that would require the services to contribute up to 5% of annual base pay into a retirement account for each servicemember. The contribution would start at 2% for those with two years of service and increase incrementally until it reached 5% for those with five or more years of service. This plan would also vest at 10 years of service but withdrawals could not begin until age 60.
- A system of *gate* pays would be established at specified career points to retain selected personnel in specified skill areas.
- Separation pay would be used to encourage personnel in over-manned skills to separate prior to vesting at the 10-year point or becoming eligible for an immediate annuity at 20 years.

11th QRMC Recommendations

DOD submitted the 11th QRMC final report in 2012. While this QRMC did not have the same focus on the entire retirement system as the previous QRMC, DOD recommended more closely aligning active and reserve retirement systems with the goal of eventually transitioning to a *total force* single-system approach for both the active and reserve components. The report recommended the following modification to the reserve retirement system:[63]

Reserve component members who have attained 20 qualifying years for retirement benefits could begin receiving retired pay on the 30th anniversary of their service start date or at age 60, whichever comes first. Reserve members would receive one retirement point for each day of service, and the points needed for a qualifying year would be reduced from the current 50-point requirement to 35.

---

[63] Report of the 11th Quadrennial Review of Military Compensation, June 2012.

Military Compensation and Retirement Modernization Commission (MCRMC)

The National Defense Authorization Act (NDAA) for FY2013 (P.L. 112-239) established a Military Compensation and Retirement Modernization Commission (MCRMC) to provide the President and Congress with specific recommendations to modernize pay and benefits for the armed services. In terms of retirement, the commission was mandated to provide recommendations to "Modernize and achieve fiscal sustainability for the compensation and retirement systems for the Armed Forces and the other Uniformed Services for the 21st century."[64] Notably, Section 674 of P.L. 112-239 mandated that the commission comply with conditions that would grandfather existing servicemembers and retirees into the existing retirement system, stating:

> (i) For members of the uniformed services as of such date, who became members before the enactment of such an Act, the monthly amount of their retired pay may not be less than they would have received under the current military compensation and retirement system, nor may the date at which they are eligible to receive their military retired pay be adjusted to the financial detriment of the member.
>
> (ii) For members of the uniformed services retired as of such date, the eligibility for and receipt of their retired pay may not be adjusted pursuant to any change made by the enactment of such an Act.

The commission delivered its final report and recommendations to Congress on January 29, 2015. Congress adopted many of the MCRMC's recommendations in the FY2016 NDAA. Several of the most prominent changes include, reduction of the retired pay multiplier, government matching contributions, and the lump sum option.

The MCRMC did not make any recommendations changing the 20-year eligibility for retirement; however, it recommended that the Secretary

[64] National Defense Authorization Act for FY2013, P.L. 112-239 subtitle H, 126 Stat. 1632, 1787 (2013).

of Defense be given authority to modify the years-of-service requirement to shape the force profile as long as it does not impose involuntary changes on existing servicemembers. DOD expressed opposition to this proposal and Congress did not adopt a provision based on this MCRMC recommendation. The 20-year eligibility remains in current law.

In: Retirement
Editor: Thomas M. Osborne

ISBN: 978-1-53615-703-1

Chapter 10

MILITARY RETIREMENT: SERVICE CONTRIBUTIONS DO NOT REFLECT SERVICE SPECIFIC ESTIMATED COSTS AND FULL EFFECT OF PROPOSED LEGISLATION IS UNKNOWN*

United States Government Accountability Office

The Honorable James M. Inhofe
Chairman

The Honorable Jack Reed
Ranking Member
Committee on Armed Services United States
Senate

* This is an edited, reformatted and augmented version of U.S. Government Accountability Office, Accesible Version, Publication No. GAO-19-195R, dated December 4, 2018.

The Honorable Mac Thornberry
Chairman

The Honorable Adam Smith
Ranking Member
Committee on Armed Services
House of Representatives

As of fiscal year 2016, the Department of Defense (DOD) has approximately 1.4 million active-duty servicemembers and 735,000 reserve component servicemembers with the potential to receive future retirement benefits.[1] In fiscal year 2016 the Military Retirement System, to which DOD contributes, paid approximately $57.2 billion in retirement benefits to approximately 2.3 million participants. As of the end of fiscal year 2016, the Military Retirement System had a present value of future benefits of over $1.6 trillion. Military retirement benefits, including funding for survivors of deceased servicemembers, are funded through the Department of Defense Military Retirement Fund (Fund).[2] Since fiscal year 1984, the Fund has operated under a financing procedure where DOD makes monthly contributions based on percentages of basic pay—one for all active duty and one for Select Reserve duty servicemembers—and the total amount of basic pay accrued that month for the same population.[3] We refer to these monthly contributions as DOD's share of the retirement

---

[1] Throughout this chapter we will refer to active duty members as well as full-time reservists (including full-time National Guard) as "active duty" servicemembers and selected reserve duty as "reserve component" servicemembers. Military retired pay is based on "basic pay." This is the principal element of military compensation that all members receive. Other elements of the military compensation package include allowances for housing and subsistence and special and incentives pays.

[2] Thrift Savings Plan matching within the Blended Retirement System is funded outside of the Department of Defense Military Retirement Fund.

[3] *Department of Defense Authorization Act, 1984*, Pub. L. No. 98-94 (1983). Throughout this chapter we will refer to active duty members as well as full-time reservists (including full-time National Guard) as "active duty" servicemembers and select reserve duty as "reserve component" servicmembers. Military retired pay is based on "basic pay." This is the principal element of military compensation that all members receive. Other elements of the military compensation package include allowances for housing and subsistence and special and incentives pays.

system's "normal cost."[4] Additionally, a lump sum payment is made to the Fund each year by the Department of the Treasury to amortize existing unfunded accrued liabilities.[5]

Section 1002 of S. 1519 (Section 1002), a bill for the National Defense Authorization Act for Fiscal Year 2018, proposed that the monthly contribution rate be percentages of basic active duty pay and reserve component pay specific to each uniformed service, rather than aggregated, and applied across all uniformed services. Section 1002 would amend 10 U.S.C. § 1465, the statute that directs the determination of contributions into the Military Retirement Fund. The provision was not adopted.

Conference Report 114-404 accompanying H.R. 2810, a bill for the National Defense Authorization Act for Fiscal Year 2018, contained a provision for us to assess the effect of the change proposed in Section 1002. Specifically, this chapter addresses whether the current method used to calculate DOD retirement contributions reflects estimated service retirement costs, and what effects, if any may result from the change proposed in Section 1002.

For our objective, we reviewed and analyzed relevant Military Retirement Fund documents, budget documents, documents related to military retirement fund contributions, relevant statutes, and proposed statutory changes. In addition, we reviewed a previous DOD effort that identifies how a potential change from a single-level, aggregate percentage rate would affect service financial contributions to the Military Retirement Fund.[6] Further, we reviewed a 2017 RAND Corporation report on military retirement contributions as contained in the conference report provision.[7]

---

[4] The DOD Board of Actuaries defines "normal cost" as the percentage of basic pay that would be necessary to finance the benefits payable to a group of new entrants into military service, assuming it is paid into a fund during each year of service and the fund is invested in interest-bearing securities. Besides DOD's share of the normal cost, the Department of the Treasury contributes the portion of the normal cost attributable to "concurrent receipt" benefits.

[5] The DOD Board of Actuaries defines "accrued liability" as the theoretical amount that would be in the fund at any given time for a group of participants if normal costs had been paid throughout all past years of service and all demographic and economic assumptions had been realized. Advance funding was not done before October 1, 1984. The accrued liability on that date is called the initial unfunded accrued liability.

[6] From here forth we refer to "single-level" contribution rate as a "single" contribution rate.

[7] RAND Corporation, *Toward Efficient Military Retirement Accrual Charges* (2017).

We also interviewed officials from the DOD Board of Actuaries, the DOD Office of the Actuary, the Office of the Under Secretary of Defense (Comptroller), the Army, Marine Corps, Navy, and Air Force, and RAND Corporation to gain their perspectives related to the current single, aggregate percentage rate and service specific contributions to the Military Retirement Fund. Finally, we reviewed and analyzed annual DMDC data on servicemembers' years of service for the period from fiscal years 1978 to 2017. We used this data to calculate annual continuation rates, from which we estimated average probabilities of servicemembers completing 20 years or more of service to be eligible for retirement, for DOD as a whole and separately for each service.[8] Continuation rates reflect a key input into the determination of a service's retirement liabilities. To assess the reliability of military retirement fund contribution data we reviewed relevant documentation about how these data are collected and interviewed the DOD Office of the Actuary about these data, and we determined the data to be sufficiently reliable for our purposes. To assess the reliability of the DMDC data on annual service cohort length of service, from 1978 through 2017, we reviewed relevant documentation and interviewed officials about the quality of these data, and determined the data to be sufficient for the purpose of estimating the probabilities of reaching 20 years of service. Enclosure I provides more detail on our objective, scope, and methodology.

We conducted this performance audit from February 2018 to November 2018 in accordance with generally accepted government auditing standards. Those standards require that we plan and perform the audit to obtain sufficient, appropriate evidence to provide a reasonable basis for our findings and conclusions based on our audit objectives. We believe that the evidence obtained provides a reasonable basis for our findings and conclusions based on our audit objectives.

---

[8] A continuation rate is the probability of continuing a state or activity. For our purposes the continuation rate for a servicemember is the probability that the servicemember will remain in military service from one year to the next. One reason why military retirement costs are so sensitive to continuation rates is that the defined benefit portion of the Military Retirement System uses 20-year "cliff vesting," whereby only those servicemembers who serve 20 years get any defined benefit pension.

BACKGROUND

DOD Military Retirement Funding

The *Department of Defense Authorization Act of 1984* changed the method of military retirement benefit funding.[9] Prior to 1984, military retirement benefits were funded on a "pay-as-you-go" basis. "Pay-as-you-go" basis is a method of funding where the costs of retirement benefits are paid for when owed to plan participants. The *Department of Defense Authorization Act of 1984* established an accrual funding system for the Military Retirement System. Accrual funding is a method of setting aside funds from current budgets for retirement annuities that eventually will be received by military personnel who are in current service. Military retirement pension benefits, including benefits for survivors of deceased servicemembers, are paid out of the Department of Defense Military Retirement Fund.

Under the current accrual funding system, a percentage of the annual appropriation for basic pay for members of the armed forces is transferred to the Department of Defense Military Retirement Fund in order to defray the future costs of retirement benefits earned during the year covered by the appropriation. Funds transferred to the Military Retirement Fund are invested until disbursed to plan participants.

The *Department of Defense Authorization Act of 1984*, as amended also mandates the actuarial cost method for developing retirement contribution rates for funding the Military Retirement Fund. The law mandates that DOD utilize the "aggregate entry-age normal" actuarial cost method for funding.[10] The law requires DOD to develop a single contribution rate across the department for active duty personnel and a single rate for reserve component personnel. The contribution rate is the

---

[9] Pub. L. No. 98-94 (1983), *codified at* 10 U.S.C. §§461-1467.

[10] An actuarial cost method is a method for allocating the cost of future retirement benefits over some period of time, generally over the working years of those expected to become eligible for benefits. The Actuarial Standards Board defines an actuarial cost method as a procedure for allocating the actuarial present value of projected benefits (and expenses, if applicable) to time periods, usually in the form of a normal cost and an actuarial accrued liability.

estimated percentage of basic pay that must be contributed over the entire active career of a typical group of new entrants to pay for all the future retirement and survivor benefits of that group. Mathematically, a contribution rate is calculated by dividing the present value of future benefits for the entire cohort by the present value of future basic pay, evaluated at an assumed interest rate.[11]

In other sectors of United States employment—in particular, for private sector and state and local government sector pension plans—to the extent that use of a particular actuarial cost method is required, the actuarial cost method generally differs from that required to be used for funding the Military Retirement System. See Enclosure II for more information regarding United States pension requirements in the private, state, and local government sectors.

In addition to DOD's contribution to the Military Retirement Fund, the Department of the Treasury is required to make an annual contribution to cover, over time, the fund's initial unfunded liability, the cost of changes to Military Retirement System benefit provisions, the cost of changes in actuarial assumptions and actuarial gains or losses, and the normal cost for "concurrent receipt" benefits. "Concurrent receipt" refers to Combat Related Special Compensation and Concurrent Retirement and Disability Pay program where certain retirees can receive both retirement pay and disability pay.[12] The Military Retirement Fund's initial unfunded liability is equal to the amount of liabilities owed when retirement benefit funding changed from a "pay-as-you-go" basis to an accrual funding basis.

DOD Board of Actuaries

The DOD Board of Actuaries consists of three members appointed by the Secretary of Defense to staggered 15-year terms.[13] The DOD Board of

[11] Present value calculations reflect the time value of money, based on the assumption that a dollar in the future is worth less than a dollar today because the dollar today can be invested and earn interest. Thus, a present value calculation uses an assumed interest rate.

[12] 10 U.S.C. § 1414§§ 1413a and 1414.

[13] 10 USC § 183.

Actuaries consists of qualified professional actuaries who are members of the Society of Actuaries. They are private sector civilians and act in a federally mandated oversight role. Each year, the DOD Board of Actuaries reviews and approves actuarial assumptions and methods to consider possible revisions, among other duties. The DOD Board of Actuaries is required to report at least once every four years to the President and Congress on the status of the Military Retirement Fund and may include relevant recommendations the DOD Board of Actuaries believes appropriate and necessary to maintain the funds on a sound actuarial basis.[14]

DOD Office of the Actuary

The DOD Office of the Actuary provides actuarial expertise on all matters relating to military compensation and benefits.

Table 1. Department of Defense Military Retirement Fund Contributions from Fiscal Years 2012 through 2016 (dollars in billions)

Fiscal year	Active	Reserve component	Total DOD contributions
2012	$19.7	$2.2	$21.9
2013	$18.3	$2.2	$20.5
2014	$18.5	$2.1	$20.5
2015	$18.0	$1.9	$19.9
2016	$17.7	$1.9	$19.5

Source: Department of Defense (DOD). | GAO-19–195R.

Note: The Department of Treasury also pays annual contributions to the Military Retirement Fund to cover the unfunded liability and the normal cost for concurrent receipts benefits. For purposes of this table, we will refer to active duty members as well as full-time reservists (including full-time National Guard) as “active duty” servicemembers and select reserve duty as “reserve component” servicemembers.

---

[14] The most recent DOD Board of Actuaries report was submitted in December 2016. *See*, DOD Board of Actuaries, *2016 Report to the President and Congress* (December 2016).

The DOD Office of the Actuary works in support of the DOD Board of Actuaries. The DOD Office of the Actuary performs annual valuations of the military retirement system and other benefits accruing to the military retired population and others. The valuations include calculating annual DOD contribution costs, as well as determining program unfunded liabilities and their amortizations.

The DOD Office of the Actuary reports DOD and Treasury contributions to the Military Retirement Fund in its Annual Valuation of the Military Retirement System reports. From fiscal year 2012 through 2016, DOD's retirement fund contributions have decreased slightly as shown in Table 1.[15]

SINGLE RETIREMENT CONTRIBUTION PERCENTAGE REQUIRED UNDER CURRENT LAW DOES NOT REFLECT ESTIMATED SERVICE SPECIFIC RETIREMENT COSTS, AND FULL EFFECT OF PROPOSED SECTION 1002 IS UNKNOWN

Current Law Requires a Single Percentage Be Applied Across Services for Retirement Contribution Calculation Purposes

Since fiscal year 1984, the "normal cost" of Military Retirement System benefits has been funded in part through monthly DOD contributions computed using a single percentage of basic pay.[16] For example, in fiscal year 2017 the military retirement contribution rate was

[15] Note that a decrease in DOD Military Retirement Fund contributions may not necessarily reflect a decrease in future retirement liabilities. Other factors are considered when developing military contributions such as the level of gains or losses due to investment performance.

[16] The DOD Board of Actuaries defines "normal cost" as the percentage of basic pay that would be necessary to finance the benefits payable to a group of new entrants into military service, assuming it is paid into a fund during each year of service and the fund is invested in interest-bearing securities. As noted earlier, the Department of the Treasury funds the normal cost of concurrent receipts benefits. For the purpose of this chapter active duty personnel include active duty members as well as full-time reservists. Reserve component personnel include part-time reservists.

28.9 percent for active duty personnel and 22.8 percent for reserve component personnel. Each rate was multiplied by the military services' respective basic pay to determine the service retirement contribution for the fiscal year. In total, the military services contribute to the Military Retirement Fund in order to meet an aggregate funding level for DOD. See Table 2 for contribution rates from fiscal years 2012 through 2017.

Table 2. Department of Defense Military Retirement Fund Contribution Rates of Basic Pay from Fiscal Years 2012 through 2017

Fiscal year	Active duty	Reserve component
2012	34.3	24.3
2013	32.1	24.4
2014	32.4	24.5
2015	32.2	22.5
2016	31.4	23.0
2017	28.9	22.8

Source: Department of Defense (DOD) data. | GAO-19–195R.

Note: The Department of Treasury also pays annual contributions to the Military Retirement Fund to cover the unfunded liability and the normal cost for concurrent receipts benefits. For the purpose of the report active duty personnel include active duty members as well as full-time reservists. Reserve component personnel include part-time reservists.

Continuation Rates Vary by Service, Indicating Retirement Contributions Do Not Reflect Service Specific Costs

Our analysis of continuation rates for active component servicemembers shows that the rate of reaching 20 years of service, or the minimum service time for retirement eligibility, varies substantially among the military services. Based on our analysis, this indicates that the mandated single, aggregate contribution rate does not reflect service specific retirement costs.[17]

[17] However, in aggregate, the single contribution rate reflects estimated retirement costs at the DOD-wide level. A continuation rate is the probability of continuing a state or activity. For our purposes the continuation rate for a servicemember is the probability that the servicemember will remain in military service from one year to the next. One reason why military retirement costs are so sensitive to continuation rates is that the defined benefit

Economic and non-economic assumptions are used in the development of the military retirement contribution rates:

- *Economic assumptions:* These include inflation, interest, and across-the-board basic pay increases. Changes in economic assumptions are generally global in that inflation, interest, and basic pay increases are not specific to any single military service.
- *Non-economic assumptions:* These include continuation rates and mortality, among others. The most important non-economic variable in the development of military retirement contribution rates are continuation rates.

In general, the actuarial valuation results that go into the development of military retirement contribution rates are most sensitive to changes in economic (e.g., long-term interest assumption) and retention assumptions (i.e., the active and reserve duty probabilities of continuation in service).

Our analysis shows that for active component servicemembers entering military service in 1992, the estimated probability of reaching 20 years of service was almost 15 percentage points higher—and more than three times higher—for the Air Force than the Marine Corps.[18] See Figure 1 for the results of our continuation rates analysis.[19] DOD Office of the Actuary officials have stated that they agree that the current mandated single, aggregate percentage does not reflect retirement costs at the individual service level, but that the method used is in compliance with statute and produces a reasonable estimate of costs at the DOD-wide level, and that

portion of the Military Retirement System uses 20-year "cliff vesting," whereby generally only those servicemembers who serve 20 years get any defined benefit pension.

[18] All of our estimated probabilities of reaching 20 years of service are based on having already completed one year of service.

[19] This analysis used data on continuation rates over time to track different cohorts entering military service in each year from 1978 through 1998 – sometimes referred to as a "longitudinal" analysis. We also performed a "cross sectional" analysis whereby we examined one-year continuation rates in a single fiscal year for servicemembers with different amounts of cumulative service years, using this data to calculate estimated probabilities of reaching 20 years of service based on the data from that fiscal year alone. We performed this additional analysis for each of fiscal years 1979 through 2017, and again found significant differences in estimated probabilities among the four service branches.

the goal of the current method is to fund military retirement liabilities at the aggregate, or DOD-level.

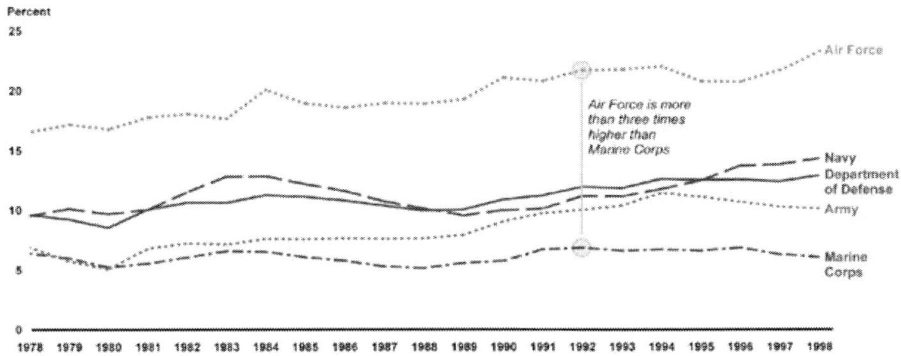

Source: GAO analysis of Department of Defense data, based on having completed one year of service. GAO-19-195R.

Figure 1. Active Component Historical Estimated Probabilities of Reaching 20 Years of Service by Entrant Cohort.

DOD's Office of Cost Assessment and Program Evaluation (CAPE) led an assessment of the current retirement contribution method as part of a larger effort and identified several positive attributes and several concerns. Among the positive attributes identified in the CAPE-led assessment are that the contribution calculations are easily auditable, and contributions to DOD's retirement liabilities are determined in an actuarially sound manner that recognizes retirement costs at the DOD level. However, the CAPE-led assessment concluded that among the concerns are that the current contribution method (1) produces "inaccurate" marginal cost estimates at the service level; (2) creates large cross-subsidies among the services; (3) generates inefficiencies in the allocation of resources; and (4) does not provide clear signals and incentives for shaping an efficient experience mix of personnel. The CAPE-led assessment did not make any recommendations and DOD Office of the Actuary officials stated that the CAPE-led assessment was put on hold, deferring reaching a Department-wide conclusion on the feasibility and desirability of service-specific contribution rates, because of other priorities such as the implementation of the Blended Retirement System.[20]

Further, a 2017 RAND study found that the current retirement contribution method tends to distort marginal costs by diluting the effect of any one service's change in force shape so that the service does not realize the full consequences of its own incremental personnel decisions that affect experience mix.[21] The RAND report presents this finding through a theoretical and empirical model, concluding that the single accrual charge rate produces "inaccurate" estimates of each service's total accrual charge, i.e., charges that are higher, or lower, than a service's actual accruing retirement liability.

Proposed Section 1002 Would Change Service Retirement Contributions but the Full Effect Is Unknown

Proposed Section 1002 would change individual military service retirement contributions to reflect service retirement costs, but the full effect of these proposed changes is unknown. Section 1002 of FY 2018 NDAA proposes separate percentages of basic pay for active duty and selected reserve for each armed force. The proposed amendment would change the calculation of the single percentage applied to basic pay with respect to the required monthly deposits into the Military Retirement Fund to separate rates for each military service, rather than the single percentage required under 10 U.S.C. § 1465.[22] The purpose of the proposed service

[20] The *National Defense Authorization Act of Fiscal Year 2016* established the Blended Retirement System, which includes a reduced defined benefit plan and a new defined contribution plan. Pub. L. No. 114-92 (2015). Under the Blended Retirement System, servicemembers may elect to contribute a portion of their salary to a portable Thrift Saving Plan, while the system provides a reduced defined benefit upon retirement. Thrift Savings Plan vesting occurs after two years of military service. All members who join the uniformed services on or after January 1, 2018 are required to participate in the new retirement system. Servicemembers who have served for fewer than 12 years as of December 31, 2017 also have the option to opt in via an irrevocable election during calendar year 2018.

[21] RAND Corporation, *Toward Efficient Military Retirement Accrual Charges* (2017).

[22] Note that "active duty" includes active component, Army National Guard and Air National Guard members on full-time duty.

specific approach is to increase budgetary transparency with respect to the relative long-term costs associated with changes in end strength and benefits among the military services. The proposed change contains the same actuarial cost method DOD is currently mandated to use, but at the military service level instead of one rate DOD-wide for active and reserve servicemembers.

However, what actual service-specific retirement contribution rates would be is not known. According to officials from DOD's Office of the Actuary, it would take an estimated 2 to 3 years to develop and implement service specific retirement contribution rates. In addition to the estimated 2 to 3 years to develop and implement service specific retirement rates, DOD's Office of the Actuary estimated that additional personnel would be required as well as additional technology resources to handle the increased workload of developing additional contribution rates.

Prior to the proposal of Section 1002, CAPE led an assessment of the potential effects of service specific retirement contribution rates for active component servicemembers. The CAPE-led assessment utilized continuation rate data analyzed by the DOD Office of the Actuary. The CAPE led assessment concluded service specific retirement contribution rates would likely increase the Air Force's and Navy's contributions and decrease the Army and Marine Corps contributions. Officials estimated two possible service contribution rate changes based on analysis of different historical continuation data, but actual service contribution rate changes are not known. See Table 3 for estimates of potential service retirement contribution changes.

Military service officials acknowledged that service specific retirement contribution rates would likely change respective service contributions but stated that their workforce decision making processes would not change.[23] However, on the other hand, the RAND report opined that service specific retirement contribution rates could enhance resource allocation efficiency among the services and, within the services, improve the efficiency of

[23] This refers to the decision making process to determine whether functions will be performed by civilian, military, or contractors.

personnel decisions and budget choices between personnel and other resources.

Table 3. Estimated Service Retirement Contribution Changes for Fiscal Year 2014 - Applied to Active Component Servicemembers

Category	Service	Retirement contribution rate	Contributions (mil)[a]	Estimated service specific[b]	Difference (mil)[b]	Percent dollar difference[c]
Potential changes based on 10 years of historical data	Army	32.4%	$6,688	31.1%	-$250	-3.7%
Potential changes based on 10 years of historical data	Air Force	32.4%	$4,359	38.2%	$800	18.4%
Potential changes based on 10 years of historical data	Navy	32.4%	$4,057	32.4%	$10	0.2%
Potential changes based on 10 years of historical data	Marine Corps	32.4%	$2,094	23.3%	-$560	-26.7%
Potential changes based on 5 years of historical data	Army	32.4%	$6,688	30.8%	-$380	-5.7%
Potential changes based on 5 years of historical data	Air Force	32.4%	$4,359	39.2%	$940	21.6%
Potential changes based on 5 years of historical data	Navy	32.4%	$4,057	33.7%	$160	3.9%
Potential changes based on 5 years of historical data	Marine Corps	32.4%	$2,094	21.1%	-$720	-34.4%

Source: Department of Defense (DOD) and GAO analysis of DOD data. | GAO-19–195R.

Note: Ten years of historical data is data from fiscal years 2005 through 2014. Five years of historical data is continuation rate data from fiscal year 2010 through 2014. Numbers may not total due to rounding.

[a]Based on Military Service fiscal year 2014 budget request.

[b]Indicates developed by a DOD Cost Analysis and Program Evaluation – led assessment of the potential effects of service specific retirement contribution rates for active component servicemembers.

[c]Calculation based on a DOD Cost Analysis and Program Evaluation-led assessment dollar difference and the Military Service fiscal year 2014 budget request.

In addition, the CAPE-led assessment also identified several positive attributes and several concerns during its effort to evaluate service specific retirement contribution rates. Among the positive attributes identified were that service specific retirement contribution rates, at the military service level, would:

- enforce good governance by providing more "accurate" budget estimates;
- provide appropriate incentives to make better tradeoffs in defense management and improve personnel policy decisions; and
- result in more accurate evaluations at the service level of long-range budgetary effects of prospective modifications to the retirement system.

Among the concerns identified are the significant effort within existing Office of the Actuary and Defense Finance and Accounting Service systems to implement service specific contribution rates, a possible increase in operational risk from disaggregating funding requirements, and a weak relationship between accrual charges and incentives to allocate resources efficiently.

AGENCY COMMENTS

We provided a draft of this chapter to DOD for review and comment. DOD informed us in an email that they had no comments.

Brenda S. Farrell
Director
Defense Capabilities and Management

Frank Todisco
Chief Actuary

APPLIED RESEARCH AND METHODS

Objective, Scope and Methodology

This chapter addresses whether the current method used to calculate Department of Defense (DOD) retirement contributions reflects estimated service retirement costs and what effects, if any, may result from proposed changes in Section 1002 of S. 1519, a bill for the National Defense Authorization Act of Fiscal Year 2018. In addition we are providing information on alternative actuarial methods we identified during this review.

For our objective, we reviewed and analyzed relevant Military Retirement Fund documents, budget documents, and documents related to Military Retirement Fund contributions. In addition, we reviewed a previous DOD effort that identifies how a potential change from a single, aggregate percentage rate would affect service financial contributions to the Military Retirement Fund. Further, we reviewed a 2017 RAND report on retirement contributions.[24] We also interviewed officials from the DOD Board of Actuaries, DOD Office of the Actuary, Office of the Under Secretary of Defense (Comptroller), the Army, Marine Corps, Navy, and Air Force, and RAND Corporation to gain their perspectives related to the current single, aggregate percentage rate and service specific contributions to the Military Retirement Fund.

Finally, we reviewed and analyzed annual Defense Manpower Data Center (DMDC) data on active component servicemembers' years of service for the period from fiscal years 1978 to 2017. We used this data to calculate annual continuation rates, from which we estimated the average probabilities of servicemembers completing 20 years or more of service to be eligible for retirement, for DOD as a whole and separately for each service. Continuation rates reflect a key input into the determination of a service's retirement liabilities.

---

[24] RAND Corporation, *Toward Efficient Military Retirement Accrual Charges* (2017).

For each service and fiscal year, we first calculated annual continuation rates, meaning the fraction of service members who completed each additional year of service (the data started with servicemembers who had already completed at least one year of service). For example, we calculated the fraction of servicemembers who completed their second year of service, the fraction of servicemembers who completed their third year of service, and so on through the fraction of servicemembers who completed their twentieth year of service. Then, we multiplied the fraction of servicemembers who completed their second year of service in one year by the fraction of servicemembers who completed their third year of service in the following year, and so on through the fraction of servicemembers who completed their twentieth year of service 19 years after the initial year. For example, to estimate the probability that servicemembers who started their service in 1990 (and then served one year) served until 2010 or later, we multiplied the fraction of servicemembers who completed their second year of service in 1992 by the fraction of servicemembers who completed their third year of service in 1993, and so on through the fraction of servicemembers who completed their twentieth year of service in 2010. In this analysis, we used data on continuation rates over time to track different cohorts entering military service in each year from 1978 through 1998 – sometimes referred to as a "longitudinal" analysis. We also performed a "cross sectional" analysis whereby we examined annual continuation rates in a single fiscal year for servicemembers with different amounts of cumulative service years, using this data to calculate estimated probabilities of reaching 20 years of service based on the data from that fiscal year alone. We performed this additional analysis for each of fiscal years 1978 through 2017.

While our estimates can shed light on differences across services in the estimated probability of serving for 20 years or more, they are subject to limitations and should be interpreted with caution. They should not be regarded as best estimates of probabilities going forward, which would depend on multiple facts, circumstances, and judgments. However, these estimates can be indicative of the likelihood of potentially significant differences across services in the retention of servicemembers over multiple years of service.

To assess the reliability of military retirement fund contribution data we reviewed relevant documentation about how these data are collected and interviewed the DOD Office of the Actuary about these data and we determined the data to be sufficiently reliable for the purposes of (1) describing total DOD annual contributions from 2012 to 2016, (2) describing the active duty and reserve components contributions as a percentage of basic pay from 2012 to 2017, and (3) making general estimates of potential differences in contributions by the services if specific changes had been made in 2014.

To assess the reliability of the DMDC data on annual service cohort length of service, from 1978 through 2017, we reviewed relevant documentation and interviewed officials about the quality of these data, and determined the data to be sufficient for the purpose of estimating the probabilities of reaching 20 years of service.

We conducted this performance audit from February 2018 to November 2018 in accordance with generally accepted government auditing standards. Those standards require that we plan and perform the audit to obtain sufficient, appropriate evidence to provide a reasonable basis for our findings and conclusions based on our audit objectives. We believe that the evidence obtained provides a reasonable basis for our findings and conclusions based on our audit objectives.

Additional Information on Pension Funding and Financial Reporting Requirements in the United States

Most pension funding and financial reporting requirements in the United States, to the extent they have required use of a particular actuarial cost method, have generally required methods other than the aggregate entry age normal method that the Department of Defense (DOD) is required by statute to use for determining contribution rates to the Military Retirement System. For employers providing pension coverage to their employees, a distinction can be made between "funding" and "financial reporting." Funding refers to the employer's obligation to contribute to the plan in accordance with applicable law or regulation. Financial reporting refers to the measures of plan costs and obligations reported in the employer's financial statements in accordance with applicable accounting standards. Measurements for both funding and financial reporting purposes typically involve actuarial calculations that will vary based on, among other factors, the particular actuarial cost method and actuarial assumptions (such as an interest rate assumption) used. Because funding and financial reporting are governed by different laws, regulations, or standards, often requiring different actuarial methods or assumptions, actuarial measurements—such as normal cost or accrued liability—for funding purposes will often differ from actuarial measurements for financial reporting purposes.

As previously discussed, the methodology that DOD uses for funding purposes—i.e., to determine its contribution rates to the Military Retirement Fund—is governed by the *Department of Defense Authorization Act of 1984*.[25] The methodology that DOD uses for financial reporting purposes—for example, in its agency financial statements—is governed by applicable accounting standards issued by the Federal Accounting Standards Advisory Board (FASAB). An actuarial cost method is a method for allocating the cost of future retirement benefits over time, generally in some manner over the working years of those expected to become eligible for benefits.[26] Attributes of different actuarial cost methods include whether the calculation methodology is "individual" or "aggregate"; and whether costs are allocated as a percentage of pay, as an amount per active participant, or in a pattern that matches some aspect of the plan's benefit formula.

---

[25] Pub. L. No. 98-94 (1983).

[26] The Actuarial Standards Board defines an actuarial cost method as a procedure for allocating the actuarial present value of projected benefits (and expenses, if applicable) to time periods, usually in the form of a normal cost and an actuarial accrued liability.

In 1984, Congress mandated DOD to utilize a method known as the aggregate entry-age normal actuarial cost method for funding purposes.[27] However, most pension funding and financial reporting requirements in the United States, to the extent they have required use of a particular actuarial cost method, have generally required actuarial cost methods other than the aggregate entry age normal method. Actuarial cost methods are applicable for pension plans in different sectors of the U.S. economy, such as for private sector pension plans, state and local government sector pension plans, and federal pension plans. In particular, outside of federal pension plans, to the extent a method is required, individual rather than aggregate actuarial cost methods have often been required. For example, for the funding of single-employer private sector plans, the *Pension Protection Act of 2006* (PPA) requires the use a particular individual type of actuarial cost method.[28]

For private sector employers sponsoring pension plans, the Financial Accounting Standards Board (FASB) provides applicable generally accepted accounting principles. For this purpose, FASB standards issued in 1985 require the use of a particular individual type of actuarial cost method.[29] For state and local government pension plans, each state has its own funding laws or regulations, but the Governmental Accounting Standards Board (GASB) provides applicable generally accepted accounting principles for state and local entities. GASB issued revised standards for pension accounting in 2012, in which it specified that the actuarial cost method should be the entry age normal method, but specifying that it should be applied on an individual basis (meaning, the

---

[27] This method is an "aggregate" type of actuarial cost method. "Individual" actuarial cost methods take into account the particular demographic characteristics and benefit entitlements of each individual participant in a plan. In contrast, the aggregate entry age normal method utilizes group averages, which can produce a reasonable overall result but can also result in less precise measures, including when measuring costs for subgroups of plan participants. The aggregate entry age normal actuarial cost method has an "individual" counterpart known as the individual entry age normal actuarial cost method.

[28] Pub. L. No. 109-280 (2006). Specifically, PPA requires the use of a method known as the Unit Credit actuarial cost method.

[29] Specifically, the FASB directs the use of a method known as the Projected Unit Credit actuarial cost method.

individual entry age normal method and not the aggregate entry age normal method that is required to be used by DOD).

In contrast, the Federal Accounting Standards Advisory Board (FASAB), which provides applicable generally accepted accounting principles for federal entities, generally directs use of the aggregate entry age normal method. One of the reasons cited by the FASAB for utilizing this method is that the method is already used for funding purposes by the Military Retirement System and other major federal retirement systems, such as the Federal Employees Retirement System (FERS) and the Civil Service Retirement System (CSRS). The FASAB also viewed the aggregate entry age normal method as a reasonable method.

One entity that used the aggregate entry age normal actuarial cost method was the New York City Office of the Actuary. However, New York City Office of the Actuary officials stated that after the current Chief Actuary arrived, the New York City Office of the Actuary began transitioning away from the aggregate entry-age normal cost method and switching to the individual entry age normal cost method for its five major actuarially-funded retirement and pension systems.[30] Officials stated that they transitioned away from the aggregate entry-age normal actuarial cost method because they found it to be less accurate for purposes of determining the costs for a specific subgroup of the population. Officials stated that their newly implemented actuarial cost method provides more accurate valuation results for purposes of determining the costs for a specific subgroup of the population, such as for a particular employer within their system; they also cited the pension plans' multiple tiers of retirement benefits. They noted that when measuring the cost impact of a plan change for a specific subpopulation

---

[30] The New York City Office of the Actuary provides actuarial information and services for the five major actuarially-funded New York City Retirement Systems and Pension Funds resulting in an annual determination of New York City's and obligors' contributions to these retirement systems and pension funds. These systems include the New York City Employees' Retirement System (NYCERS), the Teachers' Retirement System of the City of New York (TRS), New York City Board of Education Retirement System (BERS), New York City Police Pension Fund, and the New York City Fire Pension Fund. According to the New York City Office of the Actuary collectively, in 2018, this equates to the fourth largest public pension system in the United States.

of plan participants, the aggregate entry age normal method could produce anomalous results because of its use of group averages, where an individual method would be more accurate. In addition, officials stated that advances in technology and computing processes now allow for more precise and more granular methodologies, but also noted that the New York City Office of the Actuary had adequate technological resources in place to support the actuarial cost method change and therefore the change required a minimum effort in resources and personnel.

DOD is required by statute to use the aggregate entry age normal actuarial cost method for funding purposes, and directed by FASAB accounting standards to use this same method for financial reporting purposes. However, the DOD Board of Actuaries has stated that alternative actuarial cost methods may provide more transparency of retirement costs. Specifically, in its most recent quadrennial report to the President and Congress, the DOD Board of Actuaries recommended that Congress should consider alternative actuarial cost methods.[31] The Board opined that the aggregate entry-age normal cost method is a valid cost method, but stated that it is rarely used. The Board also stated that with advancements in computing capabilities, "individual" actuarial cost methods have become much more popular and do a better job of reflecting plan and assumption changes that might apply to select groups of members. The Board concluded that moving to an individual actuarial cost method would improve the overall actuarial valuation results. The Board of Actuaries also stated in its report that DOD does not currently have the software necessary for alternative methodologies and that upgrading DOD systems could be costly.

DOD Office of the Actuary officials stated that while they use the statutorily required aggregate entry age normal actuarial cost method, they

---

[31] In addition to this recommendation, the Department of Defense Board of Actuaries has also recommended that all costs of changes to military retirement benefit provisions be recognized and borne by the Department of Defense, including the portion of normal cost percentage attributable to concurrent receipts benefits, which is currently borne by the Department of the Treasury. Department of Defense Board of Actuaries, *2016 Report to the President and Congress* (December 2016).

apply it in an actuarially sound way that avoids certain problems that they stated may have contributed to the method falling out of favor.[32] They also noted that the aggregate entry age actuarial cost method, as used by the Office of the Actuary within the framework specified by current law, has an advantage to DOD in that it supports advance budgeting requirements and the need for a normal cost expressed as a costof-labor type rate, in this case as a percentage of basic pay.

In addition, significant changes have occurred external and internal to the DOD Military Retirement Fund since 1984. As mentioned above, for non-federal pension plans, actuarial cost methods other than the aggregate age entry normal method are often required for certain purposes. In addition, DOD's Office of the Actuary has made several changes to its actuarial calculations, most recently as required by the *National Defense Authorization Act of Fiscal Year 2016*, which established the "Blended Retirement System" (BRS), a major reform to military compensation.[33] Implemented in 2018, the Blended Retirement System provides a reduced defined benefit plan and is supplemented with a portable Thrift Savings Plan with matching contributions from DOD. The BRS provides a new tier of retirement benefits and changes retired pay distribution options. DOD Office of the Actuary Officials stated that the current actuarial cost method handles BRS implementation in actuarially appropriate manner. However, such a major change to the military retirement system could potentially result in future measurement needs that could be better met by an individual type of actuarial cost method. Moreover, there have been significant advances in technology and computing power since 1984, making alternative actuarial cost methods more feasible.

---

[32] DOD Office of the Actuary officials told us that they first calculate separate normal cost percentages for each historical entry-period-based tier of plan members, and then determine the required single normal cost percentage by weighting the tier-appropriate normal cost percentages by the percentage of payroll expected to be paid to plan members under that tier. They contrasted their approach with a different approach that would base the normal cost percentage solely on the most recent tier of benefits.

[33] Pub. L. No. 114-92 (2015).

INDEX

C

D

E

F

R

S

T

U

V

W

T

U

V

W

Related Nova Publications

INCOME REPLACEMENT AND SPENDING IN RETIREMENT: ANALYSES, ISSUES, RECOMMENDATIONS

EDITOR: Katrina Dixon

SERIES: Retirement Issues, Plans and Lifestyles

BOOK DESCRIPTION: This book examines whether and how spending patterns vary by age; key factors used to develop target replacement rates; and the usefulness of information on such rates provided by DOL.

HARDCOVER ISBN: 978-1-53610-193-5
RETAIL PRICE: $150

FIRM BANKRUPTCY AND RETIREE BENEFITS: EFFECTS AND PROTECTIONS, IN BRIEF

EDITOR: Joshua H. Saunders

SERIES: Retirement Issues, Plans and Lifestyles

BOOK DESCRIPTION: This book explores the protections of benefits awarded retirees and future retirees of bankrupt private-sector employers under current law.

SOFTCOVER ISBN: 978-1-63485-589-1
RETAIL PRICE: $62

To see complete list of Nova publications, please visit our website at www.novapublishers.com